Table of Contents

Top 50 Reading Skills

Critical Thinking Skills

Interpreting Fiction

Interpreting Poetry

Interpreting Drama

Interpreting Nonfiction

T0204590

Acknowledgments

Excerpt on page 2 from "Mother" from *Later the Same Day* by Grace Paley, 1985.

Poem on page 4 "Nikki Rosa" from *Black Feeling, Black Talk, Black Judgment* by Nikki Giovanni. Copyright © 1968, 1970 by Nikki Giovanni. Reprinted by permission of HarperCollins Publishers, William Morrow.

Excerpt on pages 6–7 from *The Bishop's Boys: A Life of Wilbur and Orville Wright* by Tom Crouch. Copyright © 1989 by Tom D. Crouch. Used by permission of W. W. Norton & Company, Inc.

Cartoon on page 6 reprinted by permission of Joe Martin.

Play excerpt on page 8 from "Relative Strangers" by Sheri Wilner. Reprinted by permission of the author.

Excerpt on page 10 from *Sons and Lovers* by D. H. Lawrence, copyright 1913 by Thomas Seltzer, Inc., renewed © 1948 by Frieda Lawrence Ravagli. Used by permission of Viking Penguin, a division of Penguin Group (USA) Inc.

Article and chart on page 14 from "Can Extreme Poverty by Eliminated?" by Jeffrey D. Sachs, *Scientific American*, September 2005. Reprinted by permission of Scientific American, Inc. All rights reserved.

Excerpt on page 21 from James W. Loewen, *Lies My Teacher Told Me*, New York: W. W. Norton & Company, 1995, p. 201–202.

Short story on page 23 "Night" is reprinted with the permission of the author, Bret Lott.

Excerpt on page 26 from "A Loss of Drive" by Jeanne Marie Laskas. Originally published in *The Washington Post Magazine* by Jeanne Marie Laskas. Used by permission.

Political ad on page 37 from The Brady Campaign to prevent gun violence. Reprinted by permission.

Excerpt on page 41 from *Hunger, A Novella and Stories* by Lan Samantha Chang, 1998.

Excerpt on page 47 from *The Rarest of the Rare: Vanishing Animals, Timeless Worlds* by Diane Ackerman, copyright © 1995 by Diane Ackerman. Used by permission of Random House, Inc.

Excerpt on page 53 from *You Just Don't Understand* by Deborah Tannen. Copyright © 1990 by Deborah Tannen. Reprinted by permission of HarperCollins Publishers, William Morrow.

Excerpt on page 53 from *Merrill Markoe's Guide to Love* by Merrill Markoe, 1997. Reprinted by permission of Atlantic Monthly.

Excerpt on page 54 Terry Tempest Williams, *Desert Quartet*. New York: Pantheon Books, 1995, p. 41–42.

Excerpt on page 55 "Caring for the Woods" from *Audubon*, 1995 by Barry Lopez. Reprinted by permission of Sterling Lord Literistic, Inc. Copyright by Barry Lopez.

Excerpt on page 57 from *American Chica* by Marie Arana, copyright © 2001 by Marie Arana. Used by permission of The Dial Press/Dell Publishing, a division of Random House, Inc.

Excerpt on page 58 from "Indian Camp." Reprinted with permission of Scribner, an imprint of Simon & Schuster Adult Publishing Group, from *In Our Time* by Ernest Hemingway. Copyright 1925 by Charles Scribner's Sons. Copyright renewed 1953 by Ernest Hemingway.

Excerpt on page 60 from "The Voyagers" by Linda Hogan. As appeared in *Parabola: A Magazine of Myth & Tradition* and *Dwellings: A Spiritual History of the Living World* by Linda Hogan, (W.W. Norton, 1995). Reprinted by permission of the author.

Short story on page 65 "The Paring Knife" by Michael Oppenheimer as appeared in *Sundog*, Vol. 4, No. 1, 1982.

Excerpt on page 66 from *Madame Bovary* by Gustave Flaubert, translated by Francis Steegmuller, copyright © 1957 by Francis Steegmuller. Used by permission of Random House, Inc.

Excerpt on page 68 from "Glass Bottle Trick" from *Whispers from the Cotton Tree Root* by Nalo Hopkinson, 2000. Used by permission of Invisible Cities Press.

Short story on page 73 from "A Quartet of Mini-Fantasies" by Arthur Porges. Copyright Arthur Porges. Reprinted by permission.

Excerpt on page 74 from "The Star" by H. G. Wells. Reprinted by permission of A P Watt Ltd on behalf of The Literary Executors of the Estate of H. G. Wells.

Excerpt on page 75 from "The Catbird Seat" by James Thurber. © 1942 James Thurber. © renewed 1970 Rosemary Thurber. All Rights Reserved. Used with Permission.

Excerpt on page 75 from *Waltzing the Cat* by Pam Houston. Copyright © 1998 by Pam Houston. Used by permission of W. W. Norton & Company, Inc.

Excerpt on page 77 from *Cat's Eye* by Margaret Atwood, copyright © 1988 by O. W. Toad, Ltd. Used by permission of Doubleday, a division of Random House, Inc.

Excerpt on page 78 from *New Islands and Other Stories* by Maria Luisa Bombal. Translation copyright © 1982 by Farrar, Straus & Giroux, Inc. Reprinted by permission of Farrar, Straus & Giroux LLC.

Excerpt on page 79 from "The Tournament at Surreptitia" by John Morressy as appeared in *The Magazine of Fantasy & Science Fiction*, July 2005. Copyright © by John Morressy. Reprinted by permission.

Excerpt on page 80 from *The Rosewood Casket* by Sharyn McCrumb, copyright © 1996 by Sharyn McCrumb. Used by permission of Dutton, a division of Penguin Group (USA) Inc.

Excerpt on page 80 from *The Namesake* by Jhumpa Lahiri. Copyright © 2003 by Jhumpa Lahiri. Reprinted by permission of Houghton Mifflin Company. All rights reserved.

Excerpt on page 81 from *Jonathan Strange & Mr. Norrell* by Susanna Clarke, 2004. Copyright © 2004 by Susanna Clarke. Reprinted by permission of Bloomsbury USA, LLC.

Excerpt on page 84 from *Charlie and the Chocolate Factory* by Roald Dahl, copyright text and illustrations copyright © 1964, renewed 1992 by Roald Dahl Nominee Limited. Used by permission of Alfred A. Knopf, an imprint of Random House Children's Books, a division of Random House, Inc.

Excerpt on page 84 from *The Djinn in the Nightingale's Eye* by A. S. Byatt, copyright © 1994 by A. S. Byatt. Used by permission of Random House, Inc. Also reprinted by permission of Sterling Lord Literistic, Inc.

Excerpt on page 85 from *The God of Small Things* by Arundhati Roy, copyright © 1997 by Arundhati Roy. Used by permission of Random House, Inc.

Excerpt on page 87 from *How the Garcia Girls Lost Their Accents*. Copyright © 1991 by Julia Alvarez. Published by Plume, an imprint of Dutton Signet, a division of Penguin USA, Inc., and originally in hardcover by Algonquin Books of Chapel Hill. Reprinted by permission of Susan Bergholz Literary Services, New York. All rights reserved.

Short story on pages 88–89 "Faded Roses" by Karen Joy Fowler, first published in *Omni Magazine*, November 1989. Used by permission of General Media International.

Excerpt on page 91 from *Mrs. Dalloway* by Virginia Woolf, copyright 1925 by Harcourt, Inc. and renewed 1953 by Leonard Woolf, reprinted by permission of the publisher.

Excerpt on page 93 from J. R. R. Tolkien, *The Hobbit*, London: Allyn & Unwin, 1937.

Excerpt on page 93 from "Introduction" to 1976 edition of *The Left Hand of Darkness* by Ursula K. Le Guin. Copyright © 1969, 1997 by Ursula K. Le Guin. Reprinted by permission of the author and the author's agent; the Virginia Kidd Agency, Inc.

Excerpt on page 93 from the *The Left Hand of Darkness* by Ursula K. Le Guin. Copyright © 1969, 1997 by Ursula K. Le Guin. Reprinted by permission of the author and the author's agent; the Virginia Kidd Agency, Inc.

Poem on page 95 "Not Waving but Drowning" by Stevie Smith from *Collected Poems of Stevie Smith*, copyright © 1972 by Stevie Smith. Reprinted by permission of New Directions Publishing Corp.

Excerpted poem on page 97 from "Poetry Workshop at the Homeless Shelter" from *Boneshaker*, by Jan Beatty, © 2002. Reprinted by permission of the University of Pittsburgh Press.

Poem on page 98 "Milk-Bubble Ruins" from *The Wellspring* by Sharon Olds, copyright © 1996 by Sharon Olds. Used by permission of Alfred A. Knopf, a division of Random House, Inc.

Poem on page 99 "Those Winter Sundays." Copyright © 1966 by Robert Hayden, from *Collected Poems of Robert Hayden* by Robert Hayden, edited by Frederick Glaysher. Used by permission of Liveright Publishing Corporation.

CONTEMPORARY'S

Top 50 Reading Skills

for GED SUCCESS

Wright Group

JUDITH GALLAGHER

*poetry.foundation.org/
learning/poem*

Executive Editor: Linda Kwil
Cover Design: Tracey Harris-Sainz
Interior Design: Linda Chandler

ISBN: 0-07-704481-9
ISBN: 0-07-704482-7 (with CD-ROM)

Send all inquiries to:
Wright Group/McGraw-Hill
130 E. Randolph Street, Suite 400
Chicago, IL 60601

5 6 7 8 9 POH/POH 10 09

The **McGraw·Hill** Companies

How to Use This Book

Test Overview and Contents of This Book

The actual GED Language Arts, Reading Test contains 40 multiple-choice questions to be completed in 65 minutes. Reading passages include fiction, poetry, drama, literary nonfiction, and informational nonfiction, such as business documents and consumer letters. The 50 skills chosen for this book are those most representative of the type and difficulty level of skills tested on the GED Language Arts, Reading Test.

Top 50 Reading Skills for GED Success is divided into four main sections:

- **Pretest:** The Pretest and Pretest Evaluation Chart help instructors and learners identify the exact skills learners need to work on. Each of the 50 questions addresses a particular reading skill.
- **Top 50 Skills:** Lessons provide instruction on the top 50 skills needed for success on the GED Language Arts, Reading Test. Learners may complete only those skills they have identified on the Pretest, or they may work through all the skills to ensure complete understanding. GED Readiness exercises for each skill provide immediate practice and reinforcement. Related skills listed at the bottom of left-hand pages help the learner understand how various skills work together in reading.
- **Posttest:** Use the Posttest for practice under test-like conditions to show readiness for the GED Language Arts, Reading Test. The Posttest Evaluation Chart helps to determine which skills need additional review and reinforcement. Correlations to Contemporary's *GED Language Arts, Reading* give further instruction and practice if needed.
- **Supporting Material:** Also included are a complete Answer Key, a glossary of important reading terms, and an index.

To the Instructor

Top 50 Reading Skills for GED Success is instructor-friendly, organizing for you in 50 lessons a core of reading skills to help your learners pass the GED Language Arts, Reading Test. Each lesson addresses a single skill and provides follow-up practice. One or more lessons can be completed in a single study period.

To the Learner

Follow these steps to use *Top 50 Reading Skills for GED Success* to maximum advantage:

- Take the Pretest to determine your strengths and weaknesses. Then use the Pretest Evaluation Chart to determine the skills you need to review.
- Review the lesson for each skill identified on the Pretest Evaluation Chart, or go through all of the skills in order. Use the Answer Key to review your answers to each question in the GED Readiness exercises.
- Take the Posttest. For best results, take the test under timed, test-like conditions. The Answer Key allows you to check your answers, and the Posttest Evaluation Chart tells you which skills you need to review again.

About the Pretest

This Pretest is an overview of 50 skills you are most likely to see addressed on the GED Language Arts, Reading Test. The GED Test will include approximately seven passages with a series of multiple choice questions for each passage. The passages will include

- one poem
- one excerpt from drama
- several excerpts from literature
- some nonfiction excerpts, with at least one business or consumer document

The question types will include

- 20% comprehension
- 15% application
- 30 to 35% analysis
- 30 to 35% synthesis

For the actual GED Language Arts, Reading Test, you will have 65 minutes to read the passages and answer the 40 questions. However, this Pretest is not a timed test. In fact, you should take as much time as you need to answer each question. This Pretest is designed to help you identify specific skills in which you need more practice.

Answer every question on this Pretest. If you are not sure of an answer, put a question mark by the item number to note that you are guessing. Then make your best guess. You may return to this question later if you wish. On the actual GED Test, an unanswered question is counted as incorrect, so making a good guess is an important skill to develop.

When you are finished, turn to the Answer Key on page 17 to check your answers. Then use the Pretest Evaluation Chart (pages 16–17) to figure out which skills to focus on in the instruction section of the book (pages 18–153).

After working through the instruction section, take the Posttest on pages 156–169. Your success on the Posttest will indicate your readiness to take the actual GED Language Arts, Reading Test.

Pretest

Directions: Choose the <u>one best answer</u> to each question.

Questions 1 through 8 refer to the following short story.

WHO DOES THE NARRATOR MISS?

1   One day I was listening to the AM radio. I heard a song: "Oh, I Long to See My Mother in the Doorway." By God! I said, I understand that song. I have often longed to see my mother in the doorway. As a matter of fact, she did stand frequently in various doorways looking at me. She stood one day, just so, at the front door, the darkness of the hallway behind her. It was New Year's Day. She said sadly, If you come home at 4 a.m. when you're seventeen, what time will you come home when you're twenty? She asked this question without humor or meanness. She had begun her worried preparations for death. She would not be present, she thought, when I was twenty. So she wondered.

2   Another time she stood in the doorway of my room. I had just issued a political manifesto attacking the family's position on the Soviet Union. She said, Go to sleep for godsakes, you damn fool, you and your Communist ideas. We saw them already, Papa and me, in 1905. We guessed it all.

3   At the door of the kitchen she said, You never finish your lunch. You run around senselessly. What will become of you?

4   Then she died.

5   Naturally for the rest of my life I longed to see her, not only in doorways, in a great number of places—in the dining room with my aunts, at the window looking up and down the block, in the country garden among zinnias and marigolds, in the living room with my father.

6   They sat in comfortable leather chairs. They were listening to Mozart. They looked at one another amazed. It seemed to them that they'd just come over on the boat. They'd just learned the first English words. It seemed to them that he had just proudly handed in a 100 percent correct exam to the American anatomy professor. It seemed as though she'd just quit the shop for the kitchen.

7   I wish I could see her in the doorway of the living room.

8   She stood there a minute. Then she sat beside him. They owned an expensive record player. They were listening to Bach. She said to him, Talk to me a little. We don't talk so much anymore.

9   I'm tired, he said. Can't you see? I saw maybe thirty people today. All sick, all talk talk talk talk. Listen to the music, he said. I believe you once had perfect pitch. I'm tired, he said.

10   Then she died.

—"Mother" by Grace Paley

1 How many characters are in this story?

   ① one
   ② two
   ③ three
   ④ four

2 The mother is so worried about her daughter because she thinks

   ① she won't live to be there for her daughter
   ② she hasn't been a good role model so far
   ③ her daughter doesn't have any friends
   ④ her daughter has an eating disorder

3 What can you conclude about the narrator's father from paragraphs 6–10?

   ① He likes swing music.
   ② He likes to hear himself talk but not his wife.
   ③ He's a student in anatomy class.
   ④ He's a better doctor than he is a husband.

4 From whose point of view is this story told?

   ① the mother's
   ② the father's
   ③ the daughter's
   ④ an omniscient narrator's

5 How does this story's use of dialogue differ from the normal use?

   ① The dialogue doesn't sound much like real people.
   ② The dialogue isn't enclosed in quotation marks.
   ③ The dialogue doesn't advance the plot.
   ④ There isn't enough dialogue.

6 What do the various settings mentioned in the story have in common?

   ① They all begin in doorways.
   ② They're all dark and depressing.
   ③ They're all on New Year's Day.
   ④ They're all in the Soviet Union.

7 The author's style is marked by

   ① an angry tone
   ② similes and metaphors
   ③ long, difficult words
   ④ informal, conversational language

8 Which statement best summarizes paragraph 1?

   ① The song "Oh, I Long to See My Mother in the Doorway" makes me long to see my mother, who stood frequently in doorways looking at me and worrying because she was dying and she wouldn't be there for me.
   ② My mother stood one New Year's Day at the front door and said sadly, If you come home at 4 a.m. when you're seventeen, what time will you come home when you're twenty? She would not be present, she thought, when I was twenty.
   ③ One day I was listening to the AM radio. I heard a song: "Oh, I Long to See My Mother in the Doorway." By God! I said, I understand that song. My mother stood frequently in various doorways looking at me. She would not be present, she thought, when I was twenty. So she wondered.
   ④ One day I heard a song: "Oh, I Long to See My Mother in the Doorway." I understood that song. My mother did stand in various doorways looking at me. One day she said sadly, If you come home at 4 a.m. when you're seventeen, what time will you come home when you're twenty? She would not be present, she thought, when I was twenty.

WHAT MATTERS MOST TO THE SPEAKER?

Nikki Rosa

childhood memories are always a drag
if you're Black
you always remember things like living in Woodlawn
with no inside toilet
5 and if you become famous or something
they never talk about how happy you were to have
your mother
all to yourself and
how good the water felt when you got your bath
10 from one of those
big tubs that folk in Chicago barbeque in
and somehow when you talk about home
it never gets across how much you
understood their feelings
15 as the whole family attended meetings about Hollydale
and even though you remember
your biographers never understand
your father's pain as he sells his stock
and another dream goes
20 And though you're poor it isn't poverty that
concerns you
and though they fought a lot
it isn't your father's drinking that makes any difference
but only that everybody is together and you
25 and your sister have happy birthdays and very good
Christmases
and I really hope no white person ever has cause
to write about me
because they'll never understand
30 Black love is Black wealth and they'll
probably talk about my hard childhood
and never understand that
all the while I was quite happy

by Nikki Giovanni

9 Who is the speaker in this poem?

   ① a white child
   ② a black child
   ③ a famous adult who had an unhappy childhood
   ④ a famous adult who had a happy childhood

10 Which best represents the poem's theme?

   ① Childhood memories are a drag.
   ② Another dream goes away.
   ③ They'll never understand.
   ④ Black love is Black wealth.

11 The form of this poem is

   ① in two stanzas
   ② in 33 lines
   ③ concrete form
   ④ free form

12 The rhythm of this poem is

   ① metrical
   ② repetitive
   ③ regular
   ④ irregular

13 The words *white* and *write* in lines 27–28 are an example of

   ① internal rhyme
   ② end rhyme
   ③ assonance
   ④ alliteration

14 An example of imagery is found in

   ① lines 1–2
   ② lines 9–11
   ③ lines 20–21
   ④ lines 27–29

15 What is the speaker's mood today?

   ① happy
   ② vengeful
   ③ afraid
   ④ annoyed

16 The poet contrasts her view of her childhood with the viewpoint of

   ① Black wealth
   ② people from Chicago
   ③ a white biographer
   ④ her father

17 What can you conclude about the speaker's father?

   ① He knew how to handle disappointment.
   ② He was unkind to his children.
   ③ He had money but didn't share it with his family.
   ④ He discouraged the speaker from following her dreams.

Boffo by Joe Martin, 1986

1 WHAT DID THE WRIGHT BROTHERS INVENT?

Wilbur walked back to the men with a final request—"not to look too sad, but to . . . laugh and holler and clap . . . and try to cheer Orville up when he started." The elder brother then strode to the right wingtip, removing the small wooden bench that had been supporting that

2 side of the aircraft.

At about 10:35 [on December 17, 1903], Orv shifted the lever to the left. Slowly, much more slowly than on December 14, the machine began to move down the rail into the teeth of a wind that was now gusting up to 27 miles an hour. Wilbur had no trouble keeping up with the craft, which rose from the track after only a forty-foot run. Daniels snapped the photo catching Will in mid-stride, apparently a bit startled by what was happening. He is the center of attention, the object to which the eye

3 is drawn. That is as it should be.

The lifesavers broke into a ragged cheer. Bob Westcott, still watching through his telescope, let out a whoop of his own. The griddle cakes he was preparing for lunch that day were burned.

4 It was over very quickly. The airplane floundered forward, rising and falling for 12 seconds until it struck the sand only 120 feet from the point at which it had left the rail. You could have thrown a ball farther but, for the Wrights, it was enough. For the first time in history, an airplane had taken off, moved forward under its own power, and landed at a point at least as high as that from which it had started—all under the complete control of the pilot. On this isolated, windswept beach, a man had flown.

5 The small group ran forward to congratulate Orv. Then it was back to work, carrying the machine to the starting point for another trial. But first the Wrights invited everyone inside for a bit of warmth. When they reemerged at 11:20, Will took his place for a flight of 195 feet. Twenty minutes later, Orv was back in the cradle, covering 200 feet in 15 seconds. At about noon, Will tried again, with spectacular success: he flew 852 feet in 59 seconds, demonstrating beyond any doubt that the machine was capable of sustained flight.

6   The distance for the men carrying the machine back to the starting point was longer this time. When it was done, they paused for a moment to catch their breath. The brothers, confident now, discussed the possibility of a really long flight—perhaps all the way down the beach to the telegraph at the Kitty Hawk weather station.

7   Suddenly, a gust of wind raised one wingtip high into the air. Daniels, who was standing closest, jumped to catch a strut and was carried along. The engine broke loose as the disintegrating machine rolled over backward to the accompaniment of Daniels's screams and the sound of snapping wires and splintering wood. When the dust settled, the world's first airplane lay transformed into a twisted mass of wreckage. Daniels, at least, was uninjured. For the rest of his life, he would remind anyone willing to listen that he had survived the first airplane crash.

—Excerpted from *The Bishop's Boys: A Life of Wilbur and Orville Wright* by Tom Crouch

18 This passage is an example of

① a biography
② an autobiography
③ an essay
④ a letter

19 Which heading in the index would be most likely to direct you to this passage?

① first flight
② Bishop Wright
③ Tom Crouch
④ lifesavers

20 How is this passage organized?

① chronological order
② cause and effect
③ comparison and contrast
④ order of importance

21 The author's primary purpose is to

① entertain
② persuade
③ evoke emotions
④ inform

22 What is the main idea of this passage?

① The Wright brothers invented powered flight.
② Wilbur Wright piloted the first flight.
③ You could throw a ball farther than the first airplane flew.
④ The first airplane flight lasted only 12 seconds.

23 What can you infer from paragraph 7 about the first airplane?

① It flew during excellent weather.
② It had no engine.
③ It was not very sturdy.
④ It injured a bystander.

24 Read what the pilot in the cartoon is saying. What is the passenger probably thinking?

① "I didn't know we'd be so high up."
② "This is so exciting!"
③ "Hey, aren't those poplar trees up ahead?"
④ "But the wings are wider than my arms!"

HOW WELL DO THE TWO MARIES GET ALONG?

Characters
Marie Barrett, 25 years old
Marie Harvey, 49 years old
Virginia, 35–45 years old. Head flight
5 attendant. Speaks with a Southern accent.

Setting
On board an airplane flying from New York City to Charleston, South Carolina.

MARIE BARRETT: There's something
10 unbelievable to me about a mother and a daughter not getting along.

MARIE HARVEY: It's unbelievable to me that any do. If the truth be told, you've asked me more questions in the past ten minutes than
15 my own daughter has asked me in the past ten years. I'm not as adept [skilled] at mothering as you'd think.

MARIE BARRETT: I don't care. In fact, I prefer it that way. If you've been waiting ten years for
20 someone to ask you for advice, you must have a lot of it to give. Right?

[Marie Harvey laughs.]

Hey, and just think, you'd be getting me at the best possible time. No teething, no toilet
25 training . . . I've had all my shots.

[Virginia returns with a pillow and a glass.]

VIRGINIA: Here's your second drink. FYI, regulations do not permit us to serve more than three.

30 MARIE HARVEY: Thank you.

[Marie Harvey pays Virginia for the drink.]

VIRGINIA: My hands are full. Would you put this behind her?

[Handing Marie Harvey the pillow.]

35 *[To Marie Barrett.] Lean forward honey.*

[Marie Barrett leans forward. Marie Harvey fluffs up the pillow and then puts it behind her. Virginia watches happily.]

So, is it settled? Are you two gonna go out and
40 buy matching outfits?

MARIE HARVEY: Go away. Shoo.

VIRGINIA: Don't blow this.

MARIE BARRETT: You did tell me that all you have are lawyer bills and a tan line. When you
45 said that, you reminded me of this quote I use to describe how I feel: "Life has not yet offered me a trinket of the slightest value." It's from Virginia Woolf—Mrs. Dalloway. Except for the *yet.* I added that—I try to be optimistic. "Life
50 has not yet offered me a trinket of the slightest value." That's how you feel, too, isn't it?

MARIE HARVEY: Well, like I said . . . I paint. That's my trinket.

MARIE BARRETT: *[Disappointed.]* Maybe I'll
55 buy some watercolors.

MARIE HARVEY: I'm sure you have something.

MARIE BARRETT: Books, I guess. Virginia Woolf, Willa Cather, George Eliot. Anything
60 written by a woman, I've read. But Virginia, Willa, and George, God bless 'em, have little to say about yeast infections and monthly mood swings. I can't find my mother in a book.

MARIE HARVEY: So now you're looking for
65 her on airplanes?

—Excerpted from *Relative Strangers*
by Sheri Wilner

25 Lines 2–5 are

① a cast list
② a comedy
③ dialogue between the two Maries
④ stage directions

26 How would lines 32–35 look if they were in a novel?

① Virginia: My hands are full. Would you put this behind her? She handed Marie Harvey the pillow and said to Marie Barrett: Lean forward honey.

② Virginia said, *"My hands are full. Would you put this behind her?"* She handed Marie Harvey the pillow and said to Marie Barrett, *"Lean forward honey."*

③ Virginia said, "My hands are full. Would you put this behind her?" She handed Marie Harvey the pillow and said to Marie Barrett, "Lean forward honey."

④ Virginia: "My hands are full. Would you put this behind her?" She *[hands Marie Harvey the pillow and says to Marie Barrett]* "Lean forward honey."

27 The main conflict here is

① within Marie Barrett
② within Marie Harvey
③ within Virginia
④ between the two Maries

28 Virginia is trying to

① help Marie Harvey with her drinking problem
② make Marie Harvey act like a mother toward Marie Barrett
③ become friends with Marie Barrett
④ find a better job

29 How can you tell that the connotation of *advice* in line 20 is positive?

① It's a homonym.
② Marie Barrett seems sincere in requesting it.
③ Marie Harvey has been waiting ten years to be asked for it.
④ Virginia brings a pillow and a glass.

30 What do you predict will happen next?

① Marie Harvey will put on headphones and ignore her seatmate the rest of the trip.
② Virginia will yell at Marie Barrett for being so needy.
③ Marie Barrett will start asking Virginia for advice.
④ Marie Harvey will warm up to Marie Barrett.

HOW DOES MIRIAM FEEL?

1   And gradually the intimacy with the family concentrated for Paul on three persons—the mother, Edgar, and Miriam. To the mother he went for that sympathy and that appeal which seemed to draw him out. Edgar was his very close friend. And to Miriam he more or less condescended, because she seemed so humble.

2   But the girl gradually sought him out. If he brought up his sketchbook, it was she who pondered longest after the last picture. Then she would look up at him. Suddenly, her dark eyes alight like water that shakes with a stream of gold in the dark, she would ask:

3   "Why do I like this so?"

4   Always something in his breast shrank from these close, intimate, dazzled looks of hers.

5   "Why do you?" he asked.

6   "I don't know. It seems so true."

7   "It's because—it's because there is scarcely any shadow in it; it's more shimmery, as if I'd painted the shimmering protoplasm [the living cells] in the leaves and everywhere, and not the stiffness of the shape. That seems dead to me. Only this shimmeriness is the real living. The shape is a dead crust. The shimmer is inside really."

8   And she, with her little finger in her mouth, would ponder these sayings. They gave her a feeling of life again, and vivified [brought to life] things which had meant nothing to her. She managed to find some meaning in his struggling, abstract speeches. And they were the medium through which she came distinctly at her beloved objects.

9   Another day she sat at sunset while he was painting some pine trees which caught the red glare from the west. He had been quiet.

10   "There you are!" he said suddenly. "I wanted that. Now, look at them and tell me, are they pine-trunks or are they red coals, standing-up pieces of fire in that darkness. There's God's burning bush for you, that burned not away."

11   Miriam looked, and was frightened. But the pine-trunks were wonderful to her, and distinct. He packed his box and rose. Suddenly he looked at her.

12   "Why are you always sad?" he asked her.

13   "Sad!" she exclaimed, looking up at him with startled, wonderful brown eyes.

14   "Yes," he replied. "You are always, always sad."

15   "I am not—oh, not a bit!" she cried.

16   "But even your joy is like a flame coming off of sadness," he persisted. "You're never jolly, or even just all right."

17   "No," she pondered. "I wonder—why."

18   "Because you're not; because you're different inside, like a pine-tree, and then you flare up; but you're not just like an ordinary tree, with fidgety leaves and jolly—"

19   He got tangled up in his own speech; but she brooded on it, and he had a strange, roused sensation, as if his feelings were new. She got so near him. It was a strange stimulant.

—Excerpted from *Sons and Lovers*
by D. H. Lawrence

31 The genre of this passage is

① fiction
② nonfiction
③ drama
④ poetry

32 The main conflict here is

① within Paul
② within Miriam
③ between Paul and Miriam
④ between Edgar and Miriam

33 Paragraph 10 is an example of

① sensory details
② vivid verbs
③ simile
④ personification

34 The author uses *shimmer* in paragraph 7 to symbolize

① intimacy
② life
③ art
④ pine trees

35 When Paul visits Miriam, he always plays with the family dog, Bill. Even if the dog gets too close, Paul is affectionate. Later in the novel, when Bill pushes against him, Paul says, "Go away, Bill. I don't want you."

How does this behavior suggest the way Paul will treat Miriam that day?

① He will propose to her.
② He will give her flowers.
③ He will scold her for not training the dog.
④ He will break up with her.

36 Which word or phrase from paragraph 18 is a homonym for the word *your*?

① belonging to you
② you're
③ not just
④ you are

37 If Miriam were writing a review of Paul's painting, which statement would she be most likely to use?

① "He doesn't use light very well."
② "His pictures are beautiful but false."
③ "I love the glow in his paintings, although I'm not sure why."
④ "I admire his pine trees because he captures them in accurate botanical detail."

WHAT DOES JENNA WANT?

1635 Madonna Lane
Fairfax, VA 22033

Customer Service Manager
Leading Edge Electronics
1240 Waukegan Ave.
Glenview, IL 60025

Dear Customer Service Manager:

I am writing to complain about a bad experience with one of your products. I bought your combination TV/VCR/DVD player (model #LE862) for my daughter for Christmas. She was thrilled to get it, but once we took the TV out of the box and tried to hook it up, our problems began.

The owner's manual said that a coaxial cable came with the TV, but we couldn't find one. We had to wait until the day after Christmas and make a special trip to the electronics store to get one. Then we learned the hard way that the remote control has a terrible design. Why would anyone use the same button for Stop and Eject? Tiffany is constantly pressing the button twice to make the tape stop. Instead of just stopping, though, the tape ejects, and she has to get up and walk over to the TV to push it back in. What's the point of having a remote if you have to jump up all the time?

We tried to take the TV back to the store. (I had bought it at Top Electronics on December 10. I'm enclosing a copy of the sales receipt.) They refused to take it back. They said the problem is in how Tiffany uses the remote, not how it's designed. My daughter has had a remote in her hand since she was two years old. She's now 16 and a straight A student. She's smart enough to operate a remote, I assure you.

My family has spent thousands of dollars on Leading Edge products over the years. We've always been pleased with them before—but this is an outrage. If you want our business ever again (or that of our friends and relatives), you'll fix this problem. I expect you to take back this piece of junk and refund our money. (I paid for it with my platinum MasterCard, account #5424-5424-5424-5424, expiration date March 2008.)

Frustratedly yours,

Jenna Yablonsky

Jenna Yablonsky

38 This letter is being sent to

① Jenna Yablonsky
② Leading Edge Electronics
③ Top Electronics store
④ MasterCard

39 What does the letter writer want?

① help hooking up a TV/VCR/DVD player
② an apology to her disappointed daughter
③ a TV with a better-designed remote control
④ a refund of the product's cost

40 What business document is most likely to help a customer service person know how to answer this letter?

① the company's mission statement
② the employee handbook
③ a training manual
④ a program brochure

41 This letter is an example of

① fiction
② drama
③ literary nonfiction
④ informational nonfiction

42 "This piece of junk" is an example of

① a fact
② loaded language
③ an inference
④ denotation

43 The statement "the remote control has a terrible design" is

① a fact
② an opinion
③ a generalization
④ a paraphrase

HOW CAN WE HELP THE POOREST PEOPLE IN THE WORLD?

We Can End Poverty Worldwide

More than a billion people on this planet live in "extreme poverty," defined as existing on less than $1 a day. At the United Nations Millennium Summit in 2000, nations promised to invest enough money to help poor regions improve their residents' welfare. The U.N. specified eight broad Millennium Development Goals (MDGs) to greatly reduce poverty throughout the world by 2015.

The table shows how much money wealthier nations would need to contribute for specific goals in three typical countries of tropical Africa, where the average income per person is only $330 per year. Affluent nations, including the United States, have promised to contribute 0.7 percent of their gross national product (GNP), or about $110 per capita (per person who lives in the poorer countries).

Most Americans vastly overestimate the amount of foreign aid the U.S. government gives. Most years, the U.S. contributes only $3 to $6 per African, and much of it never gets to those who need it. We need to give that money directly to villages and towns. Foreign aid is one of the best investments we can make. Helping poor countries develop their economies will save countless lives. It will greatly reduce political instability and improve our own safety. The U.N.'s Secretary-General, Kofi Annan, said, "There will be no development without security, and no security without development."

Foreign Aid: How Should the Money Be Spent?

Here is a breakdown of the needed investment for three typical low-income African countries to help them achieve the MDGs. For all nations given aid, the average total annual assistance per person would come to around $110 per year. These investments would be financed by both foreign aid and the countries themselves.

Investment Area	Average per Year, 2005–2015 ($ per capita)		
	Ghana	Tanzania	Uganda
Hunger	7	8	6
Education	19	14	15
Gender equality	3	3	3
Health	25	35	34
Water supply and sanitation	8	7	5
Improving slum conditions	2	3	2
Energy	15	16	12
Roads	10	22	20
Other	10	10	10
Total	100	117	106

Source: *Scientific American*, September 2005
Numbers do not sum to totals because of rounding.

44 What type of nonfiction is this?

1. autobiography
2. personal essay
3. editorial
4. business document

45 Which of the following is a strength of this passage's argument?

1. the explanation of MDGs
2. the specific dollar amounts discussed
3. the quote from Kofi Annan
4. all of the above

46 Which of the writer's values does this piece reveal?

1. greed
2. concern for poor people
3. math anxiety
4. mistrust of the U.N.

47 What context clue helps you figure out the meaning of *affluent* in paragraph 2?

1. the phrase "wealthier nations"
2. the reference to the table
3. the phrase "0.7 percent of their gross national product"
4. the definition of "per capita"

48 What do the numbers in the table represent?

1. numbers of poor people (in millions)
2. dollars needed (per person)
3. percentage of gross national product (GNP)
4. Americans' estimate of foreign aid

49 How is the Investment Area (left column in the table) organized?

1. chronological order
2. cause and effect
3. alphabetically
4. most important to least important

50 The author's point of view toward affluent nations is

1. implied
2. clearly stated
3. unfair
4. unforgiving

Pretest Evaluation Chart

After you complete the Pretest, check your answers with the Answer Key on page 17. Then use this chart to figure out which skills you need to focus on in the instruction section of this book. In column 1, circle the numbers of the questions you missed. The second and third columns tell you the name of the skill and its number in the instruction section of this book. Focus your preparation on these skills. The fourth column tells you the pages to study. After you complete those pages, put a check in the last column.

Question Number	Skill Name	Skill	Pages	Completed ✔
22	Main Idea and Details	1	18–19	
23	Inference	2	20–23	
17	Conclusion	3	24–27	
47	Context Clue	4	28–29	
29	Connotation and Denotation	5	30–31	
8	Summarizing and Paraphrasing	6	32–33	
43	Fact and Opinion	7	34–35	
42	Detecting Bias	8	36–37	
45	Strengths of an Argument	9	38–39	
30	Prediction	10	40–41	
20	Chronological Order	11	42–43	
2	Cause and Effect	12	44–45	
16	Comparison and Contrast	13	46–47	
49	Order of Degree	14	48–49	
36	Homonym	15	50–51	
21	Author's Purpose	16	52–53	
50	Author's Point of View	17	54–55	
7	Author's Style	18	56–59	
31	Genre	19	60–61	
1	Basic Elements of Fiction	20	62–65	
3	Characterization	21	66–69	
32	Plot and Conflict	22	70–73	
4	Point of View	23	74–75	
5	Dialogue and Narrative	24	76–77	
6	Setting, Mood, and Tone	25	78–81	
33	Descriptive Detail	26	82–85	
34	Theme and Symbol	27	86–89	
35	Extended Synthesis	28	90–93	
9	How to Read a Poem	29	94–97	
10	Subject and Theme	30	98–101	
11	The Shape of Poetry	31	102–105	
12	Rhythm and Meter	32	106–109	
13	The Sound of Poetry	33	110–113	
14	Imagery and Figurative Language	34	114–117	

Question Number	Skill Name	Skill	Pages	Completed ✔
15	Mood and Emotion	35	118–119	
25	Drama as a Literary Form	36	120–123	
26	Reading a Play or Script	37	124–125	
27	Plot and Conflict	38	126–127	
28	Characterization	39	128–129	
44	Types of Nonfiction	40	130–131	
18	Literary Nonfiction	41	132–133	
37	Commentary and Review	42	134–135	
41	Informational Nonfiction	43	136–137	
46	Editorial	44	138–139	
40	Workplace and Business Document	45	140–141	
39	Community and Consumer Document	46	142–143	
38	Business and Consumer Letter	47	144–145	
24	Cartoon	48	146–149	
48	Table and Graph	49	150–151	
19	Reference Source	50	152–153	

Answer Key

Page 3

❶ ③, ❷ ①, ❸ ④, ❹ ③, ❺ ②, ❻ ①, ❼ ④, ❽ ①

Page 5

❾ ④, ❿ ④, ⓫ ④, ⓬ ④, ⓭ ①, ⓮ ②, ⓯ ④, ⓰ ③, ⓱ ①

Page 7

⓲ ①, ⓳ ①, ⓴ ①, ㉑ ④, ㉒ ①, ㉓ ③, ㉔ ④

Page 9

㉕ ①, ㉖ ③, ㉗ ④, ㉘ ②, ㉙ ②, ㉚ ④

Page 11

㉛ ①, ㉜ ③, ㉝ ①, ㉞ ②, ㉟ ④, ㊱ ②, ㊲ ③

Page 13

㊳ ②, ㊴ ④, ㊵ ③, ㊶ ④, ㊷ ②, ㊸ ②

Page 15

㊹ ③, ㊺ ④, ㊻ ②, ㊼ ①, ㊽ ②, ㊾ ④, ㊿ ①

Finding the Main Idea and Details

Main Idea

If someone asks you what you did last night, you probably answer with a sentence or two saying where you went or what activity you did. Such a statement gives the **main idea** of your evening. The main idea is the most important idea about the topic. The **topic** is the subject of what you are talking or writing about. It can usually be summed up in a word or two: your evening, gardening tips, the latest movie.

Most of what you read has a main idea. The main idea is often stated in the title. When you read a newspaper or magazine, the headlines are probably the first things you notice.

Examples:

Patriots Win Super Bowl	**How to Avoid the Flu**
Ideas for Impatient Gardeners	**Will Jen Wed Again?**
Blizzard Causes 20-Car Pileup	**Budget Deficit Increases**

Topic Sentence and Supporting Details

The main idea of a paragraph is the **topic sentence**, which is often (though not always) the paragraph's first sentence.

Supporting details tell more about the main idea. They include reasons, facts or statistics, examples, anecdotes, how-to steps, and expert testimony.

Example:

> **WHY DID THE NATIONAL GUARD OFFER BONUSES?**
>
> <u>The National Guard introduced re-enlistment bonuses of $15,000 in December 2004.</u> That year the Guard attracted 49,000 soldiers, about 7,000 short of its goal. It was the first time in ten years the Guard had failed to meet its recruiting goals. The re-enlistment rate rose nationwide when the bonuses were offered. The catch? Soldiers must sign up for six years, a near guarantee that they'll do at least one tour of duty in Iraq.

The **main idea** is the most important idea in a paragraph or a passage.

The **topic** is the subject of what you are talking or writing about.

The **topic sentence** is the sentence that expresses a paragraph's main idea. It is often the first sentence in the paragraph.

Supporting details give you more information about the main idea, such as *who, what, when, where, how much,* and *why.*

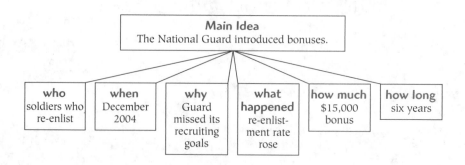

GED Readiness

Read the article and answer the questions that follow.

WHAT HAPPENED IN GRENADA?

1   Grenada is an island in the West Indies. On September 7, 2004, Ivan, the most powerful hurricane to hit Grenada in nearly a decade, killed at least 12 people, damaged most of its homes, and destroyed a prison, leaving criminals on the loose, officials said Wednesday.

2   Hurricane Ivan is expected to inflict more damage as its 140-mile-per-hour winds churn through the Caribbean. The U.S. Hurricane Center in Miami, Florida, warned it could make direct hits on Jamaica, Cuba, and the southern United States.

3   "We are terribly devastated. It's beyond imagination," said Grenadan Prime Minister Keith Mitchell, whose own home was flattened by Ivan. Mitchell said 90 percent of homes on the island were damaged. The hurricane pulverized concrete homes into rubble and tore off hundreds of roofs.

—Adapted from CNN

1 What is the main idea of paragraph 1?

  ① Grenada is an island in the West Indies.
  ② Ivan is the most powerful hurricane to hit Grenada in nearly a decade.
  ③ Ivan killed at least 12 people.
  ④ Ivan destroyed a prison, leaving criminals on the loose.

2 What is the main idea of paragraph 2?

  ① Hurricane Ivan is expected to inflict more damage.
  ② Ivan's winds hit 140 miles per hour.
  ③ The U.S. Hurricane Center is in Miami, Florida.
  ④ Ivan could make direct hits on Jamaica, Cuba, and the southern United States.

3 What is the main idea of paragraph 3?

  ① The prime minister of Grenada is Keith Mitchell.
  ② The prime minister's own home was flattened by Ivan.
  ③ Ninety percent of homes on the island were damaged.
  ④ The hurricane pulverized concrete homes into rubble.

4 What is the main idea of the entire article?

  ① Hurricane Ivan ravaged Grenada.
  ② Ivan destroyed a prison, leaving criminals on the loose.
  ③ Ivan's winds hit 140 miles per hour.
  ④ The hurricane tore off hundreds of roofs.

Reread the entire article and answer the questions that follow.

5 Write three details that support the main idea of the article.

_____

_____

_____

6 Where did the devastation take place?

_____

7 When?

_____

8 How many people died?

_____

9 Why? What killed them?

_____

Making Inferences

The main idea of a piece of writing is not always stated. Sometimes it's just suggested. In that case, you need to make inferences to figure it out.

Making inferences means using information that is stated directly to figure out a message that is unstated or hinted at. It's reading between the lines. To make inferences

- look at the supporting details
- figure out what they all relate to

You already make inferences all the time. Suppose the kids are playing in the living room while you fix dinner. If you hear a crash, you **infer** that they knocked something over.

Example:

> ### WHAT HAPPENED TO ALEX?
>
> Alex was walking home from the bus stop after work. A fire engine rushed past, siren shrieking. Alex noticed smoke billowing up to the sky a block away. As he got closer, he saw two fire engines parked in front of a house across the street from his apartment. Firefighters were spraying the house with water. What could Alex infer?

Alex would probably infer that the house across the street was on fire. These are the clues, or stated facts, that would help him make this inference:

- A fire engine rushed past, siren shrieking.
- Smoke billowed to the sky.
- Two fire engines were parked in front of the house.
- Firefighters were spraying the house with water.

A good reader uses details in a passage as clues to the author's message. The author **implies** (sends) the message. The reader **infers** (receives) it.

Ads often use buzzwords to make their products appealing. Watch for loaded language like *new and improved* or *exciting*. These words will help you understand what an ad is trying to make you infer.

Making inferences means using facts that are stated to figure out a meaning that is not stated directly.

You make inferences when you read cartoons. Two pieces of information that will help you understand cartoons are the characters and the topic. Identifying them will help you figure out the opinion, or message, the cartoonist is expressing.

Related Skills: 3, 4, 18, 29, 34, 37, and 43

GED Readiness

Read the passage and answer the questions that follow.

WHY DO MOTORISTS HONK?

Several years ago, two students of mine provided a demonstration: they drove around Burlington, Vermont, in a big, nearly new, shiny black American car (probably a Lexus would be more appropriate today) and then in a battered ten-year-old subcompact. In each vehicle, when they reached a stoplight and it turned green, they waited until they were honked at before driving on. Motorists averaged less than seven seconds to honk at them in the subcompact, but in the luxury car the students enjoyed 13.2 seconds before anyone honked. . . . Motorists of all social stations honked at the subcompact more readily.

—Excerpted from *Lies My Teacher Told Me* by James W. Loewen

❶ What can you infer that the demonstration showed?

① New cars are faster than beat-up old cars.
② Burlington is an economically deprived city.
③ Most Americans unconsciously grant respect to wealthy people.
④ All of the author's students had their driver's licenses.

❷ What clues does the author state directly that helped you infer what the demonstration showed? You may choose more than one.

① One car was a luxury car and the other was old and battered.
② When the drivers hesitated at a green light, other motorists honked at them.
③ The demonstration happened several years ago.
④ Before honking, motorists waited more than thirteen seconds for the driver of an expensive car but less than seven seconds for the driver of an old car.

❸ What can you infer from the fact that motorists of all social stations honked at the subcompact more readily?

① Even people who drive old cars respect wealthy drivers more than they respect their peers.
② All motorists are impatient whether they're rich or poor.
③ The road is a good place for poor people to let out their frustrations.
④ The motorists assumed that the driver of the cheaper car had slower reflexes than the wealthier driver.

Read the advertisement and answer the question that follows.

❹ What does this company want you to infer about its new printer?

_____

_____

Making Inferences in Fiction

Inferences are often found in fiction (novels and short stories). Rather than stating ideas about characters and events, authors often hint at them. As a reader, you can piece clues together to make sense of characters and figure out the point of a story.

Example:

HOW DID DAN'S INTERVIEW GO?

On the way home that evening, Sue wondered how Dan's job interview had gone. The minute she walked in the door, she smelled meat cooking. Dan was a wannabe vegetarian. Most nights he threw together a simple dinner of salad and bread or ramen noodles and broccoli. When he was upset, however, he craved red meat. He tried to distract himself from his mood by cooking something ridiculously complicated and bad for his health.

What two inferences might you draw from this passage?

① Sue has a job outside the home.
② Being a vegetarian is hard work.
③ Dan's job interview went badly.
④ Sue is Dan's mother.

If you picked ① and ③, you're right. The facts that Sue is coming home in the evening and that Dan usually cooks dinner support the inference that Sue works outside the home. The fact that Dan is cooking red meat suggests that his job interview went badly.

Inference ② is not supported in this passage. Being a vegetarian may challenge Dan's willpower, but you can't assume everyone reacts the same way he does. Inference ④ is not supported by the facts either. Sue may be Dan's mother, or she may be his wife or girlfriend or a roommate. You can't tell from this passage.

GED Readiness

Read the passage and answer the questions that follow.

WHAT DID HE HEAR?

1   He woke up. He thought he could hear their child's breathing in the next room, the near-silent, smooth sound of air in and out.

2   He touched his wife. The room was too dark to let him see her, but he felt her movement, the shift of blanket and sheet.

3   "Listen," he whispered.

4   "Yesterday," she mumbled. "Why not yesterday," and she moved back into sleep.

5   He listened harder; though he could hear his wife's breath, thick and heavy next to him, there was beneath this the thin frost of his child's breathing.

6   The hardwood floor was cold beneath his feet. He held out a hand in front of him, and when he touched the doorjamb, he paused, listened again, heard the life in his child.

7   His fingertips led him along the hall and to the next room. Then he was in the doorway of a room as dark, as hollow as his own. He cut on the light.

8   The room, of course, was empty. They had left the bed just as their child had made it, the spread merely thrown over bunched and wrinkled sheets, the pillow crooked at the head. The small blue desk was littered with colored pencils and scraps of construction paper, a bottle of white glue.

9   He turned off the light and listened. He heard nothing, then backed out of the room and moved down the hall, back to his room, his hands at his sides, his fingertips helpless.

10   This happened each night, like a dream, but not.

—"Night" by Bret Lott

1 What can you infer about the narrator's child?

  ① The child is at a sleepover.
  ② The child has died.
  ③ The child is staying with a relative.
  ④ The child doesn't really exist.

2 What can you infer from this sentence: "Then he was in the doorway of a room as dark, as hollow as his own"?

  ① There is a power failure in the neighborhood.
  ② The father has gotten lost in his own house.
  ③ There is no furniture in the child's bedroom.
  ④ In his heart, the father is as absent as his child.

3 What can you infer about the narrator?

  ① He misses his child.
  ② He is in a bad marriage.
  ③ He has no imagination.
  ④ He works the night shift.

4 What clues does the author state directly that help you infer the story's main idea?

  ① "The room, of course, was empty." (paragraph 8)
  ② "His fingertips [were] helpless." (paragraph 9)
  ③ "Like a dream, but not." (paragraph 10)
  ④ all of the above

Drawing Conclusions

In its simplest form, a **conclusion** is the logical outcome of a general statement plus a specific example. Here is a formula for drawing a conclusion:

General statement	+	Specific example	=	Conclusion
All power tools make noise.	+	Electric drills are power tools.	=	Electric drills make noise.

Both the general statement and the example must be true for the conclusion to be true. If either one is false, then the conclusion is not true. For example, if the example above said, "Hand-driven screwdrivers are power tools," the conclusion would be false because hand-driven screwdrivers are not power tools.

One reason general statements are often false is because they tend to start with *all*, *every*, or *only*. The world is full of exceptions to most such statements.

> In logic, a general statement plus a specific example equals a **conclusion**.

> In both fiction and nonfiction, **drawing conclusions** means combining what you read with what you already know to figure out what the text means.

GED Readiness

Read each argument. Circle any statement that is false. Write *true* or *false* on the line before the argument.

_____ ❶ All stars are balls of fire.
Our sun is a star.
Our sun is a ball of fire.

_____ ❷ Only Irish people have red hair.
Sha-lin has red hair.
Sha-lin must be Irish.

_____ ❸ All cats are stupid.
Luna is a cat.
Luna must be stupid.

_____ ❹ All birds have hollow bones.
Alligators have hollow bones.
Alligators are birds.

_____ ❺ Only humans know American Sign Language.
Koko the gorilla knows American Sign Language.
Koko must be human.

_____ ❻ Endangered species are nearly extinct.
Monk seals are endangered.
Monk seals are nearly extinct.

In a larger sense, **drawing conclusions** means combining what you read with what you already know to figure out the meaning of a piece of writing. Drawing conclusions is similar to making inferences (Skill 2), but it adds another element. If making inferences involves reading between the lines, drawing conclusions involves reading beyond the text, bringing in your own experience. Drawing conclusions tests your ability to reason.

Stated facts	+	**Implied facts**	+	**Personal experience and knowledge**	=	**Conclusion**

Example:

DO ANIMALS FEEL EMOTIONS?

For centuries, many people denied that animals felt emotions. This gave them an excuse to mistreat animals. Some farmers worked horses to death. Hunters clubbed baby seals for their fur. Even today, there are still scientists who perform painful and unnecessary tests on animals—for example, blinding rabbits to test which mascara is most waterproof.

But much evidence of animals' ability to feel has accumulated in recent years. In his book *When Elephants Weep*, psychologist Jeffrey Masson documented emotions of many species. He observed gorillas who know 200 words in sign language, elephants who paint pictures, and dogs who warn their epileptic owners several minutes before a seizure hits. He even observed bears who walk up a hill most nights to watch the sunset, apparently just because of its beauty.

What conclusion can you draw about animal emotions?

Stated facts: There are gorillas who know sign language, elephants who paint pictures, and dogs who warn their epileptic owners before a seizure.

Implied facts: Bears enjoy beautiful sunsets. Animals want to communicate.

Personal experience and knowledge: My dog is happy when I get home and sad when I leave.

Conclusion: Yes, I believe animals feel emotions.

Note that the conclusions you draw may differ depending on your personal experience and knowledge. You use your own beliefs, attitudes, and values to draw conclusions about the behavior of people you read about. The written text, whether fiction or nonfiction, is a jumping-off point, but what you bring to your reading is just as important.

GED Readiness

Read the passage. Then write the answers to the questions that follow.

WHAT HAS THE HUSBAND LEARNED TODAY?

At dinner we usually go around the table and tell one thing we've learned today, and so that's why I'm swirling my spaghetti and just finishing my remarks about chickens not needing rain. Now it's the husband's turn.

"Ahem," he says. "Today I learned that I have a dead Zip drive." This news falls upon the family with a thud. Just yesterday we ruled that it's not fair to learn the same thing several days in a row.

"All right, I'll take a look at it again," I say. Just how many times am I going to have to revive this thing? "Remember, it's drive E. Not drive B, like you were trying before."

"Drive E?" he says.

"Remember, you thought it was dead, but you were just calling it drive B?"

"Drive B?" he says.

Woe is the spouse in charge of family tech support. This is exhausting work. You are not simply the ever-chirpy computer geek agreeing to install some new software. You are *married*. You are the total emotional support service package, the shoulder to cry on as the husband stands weeping over his laptop and you urge him to *pay attention* as you demonstrate *again* the wonders of a Norton Protected Recycle Bin.

Many hours of my life have thus expired.

—Excerpted from "A Loss of Drive"
by Jeanne Marie Laskas

1 In what kind of place does this family probably live?

_____

How do you know?

_____

_____

2 Do you think this couple has children?

_____

How do you know?

_____

_____

3 Does this couple's nontraditional division of labor work?

_____

Why or why not?

_____

_____

4 What kind of job might the husband have?

_____

What makes you come to that conclusion?

_____

_____

Read the passage. Then circle the correct answers.

WHAT HAS THE NARRATOR DONE?

True!—nervous—very, very dreadfully nervous I had been and am! but why *will* you say that I am mad [insane]? The disease had sharpened my senses—not destroyed—not dulled them. Above all was the sense of hearing acute. I heard all things in the heaven and in the earth. I heard many things in hell. How, then, am I mad? Hearken! and observe how healthily—how calmly I can tell you the whole story.

It is impossible to say how first the idea entered my brain; but once conceived, it haunted me day and night. Object there was none. Passion there was none. I loved the old man. He had never wronged me. He had never given me insult. For his gold I had no desire. I think it was his eye! yes, it was this! He had the eye of a vulture—a pale blue eye, with a film over it. Whenever it fell upon me, my blood ran cold; and so by degrees—very gradually—I made up my mind to take the life of the old man, and thus rid myself of the eye forever.

—Excerpted from "The Tell-Tale Heart"
by Edgar Allan Poe

5 What is the narrator's state of mind?

  ① He is slightly nervous.
  ② He is paying close attention.
  ③ He is mentally unbalanced.
  ④ He is very calm.

6 Which statement in the passage is a clue to the narrator's state of mind?

  ① "Above all was the sense of hearing acute."
  ② "I heard many things in hell."
  ③ "I loved the old man."
  ④ "He had never given me insult."

7 How would you assess the narrator's ability to tell his story accurately?

  ① He remembers all the details accurately.
  ② He is mentally unbalanced and may not know what really happened.
  ③ He is too depressed to notice what happened.
  ④ His senses are so acute that he doesn't miss a thing.

8 Why does the narrator provide so many details?

  ① He hopes to convince readers his story is true.
  ② He's trying to make the story long enough that readers stop paying attention.
  ③ It helps him remember what happened.
  ④ His story is part of a police report that requires specifics.

9 What does the narrator say is the reason he decided to kill the old man?

  ① He hates the old man.
  ② He wants the old man's money.
  ③ He has been insulted by the old man.
  ④ He is terrified by the old man's eye.

10 What do you think is the reason he decided to kill the old man?

  ① He hates the old man.
  ② He loves the old man.
  ③ He wants the old man's money.
  ④ He's mentally ill.

Recognizing Context Clues

As you read, you'll often run into words whose meanings you don't know. However, you don't have to look up every unfamiliar word in a dictionary. You can infer the meaning of many words from **context clues**, or nearby words and sentences. Three kinds of context clues will help you understand unknown words:

- clues within nearby sentences. Notice how the underlined words give clues to the meaning of the **boldfaced** word in the following sentence.

> President Martinez rarely **digressed** in her State of the Union speech. She had five important points to make, and she <u>didn't stray</u> from those subjects. She <u>didn't discuss irrelevant details</u>.

Since President Martinez is described as not digressing, not straying, and not discussing irrelevant details, we can guess that *digress* means "to stray from the main subject."

- examples. Notice that examples are underlined in the following sentence.

> Any **ecological crisis,** such as <u>global warming or mass extinctions of plants and animals,</u> can have serious long-term consequences.

The examples "global warming" and "mass extinctions of plants and animals" give you clues. An *ecological crisis* is a serious problem (crisis) affecting plants, animals, and their environment (ecology).

- definition set off by commas. In this sentence, the underlined words define the word in **boldfaced type.**

> **Dendrologists**, or <u>people who study trees,</u> can tell a lot about weather extremes and other stresses the trees lived through.

The definition of *dendrologists* is set off by commas: "people who study trees."

Context clues are the words and sentences around a word that provide clues to its meaning.

Even when you can figure out a word from its context, it does no harm to look it up in a dictionary to verify the meaning. The dictionary definition will give you other information too, such as the origin of the word and its pronunciation.

Related Skills: 1, 2, 3, and 10

GED Readiness

Read the following sentences and circle the correct definition of each word in boldfaced type.

1 Karl is so **mercenary** that he cares more about money than family. He would sell his mother if he could make a profit.

① greedy
② angry
③ stupid
④ jealous

2 Jasmine couldn't decide whether she felt more **oppressed** by her job or by the stifling heat. She only knew that both were crushing her.

① indecisive
② challenged
③ sweaty
④ burdened

3 Olympic **track** events, from the sprint to the marathon, are great tests of an athlete's fitness.

① jumping
② running
③ throwing
④ summer

4 The **spring bulbs**, such as tulips and daffodils, are finally starting to bloom now that the temperature is warmer and the days are longer.

① bulbs that you plant in the spring
② flowers that are attached to springs
③ tulips, daffodils, and other flowers that bloom in spring
④ warm days with more sunlight

5 **Archaeology**, the study of physical evidence of past human activities, fascinates Mary Ann, who is digging for pieces of pots and jewelry in Egypt this summer.

① the study of physics
② the study of past human activities
③ the study of pots and jewelry
④ the study of physical evidence in Egypt

6 When his hands began shaking uncontrollably, Mr. Mickinak went to a **neurologist**, a doctor who treats diseases of the nervous system.

① a doctor who treats hands and feet
② an abnormality of the human nervous system
③ a patient whose hands shake
④ a doctor who specializes in the nervous system

Use context clues to figure out the meaning of each word in boldfaced type. Then write the meaning on the line.

7 **Cognitive science**, or the study of how people think and learn, is used to solve problems in many industries.

_____

8 Researchers have learned that workers can't pay attention to more than five things **consciously** at one time.

_____

9 **Disruptions** of conscious attention, such as interruptions, lead to problems.

_____

10 **Internal information**, or knowledge in the mind, is limited by memory and attention spans.

_____

11 **External information**, or knowledge in the world, reminds people of the tasks still to be done.

_____

Understanding Connotation and Denotation

Many words have two levels of meanings, their denotation and their connotation. A word's **denotation** is its basic meaning, its dictionary definition. The same word's **connotation** has to do with the positive or negative emotions the word makes us feel. Words that have the same denotation can have very different connotations.

Examples:

> The sky was silvered with clouds and the wind was brisk.
> The sky was gloomy with clouds and the wind was freezing.

Denotation is a word's basic meaning, its dictionary definition.

Connotation is the positive or negative emotions the word makes us feel.

A **euphemism** is a word with a positive connotation chosen to replace a negative one. Examples are *pre-owned* instead of *used*, *passed away* instead of *died*, and *financially challenged* instead of *broke*.

Although the denotations (the literal meanings) of both sentences are similar, their connotations are very different. The first sentence has a **positive connotation** because *silvered* and *brisk* both sound appealing. The second sentence has a **negative connotation** because *gloomy* and *freezing* both sound unpleasant.

As you read these two sentences, think about what connotation, or feeling, each sentence contains.

> He is a very determined young man.
> He is a very stubborn young man.

If you were the person being described, would you rather be called determined or stubborn? You would probably rather be called determined because the word is a compliment; it brings out positive feelings. The word *stubborn* brings out negative feelings.

Read the sentences below. Write a plus (+) next to the statement with a positive connotation and a minus (−) next to the statement with a negative connotation.

_____ Alexander Fleming discovered penicillin.

_____ Alexander Fleming stumbled onto penicillin.

The word *discovered* in the first sentence creates a more positive image than the phrase *stumbled onto* in the second sentence.

Some words are neutral. For example, if you say, "Meet me at the park," the word *park* is neither positive nor negative. It simply means "a piece of ground for ornament and recreation."

Related Skills: 4, 7, 8, 9, and 25–27

GED Readiness

Read the sentences below. Write a plus (+) next to each statement with a positive connotation, a minus (−) next to each statement with a negative connotation, and a zero (0) next to each neutral statement.

_____ **1** Anita is tongue-tied and mousy.

_____ **2** Anita is a shy, quiet person.

_____ **3** Lindsay has an overwhelming workload.

_____ **4** Lindsay has a challenging workload.

_____ **5** When her kids were at camp, Elayne experienced loneliness.

_____ **6** When her kids were at camp, Elayne experienced solitude.

_____ **7** We were served a meal last night.

_____ **8** We were served a feast last night.

Sort the following pairs of terms based on their connotations. Put the positive word from each pair in the positive connotations box (+) and the negative word from each pair in the negative connotations box (−). The first one is done for you.

arrogant, self-confident

peaceful, dull

free-spirited, unreliable

workaholic, dedicated employee

fashionable, clothes crazy

computer geek, computer expert

brave, foolhardy

moody, artistic

curious, nosy

obsessed, focused

+

self-confident

−

arrogant

Summarizing and Paraphrasing

One good way to make sure you understand the passage you are reading is to **summarize** it. A **summary** tells the main idea of a passage but leaves out most of the supporting details, so a summary is much shorter than the original passage. To summarize, ask questions like *who, what, where, when,* and *why.*

Another way to understand and retain what you read in a passage is to **paraphrase** it. When you paraphrase, you include the main idea and most of the supporting details, but you put them in simpler language. A paraphrase is nearly as long as the original passage, but it's easier to understand and remember.

Example:

> ### WHO WAS JOSEPHINE BAKER?
>
> Josephine Baker was the first African-American woman to become an international performing star. Baker was born on June 3, 1906. She became a singer and dancer who performed on stage, in movies, and on record albums. Baker refused to perform for segregated audiences. She faced so much racial prejudice in the United States that she moved to France. During World War II, she risked her life to work undercover for the French Resistance fighting the Nazis. She breathed her last in Paris in 1975 at the age of 69. She was the first American woman ever to receive French military honors at her funeral.

> **Summarizing** means telling the main idea of a passage while leaving out most of the supporting details.

> **Paraphrasing** means including not just the main idea but most of the supporting details, putting them in simpler language.

Summary: Josephine Baker was the first African-American woman to become an international singing and dancing star. To escape American racism, she moved to France where she died later at the age of 69.

Paraphrase: Josephine Baker was the first African-American woman to become an international star as a singer and dancer. Baker, who was born on June 3, 1906, would not perform for segregated audiences. She faced so much racism in the United States that she moved to France. She was a spy for the French Resistance fighting the Nazis. She died in Paris in 1975 at the age of 69 and received French military honors at her funeral.

GED Readiness

Read each passage below and circle the best summary. Then write a paraphrase of the passage. Include the main idea and important details. Be sure to state the paraphrase in your own words.

WHY DID GEORGE VI BECOME KING?

There's a saying that some people are born to greatness and others have it thrust upon them. King George VI of England never aspired to greatness. He was a shy boy who feared crowds and couldn't speak without stuttering. His brother Edward was to become king when their father died. But Edward became involved with Wallis Simpson, a woman the British government disapproved of because she was divorced and American. So Edward was forced to abdicate the throne, and George became king in time to lead his people through World War II.

❶ The best summary is

① Some people are born to greatness and others have it thrust upon them. King George VI is an example of the first kind.

② As a boy, King George VI of England was so shy that he feared crowds and couldn't speak without stuttering. He became king of England only when his brother gave up the throne.

③ George VI became king when his brother abdicated to marry a woman the British government disapproved of.

④ When his brother abdicated the throne, George VI reluctantly became king of England and led Britain to win World War II.

❷ Paraphrase:

_____

_____

_____

_____

_____

_____

WHAT IS E.T. ABOUT?

The movie E.T. has become a classic. This story of an extraterrestrial stranded on Earth is about relationships, not car chases and gun battles like so many movies about creatures from outer space. The cute little alien becomes friends with an equally cute little boy, Elliott. Along the way, the two dodge federal agents who want to study E.T. They also deal with Elliott's perplexing parents and annoying little sister. Finally, Elliott's courage and love for his alien friend help him get E.T. back to his own planet.

❸ The best summary is

① E.T. is a movie about relationships, especially that between a cute alien and a little boy who helps him get home.

② E.T. is about relationships, like those between the alien and Elliott, Elliott and his family, and E.T. and federal agents.

③ E.T. is a good movie except that it's missing the car chases and gun battles that spice up movies about creatures from outer space.

④ E.T. is a classic movie about a space alien who needs help from a little boy to dodge federal agents and get home.

❹ Paraphrase:

_____

_____

_____

_____

_____

_____

_____

Identifying Facts and Opinions

Facts

When you read critically, you analyze and question what you read. To decide whether you agree with an author, you must be able to tell which statements are facts and which are opinions. A **fact** is a statement that can be proved either by observation or by research.

Example:

> In the spring, the days grow warmer.

Opinions

Sometimes a statement can't be proved. Some people will agree with it, but others will disagree. It is an **opinion**, a statement that expresses feelings, beliefs, or personal judgments. Words like *think, believe, best, worst, wonderful,* and *should* signal opinions.

Example:

> Spring is the *most beautiful* season.

Generalizations

A **generalization,** like an opinion, is a judgment rather than a provable statement. Generalizations are false because they allow for no exceptions. Words like *all, always,* and *never* usually signal a generalization.

Example:

> *Never* trust a tall man.   *All* students should learn French.

Read the following statements. Decide which are facts, which are opinions, and which are generalizations.

> ① Pittsburgh is a beautiful city.
> ② Pittsburgh is located at the point where three rivers join.
> ③ I'd rather swim in a lake than a river.
> ④ Cities are always more interesting than small towns.
> ⑤ Pittsburgh has more bridges than any other city but Venice.

Statements ② and ⑤ are facts. These sentences can be proved. Statements ① and ③ are opinions. They state what someone *believes* is true. Statement ④ is a generalization. Notice the word *always.*

A **fact** is a statement that can be proved.

An **opinion** is a statement that expresses feelings, beliefs, or personal judgments.

A **generalization** is an opinion that allows for no exceptions.

Related Skills: 5, 8, 9, and 42

GED Readiness

Read each sentence. Write **F** for each statement of fact, **O** for each opinion, and **G** for each generalization.

① _____ Tulips are perennials—flowers that bloom again every year.

② _____ Red tulips are the most beautiful flowers.

③ _____ Jason works at a fast-food restaurant.

④ _____ George Washington lost the battle of Fort Necessity in 1754.

⑤ _____ Everyone should vote in presidential elections.

⑥ _____ An important and long overdue women's rights convention was held in Seneca Falls, New York, in 1848.

⑦ _____ Bonnie bought a gas-efficient car last month.

⑧ _____ Basketball is an exciting sport.

⑨ _____ Nobody likes brussels sprouts.

⑩ _____ The best Katherine Hepburn movie was *The Philadelphia Story*.

These statements include both facts and opinions. Rewrite them so that they express only facts.

⑪ When the Boston Red Sox won the World Series in 2004, it was the most exciting moment in baseball history. They beat the highly paid New York Yankees. They showed Yankees owner George Steinbrenner that money isn't everything.

_____

_____

_____

_____

⑫ Everyone knows that Italian food is the best. The number of different kinds of pasta dazzles the imagination. The tomatoes in spaghetti sauce are good for you because they contain lycopene, which fights cancer.

_____

_____

_____

_____

_____

⑬ Malayan sun bears live in the tropical rainforests of Sumatra. They eat insects, small rodents, and fruit. At about four feet tall, they're the smallest bears, and they're really cute.

_____

_____

_____

_____

⑭ Rembrandt van Rijn was born in 1606 in Holland. He was a talented artist who created many oil paintings, pencil sketches, and etchings. His prints about Greek myths are especially lovely.

_____

_____

_____

Detecting Bias

You can't believe everything you read. Much of what you see, from advertising to movie reviews to letters to the editor, is designed to **persuade** you. The writer wants to influence you to share his or her opinion or even to take action. This kind of writing has a **bias**, or slanted viewpoint, that the author wants you to believe.

Ads and commercials usually have a positive bias because they want you to buy the product. They often appeal to consumers' emotions and self-esteem. They don't tell you the negative side—for instance, that Glimmer doesn't work any better than a conditioner that costs half as much.

> <u>New, improved</u> Glimmer conditioner gives your hair the <u>luxurious</u> feel <u>you deserve</u>.

Persuasive writing tries to influence readers to share the writer's opinion or even to take action.

Bias is a slanted viewpoint a writer wants you to believe.

Loaded language includes words with strong positive or negative connotations. For more on connotations, see Skill 5. For more on the effects of loaded language, see Skill 9.

Biased writing may include only the facts that support its argument. Or it may include the weakest opposing arguments so it can knock them down. It often uses **loaded language**, words with strong positive or negative connotations. In a political campaign, each candidate may claim that he is "flexible" but his opponent is a "flip-flopper." Both words mean the same thing; they just have opposite connotations. Or one candidate may say she is "focused," while her opponent calls her "obsessed with unimportant details."

What does the following ad want you to believe? Underline words and phrases that show you the ad's positive or negative bias.

> ### Do Twice the Work in Half the Time with the Amazing New Think Software!
>
> Are you tired of working long hours at your computer? Don't you deserve a life? Try Think! This new software practically reads your mind. It's so efficient it will free up hours every week for you to escape your desk. At only $100, it'll be the best investment you've ever made.

Did you underline *half the time, amazing, new, you deserve a life, efficient, free up hours, escape your desk,* and *best investment ever?* This ad paints a tempting picture, but it doesn't say exactly what's new and amazing about the software. It doesn't tell you how it works so you can judge for yourself whether it would save you time. The writer hopes you'll get so caught up in its bias that you forget about the facts.

GED Readiness

Read the ad and answer the questions that follow.

**Senators, Err on the side of Life.
Don't make it easier for killers to get guns.**

While gunshots still echo around Red Lake and Milwaukee and Atlanta and speeches lauding "The Culture of Life" still echo around the halls of Congress, the Senate is nearing a vote on a bill backed by the National Rifle Association that will make it easier for killers and terrorists to get their hands on guns.

This bill, S.397, destroys the best deterrent society has against reckless gun dealers who put murder weapons in killers' hands. It destroys the right of victims to hold those reckless dealers accountable for their acts.

Tell your Senators: Practice what you preach. If every life is precious then how do we value the 30,000 lives that will be lost to gun violence this year?

Vote No on S.397.

Call your Senators at 202-224-3121. Tell them to cast their vote on the side of Life.

—Brady Campaign to Prevent Gun Violence,
Washington Post

1 Write three examples of loaded language in this ad.

_____

_____

_____

2 Write two facts you find in the ad.

_____

_____

3 Who does the headline say the ad is addressed to? Who do the last two lines say it's addressed to?

_____

_____

4 What opinion is the ad trying to persuade you to hold?

_____

_____

5 What action is the ad trying to persuade you to take?

_____

_____

Read the following sentences. Circle the words and phrases that show bias. Then write whether the bias is positive or negative.

6 WQAZ: Where to tune for the coolest tunes

_____

7 Jeb Smith is stuck on tired old solutions to Eatonville's modern problems.

_____

8 Maria Halma has the courage to fight City Hall and the experience to run our city.

_____

9 Reward your taste buds with Fizz cola.

_____

Evaluating an Argument

Evaluating a persuasive argument means judging for yourself whether it works or not. Does it use convincing facts to support the writer's opinions? Those facts may include **statistics**, **examples**, or **reasons**. Suppose a writer believes the government should do a better job of protecting people's privacy. That's just an opinion. To convince you, the writer must offer evidence. She might cite these facts: 1) Companies that collect your social security number, spending habits, and entertainment choices sell this data for millions of dollars. 2) Identity thieves have stolen data on thousands of people from these agencies.

A persuasive argument should also avoid these **errors in reasoning**.

- The **either/or fallacy** claims there are only two alternatives, when there are usually several. For example: "You can either spank your kids or let them push you around." However, there are other methods of disciplining children.
- **Circular reasoning** repeats the same statement in different words. For example: "Reading nutrition labels is important because you should know what's in the food you eat." Reading the nutrition label is the same as knowing what's in the food.
- **False analogies** compare two things that aren't really alike. For example: "Being married is like being in jail." Marriage and jail aren't at all alike.
- **Loaded language** (words with strong positive or negative connotations) should never be used to conceal the weakness of an argument. For example: "The mayor is a moron, and this is the worst idea he's ever had." Calling the mayor a moron does not explain why this idea is bad.

What errors in reasoning can you find in the following passage?

> (1) This neighborhood has gone downhill. (2) Dealers sell drugs on the street, and gunshots ring out every night. (3) The police take an hour to respond. (4) All politicians are lying hypocrites. (5) Our kids don't feel secure because they don't know what it's like to feel safe. (6) Our only choices are to move out or start carrying guns ourselves.

Sentence (4) misuses loaded language (and a generalization). To fix it, specify one or two politicians and give examples of their lies. Sentence (5) is circular reasoning. Add a real reason why the kids don't feel secure. If you move sentences (2) and (3) after this statement, you would show the reasons. Sentence (6) is an either/or fallacy. Other options include starting a neighborhood watch, pressuring the police department to patrol the streets more often, and voting for politicians who will invest in neighborhood protection.

Evaluating what you read means judging for yourself whether it works or not.

Statistics, examples, and **reasons** are types of facts writers can use to support their opinions.

Errors in reasoning include the either/or fallacy, circular reasoning, false analogies, and loaded language.

Related Skills: 5, 7, and 8

GED Readiness

Read the passage and identify the error in reasoning in each quoted statement.

HOW IMPORTANT IS MUSIC?

(1) A battle rages on between people who believe that music classes in schools are unimportant frills and those who believe that music is as important as reading, writing, and arithmetic.

(2) People who don't see the importance of music are idiots without a spark of creativity in their souls. (3) Music classes are important because they expose students to all kinds of music.

(4) "Music directly affects the oldest part of our brain, where instinct, intuition, memory, creativity, and emotion begin," explains teacher Bob Vogelsang. (5) "Have you ever come home after a hard day and put on some soothing music, or gone out dancing on a Friday and found you had twice as much energy as you thought?"

(6) Music has a huge effect on people's moods. (7) It can calm them and lower their blood pressure—or it can invigorate them, as marching music is designed to do. (8) It can get through to people with such severe cases of Alzheimer's that they no longer recognize their family members. (9) It can reach children who have been traumatized.

(10) Some studies show that singing songs, beating on a drum, or listening to classical music makes children more receptive to therapy. (11) The Australian Music Association studied the effects of music lessons in schools. (12) After eight months, students' spatial IQs had increased by nearly 50 percent. (13) Spatial IQ is an important component of the higher brain functions necessary for complex tasks like higher mathematics.

(14) Cutting music classes to save money is like cutting off your children's hands so you don't need to buy them gloves. (15) It's clear that music is important. (16) We can either take money from the athletic budget to fund music or we can just give up on our kids.

1 "People who don't see the importance of music are idiots without a spark of creativity in their souls." (sentence 2)

① either/or fallacy
② circular reasoning
③ false analogy
④ loaded language

2 "Music classes are important because they expose students to all kinds of music." (sentence 3)

① either/or fallacy
② circular reasoning
③ false analogy
④ loaded language

3 "Cutting music classes to save money is like cutting off your children's hands so you don't need to buy them gloves." (sentence 14)

① either/or fallacy
② circular reasoning
③ false analogy
④ loaded language

4 "We can either take money from the athletic budget to fund music or we can just give up on our kids." (sentence 16)

① either/or fallacy
② circular reasoning
③ false analogy
④ loaded language

5 Did the passage convince you that music is important? Why or why not? Cite specific facts from the passage that affected your opinion either for or against music classes.

_____

_____

_____

_____

10

Making Predictions

A skill you already have that can improve your reading is predicting. **Making predictions** means thinking ahead to make educated guesses about what will happen next based on your observations and your life experiences. If you're driving down the street and your *Check Engine* light comes on, and then you hear a loud rattling, you can reasonably predict that your car is about to break down. If you've lived through this before, you may also predict that soon you'll be writing a big check to the car mechanic.

When you're watching a horror movie and you think, "Don't go down into the basement!" you're making a prediction: If the teenage girl goes down into the basement (or out of the house or into the cemetery), something bad is going to happen to her. Predicting what will happen next makes watching a movie or reading a story more exciting.

When making predictions, use what you know to guess what will come next. Look for

- clues that suggest what will happen next in a series of events (chronological order)
- clues that state causes and suggest possible effects or that state effects and suggest causes
- clues that suggest how a person will behave in a given situation

Making predictions uses the same abilities as drawing conclusions (Skill 3). The difference is that you draw conclusions about what's happening now or to try to figure out what already happened. You make predictions about what will happen in the future.

Read the passage below and predict what will happen. Underline the clues that help you figure it out.

> A woman walks into an art studio. She puts on a smock. She squeezes several colors of oil paints onto a palette and puts brushes of different sizes in a glass of water. She smiles and sits down in front of an easel with a blank canvas on it.

Did you predict that the woman would start painting a picture? Did you underline the clues *art studio, smock, oil paints, palette, brushes, easel,* and *blank canvas?*

> **Making predictions** means making educated guesses about what will happen next based on your observations and your past experiences.

Related Skills: 3, 11, and 12

GED Readiness

Read the passage. Then write your answers to the questions, predicting what will happen next.

WILL ANNA LEARN ENGLISH?

Anna had trouble in school. She possessed no background in English. The teacher explained to Tian that she seemed afraid of the other children, stood apart and watched their gestures and expressions as if she could not hear.

The failure was all mine. I buried myself in Chinese novels and read the Chinese newspaper; my Chinese had formed a brick wall in my mind and only short sentences and stray phrases of English could slip through the cracks. I vowed to study my old books. I would sit for hours staring at the simple sentences on the page. *The butter is on the table. The cat is under the bed.* But none of the new words I learned seemed able to express my thoughts—I felt as if, in order to speak English, I would have to change the climate of my soul, the flavor of my tongue. I told Tian to speak to the girls in English, which he did when he had the time, but often, when he returned from a difficult day at work, we would lapse into Chinese at the dinner table, exhausted and relieved, as if we were falling into each other's arms.

Eventually the problem solved itself. One afternoon, Anna came home from school and I greeted her at the door as usual, asked her about her day. But her eyes darted past me to focus on her sister. Ruth stood behind me, a necklace of purple plastic beads dangling from her fist. They were Anna's beads. We had bought one necklace for each, pink for Ruth and purple for Anna, but Ruth had misplaced hers almost immediately.

Anna had walked out the door that morning with her "school face" on—nervous and withdrawn, a mute child. But now she stood rigid, transformed by rage.

"That's mine!" she cried. I stopped in the middle of locking the door; the English words sounded so fierce and strange as she claimed them.

"No!" Ruth cried right back at her in English. "Mine!"

—Excerpted from "Hunger"
by Lan Samantha Chang

1 What language will Anna speak at school from now on?

_____

2 What language will Ruth speak?

_____

3 What will happen to Anna's grades in school?

_____

4 Will their mother learn English? Why or why not?

_____

Read the following passages and circle the number of the most logical prediction.

5 Mona lets her cat, Luna, out of the house. Luna notices a squirrel under a maple tree. Luna slowly creeps across the yard. Two feet away from the squirrel, she crouches and watches the squirrel as it nibbles on some maple seeds. Suddenly Luna tenses up and her tail begins to twitch. What will happen next?

 ① Luna will fall asleep.
 ② The squirrel will attack Luna.
 ③ Luna will attack the squirrel.
 ④ It will begin to rain.

6 In the 1930s, the Great Plains of the Midwest was hit by droughts and dust storms. Farmers had to abandon their land because crops would not grow. Millions of people had no work and no food. They heard that farming was easy in California, where it was warm and sunny most of the time. As a result,

 ① they decided to give up farming
 ② they learned new irrigation techniques
 ③ they got jobs in the movie industry
 ④ they headed for California

11 Using Chronological Order

There are many ways a piece of writing may be organized. Nonfiction writing like how-to articles and recipes may be written in **chronological order,** or sequence. Most stories are told in chronological order—the time order in which events happened.

Understanding the order in which events happen is important to understanding anything you read. As you read, ask yourself: What happens first? next? after that? Look for **clue words** like *first, next, before, after, then,* and *finally.* For example, Thursday comes *before* Friday. Five is the number *after* four. Picture in your mind the events or steps described.

Read the passage below. Think about *when* the events happen. Underline the clue words that help you figure out the chronological order of events.

> ### WILL LUPE FIND A JOB?
>
> As soon as Lupe got her diploma, she started looking for a better job. She was tired of scrubbing other people's floors. First she went to career counseling at a local college. The counselor helped her figure out what she wanted to do. It turned out that her hobby, making wreaths out of dried flowers, could become a job. Second, the counselor helped Lupe create a resumé and make a list of companies within thirty miles of her town that might be interested in hiring her. Next, Lupe took photos of some of her best craft projects and sent copies to the five companies she liked best. She included her resumé and a cover letter. Two of the companies called her in for interviews the following week. One was a florist, Meg Brown. Meg asked if Lupe could make dried flower baskets and other crafts. Lupe said yes, and finally she was hired.

Did you underline *As soon as, First, turned out, Second, Next, the following week,* and *finally?* Those clue words make it easier to understand the way things happened in the story.

Chronological order means the time order in which events happen.

Clue words like *first, next, before, after, then,* and *finally* help show the time order of events and actions.

Other ways to organize written material:
cause and effect (Skill 12),
comparison and contrast (Skill 13), and
order of importance (Skill 14)

Related Skills: 12, 13, and 14

GED Readiness

Read the passage and answer the questions.

WHAT HAS WANGARI MAATHAI DONE?

Parts of Africa that used to be forests are turning into deserts for two reasons: forests were cleared and replaced with plantations, and wood was most families' only source of fuel for cooking and heating. As trees were cut down, women had to walk miles every day to gather enough firewood to cook dinner. A biologist named Wangari Maathai noticed the problem and came up with a solution.

In 1976 she became chair of the National Council of Women of Kenya. In 1977 she started the Green Belt Movement. Local people (90 percent of them women) began planting trees. In less than thirty years, they have planted 30 million trees, which provide fuel, food, shelter, and income for the poorest residents of Kenya's countryside. The trees also improve soil and water quality. In recognition of her work, Maathai won the Better World Society Award in 1986, the Hunger Project's Africa Prize for Leadership in 1992, and the Global 500 Award from the United Nations Environmental Protection Agency in 1997.

But the Green Belt Movement has had an even bigger impact: It encouraged Kenyans to demand a democracy. In 2002, Kenya made a peaceful transition to a democratic government. Maathai was elected to Parliament that year. Soon after that, the new president appointed her Kenya's vice minister of the environment.

Her work has spread successfully to many other African countries. In 2004, she won the Nobel Peace Prize for her contribution to social justice, democracy, environmental sustainability, and peace.

"Today we are faced with a challenge that calls for a shift in our thinking, so that humanity stops threatening its life-support system," Maathai said in her Nobel Prize acceptance speech. "We are called to assist the Earth to heal her wounds and in the process heal our own."

1 What did Wangari Maathai do in 1977?

_____

_____

2 After what events did women have to walk miles to gather firewood?

_____

_____

3 What recognition did Maathai receive in 1992?

_____

4 What happened in Kenya in 2002?

_____

_____

5 What jobs did Maathai get in 2002?

_____

6 When did Maathai win the Nobel Peace Prize?

_____

_____

Number the events from the passage in the time order in which they occur.

7 _____ The Green Belt Movement spread to other countries.

_____ Kenya adopted a democratic government.

_____ Forests were cleared and replaced with plantations.

_____ Maathai won the Nobel Peace Prize.

_____ The Green Belt Movement began.

_____ Maathai became chair of the National Council of Women of Kenya.

12 Recognizing Cause and Effect

Writing is often organized in a cause-and-effect pattern. A **cause** is an action or event that brings about other actions or events. An **effect** is the outcome of an action or event. Sometimes a cause-and-effect relationship is stated directly. Other times it is implied. It's important when you read that you understand the reasons why things happen and the effects that stem from them.

If you can use the word *because* to show that two events or facts are related, that means they have a cause-and-effect relationship.

| effect | signal word | cause |

The kitchen floor was sticky because Ted spilled juice on it.

A cause may have more than one effect.

| **Cause** | **Effects** |
| A snowstorm hit late in the spring. | There were many car accidents. The price of orange juice rose. Fruits and flowers froze. |

An effect may result from several causes.

| **Causes** | **Effect** |
| Amber had to work Friday night. Jorge had the flu. | Last week's poker game was canceled. |

Read the following passage. What causes are mentioned? What are their effects? What **signal words** give you a clue?

WHY WAS BAMIYAN AN IMPORTANT KINGDOM?

Fifteen hundred years ago, Bamiyan was a wealthy kingdom because it controlled access over the high mountain passes to trade routes from China, India, and Persia. A ruler of Bamiyan was Buddhist, so he built two huge statues of Buddha. The statues, 180 and 125 feet tall, were carved into a cliff. People came from all over the world to see them. They also came to buy and sell goods at the bazaar, which offered exotic fare like spices from India and silks from China.

The first cause mentioned is that Bamiyan controlled trade routes. The effect is that Bamiyan was wealthy. The signal word in that sentence is *because*.

The next cause is that a ruler was Buddhist; the effect is that he built two statues of Buddha. The signal word there is *so*.

Two causes (the statues and the bazaar) are given for the effect that people came from all over the world to visit Bamiyan. No signal word is used there.

A **cause** is an action or event that brings about other actions or events.

An **effect** is the outcome of an action or event.

Signal words that show a cause-and-effect relationship include *because, therefore, so, as a result, in order to,* and *if/then.*

Related Skills: 2, 4, 11, 13, and 14

GED Readiness

Read the passage. The write the answers to the questions that follow.

WHAT CAUSED THE JOHNSTOWN FLOOD?

On May 31, 1889, a huge flood nearly washed away Johnstown, a mill town located in a valley in southwestern Pennsylvania. More than 2,200 people were killed and thousands more were injured. The cleanup took five years, and bodies were still being found years after the flood.

How did this tragedy happen? The fact that it rained hard for two solid days was a factor. But more important was the fact that the dam of a manmade lake in the hills 14 miles above the town gave way. The entire lake, over 20 million tons of water, rushed through the breach. The water couldn't spread out because it was channeled through a narrow mountain pass. The 36-foot-high wall of water rolled over Johnstown at 40 miles an hour, destroying everything in its path.

The dam was part of an exclusive resort called the South Fork Fishing and Hunting Club, which was run by some of the richest, most powerful men in America. During the ten years they owned the club, they did little to maintain the South Fork Dam, which at 72 feet high and 900-plus feet long was one of the biggest earthen dams in the world. In fact, they weakened the dam by cutting its height so there was room for two carriages to pass each other driving across its top. They failed to build up the dam's center, as their own engineer had recommended. They ignored the fears of the townsfolk, who were mostly immigrant millworkers who made less than $10 a week.

All of the club members survived the flood. About one-fifth of the residents of Johnstown perished. Many more died in later weeks of a typhoid epidemic that swept through the area due to crowded conditions and lack of sanitation.

1 What caused the dam's failure?

_____

2 What were the results of the flood?

_____

3 What was the main reason the resort's owners ignored Johnstown residents' concerns?

_____

4 What caused the typhoid epidemic?

_____

Read each sentence. Then circle the correct answers to the questions.

5 Which of the following caused the other events to happen?

① Amy had to throw out all her frozen food.
② Amy stayed home from work to wait for the repairman.
③ Amy's refrigerator broke down.
④ Amy couldn't afford any extras that month.

6 Which of the following was caused by the other events?

① Ben was up very late the night before.
② Ben hit the Off button instead of the Snooze button.
③ Ben was late for work.
④ Ben woke up an hour later than usual.

7 Which of the following caused the other events to happen?

① A devastating tsunami hit Southeast Asia.
② An earthquake occurred under the Indian Ocean.
③ The shift pushed vast amounts of water ahead of it.
④ The quake made the ocean floor shift vertically.

8 Which of the following was caused by the other events?

① A Swiss chemist developed DDT.
② Condors nearly became extinct.
③ Many countries began using DDT in quantity to kill insects.
④ DDT thinned eggshells so much that the birds in them died.

Recognizing Comparison and Contrast

Writers examine two or more things or ideas by comparing and contrasting them. When you **compare**, you tell how the things are alike. When you **contrast**, you tell how they are different. This pattern is often used in writing that gives readers advice: which car to buy, which book to read, which place to go on vacation. It's important to understand the likenesses and differences between things when you read.

One way to picture comparison and contrast is with a Venn diagram like the one below. The place where the two circles intersect shows the subjects' similarities (comparison). The places where the circles are separate show the subjects' differences (contrast).

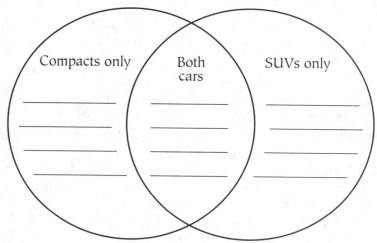

Which Car Should You Buy?

| Compacts only | Both cars | SUVs only |

Comparing two or more things means telling how they are alike.

Contrasting two or more things means telling how they are different.

Signal words like *also*, *likewise*, and *similarly* show a comparison. Words and phrases like *although*, *however*, *in contrast*, *on the contrary*, and *on the other hand* show a contrast.

Read the passage below and write the similarities in the center of the Venn diagram. Place the differences on either side of the diagram.

WHICH CAR SHOULD YOU BUY?

If you're shopping for a car, this is the year for a compact. They're the least expensive vehicles on the market, they're easy to park, and they get great gas mileage (an important consideration when gas prices are through the roof). On the other hand, SUVs are luxurious. They come with special features like DVD players. They have room for big families. They protect you better in an accident. Of course, either vehicle will get you where you're going.

You should have listed *inexpensive, easy to park, and great mileage* under "Compacts only." *Luxurious, features like DVD players, room for big families,* and *protect you in an accident* should be listed under "SUVs only." *Get you where you're going* belongs under "Both cars."

GED Readiness

Read the following passage. Then circle the correct answers.

HOW IS ALL LIFE ON EARTH SIMILAR?

A segmented worm seems radically different in shape, function, and form from a hydrangea plant, or an ocelot, or a college swim team. We picture life on earth as a feast of wildly distinct entities, but on the molecular level, they differ very little. They have cells, organs, fluids that contain similar stuffs, perform similar functions. Earth's chemicals can cancel, inflame, dilute, calm, deflect one another—as pigments do when you mix them—because, essentially, they're all composed of the same raw materials. A chimpanzee seems radically different from a human; but our genes differ from theirs by less than 1.6 percent. There is a deep-down kinship among all living things, not just spiritually, or morally, or through some accident of our being neighbors, but physically, functionally, in our habits, in our hungers, in our genes. Our common ancestor was life, and, at that, a rare form—earthlife—which developed its own basic shapes, symbioses, and motives. That will always make us more closely related to a panda than a stone.

—Excerpted from *The Rarest of the Rare* by Diane Ackerman

1 What two major categories of things are contrasted in this paragraph?

① worms and hydrangeas
② cells and organs
③ chimpanzees and humans
④ living things and nonliving things

2 How are segmented worms and hydrangeas alike?

① in shape
② in motives
③ in form
④ in molecules

3 How are chimps and humans alike?

① Their genes are nearly identical.
② They both eat worms.
③ They both fear ocelots.
④ Their habits are similar.

4 What is the author's main point?

① All living things are radically different in shape.
② All living things have more in common than we think.
③ All living things are wildly distinct.
④ All living things have something in common with stones.

For each pair, circle the details that tell how they are alike. Underline details that show how they are different.

5 an amusement park and the seashore

gravity-defying rides   family fun
relaxation   watching fish

6 seals and sharks

fish   ocean dwelling
covered with hair   good swimmer

7 playing baseball and watching baseball

rooting for your team   getting a workout
eating hot dogs   cheering home runs

8 Chicago and San Diego

big city   cold in winter
near Mexico   crowded highways

9 paint and varnish

comes in all colors   highlights wood grain
goes on drywall   is applied with a brush

10 soft drink and orange juice

quenches thirst   contains Vitamin C
rots teeth   has no nutrients

11 sandals and boots

protect from snow   come in different sizes
go on feet   are comfy in warm weather

12 crocuses and chrysanthemums

bloom in spring   flowers
have petals   bloom in fall

Using Order of Degree

To better understand a piece of writing, notice how it is organized. One of the most flexible methods of organization is **order of degree**, which is any form of arrangement or ranking. For example, ranking might be

- from most to least important
- from least to most useful
- from most to least familiar
- from least to most expensive
- from least to most popular
- from simplest to most complex
- from nearest to farthest
- from biggest to smallest
- from oldest to youngest

The topic and the goal of the writing determine what order the author uses. Starting with the most important (or most useful or most familiar) item hooks readers' attention, but ending with the most important is more persuasive. It's the point readers remember best. The author uses the order he or she believes to be most effective.

Transitional words signal that a piece of writing is using order of degree. They include *first, second, mainly, also, furthermore, finally,* and *ultimately.*

Read the passage below and identify how it is organized. Circle the transitional words the author used.

> **Order of degree** is any form of arrangement or ranking that suits the topic (for example, from most to least important).

> **Transitional words** include *first, second, mainly, also, furthermore, finally,* and *ultimately.*

HOW MANY CHILDREN DO THEY HAVE?

Linda and Haider have four children. First there's Taneesha, who is twenty years old. She's studying business administration. Next is George. He's eighteen and on his high school basketball team. Yvette is fifteen and a talented artist. Finally, the baby of the family is Jimmy. He's ten, and all he cares about is soccer.

Note that the example is organized by the children's ages—from oldest to youngest. It might have been organized from youngest to oldest. It might have been organized by interests (in which case the two athletes would be discussed together). It might even have been organized by gender (in which the girls might be mentioned first and then the boys, or vice versa). However, age is a logical way to organize a paragraph about the members of a family.

You should have located three transitional words: *First, Next,* and *Finally.*

Related Skills: 7, 11, 12, 13, and 16

GED Readiness

Read the following passage. Notice how it is organized. Then circle the correct answers.

WHAT QUALITIES MUST A STEAMBOAT PILOT HAVE?

A steamboat pilot must have a memory, but there are two much higher qualities which he must also have. He must have good, quick judgment and decision, and a cool, calm courage that no peril can shake. Give a man the merest trifle of pluck [courage] to start with, and by the time he has become a pilot he cannot be unmanned by any danger a steamboat can get into; but one cannot quite say the same for judgment. Judgment is a matter of brains, and a man must start with a good stock of that article or he will never succeed as a pilot.

—Excerpted from *Life on the Mississippi* by Mark Twain

1 What does Twain say is the least important quality a steamboat pilot must have?

  ① memory
  ② courage
  ③ judgment
  ④ calmness

2 What is the most important quality a steamboat pilot must have?

  ① memory
  ② courage
  ③ judgment
  ④ calmness

3 How much courage does a pilot need to start with?

  ① enough to be unshakable
  ② the merest trifle of it
  ③ none; he can acquire it later
  ④ a good stock of it

Read the following topics and determine which way of organizing them is most appropriate.

4 a list of top ten tourist destinations

  ① most to least popular
  ② biggest to smallest
  ③ oldest to youngest
  ④ most to least familiar

5 a description of tools a carpenter needs

  ① biggest to smallest
  ② most to least familiar
  ③ nearest to farthest
  ④ most to least useful

6 an article about the planets in our solar system

  ① most to least important
  ② oldest to youngest
  ③ simplest to most complex
  ④ nearest to farthest from the sun

7 an analysis of six car models

  ① newest to oldest
  ② most to least familiar
  ③ least to most expensive
  ④ simplest to most complex

8 a report about diseases

  ① most to least familiar
  ② most to least dangerous
  ③ least to most popular
  ④ simplest to most complex

9 a warning about endangered animals

  ① oldest to youngest
  ② most to least familiar
  ③ most to least important
  ④ least to most complex

Understanding Homonyms

As used on the GED test, a **homonym** is a word that sounds the same as another but is spelled differently. However, homonym is also a term that includes both homophones and homographs.

Homophones are words that are pronounced the same way, or nearly the same way, but are different in meaning and spelling. The meanings of some common homophones are listed below.

accept	receive willingly
except	with the exclusion of
brake	a device for stopping
break	to cut, crush, or otherwise separate
it's	contraction for *it is*
its	belonging to it
passed	went beyond
past	time gone by
their	belonging to them
there	in that place
they're	contraction for *they are*
to	toward
too	also, very
two	2
who's	contraction for *who is*
whose	possessive form of *who*
your	belonging to you
you're	contraction for *you are*

Homographs are words that are spelled alike but are different in meaning and often in pronunciation. The meanings and pronunciations of some common homographs are listed below.

bow (bō)	used to shoot an arrow
bow (baü)	forward part of a ship
console (kȧn´ sōl)	cabinet
console (kən sōl´)	ease someone's grief
buffet (bə fā´)	self-serve meal
buffet (bə´ fət)	strike
bark (bärk)	tree covering
bark (bärk)	sound a dog makes

You may need to use a dictionary for the meanings and pronunciations of homonyms if you are not sure which spelling or pronunciation to use.

Homonym is a term that includes both homophones and homographs.

Homophones are words that are pronounced the same way but are different in meaning and spelling.

Homographs are words that are spelled the same way but are different in meaning and often in pronunciation.

GED Readiness

Circle the homonym in parentheses that correctly completes each sentence.

1. Amanda is a model; the guiding (principal, principle) of her diet is, if it tastes good, spit it out.

2. Poison ivy doesn't (affect, effect) Ben at all.

3. I was (board, bored) to tears last night. Remind me never to go to one of Bob's parties again.

4. Dale went to the building (sight, site) to take some measurements.

5. Why don't you (by, buy) your mother some flowers?

6. My daughter can't decide (weather, whether) she wants to be a doctor or a firefighter.

7. Jason rides his (stationary, stationery) bike for thirty minutes a day.

8. Ron's cousin is playing the (role, roll) of Emily in the school play.

9. Dr. Wang is seeing too many (patience, patients) this week while her colleagues are on vacation.

10. The salad and the main course usually (precede, proceed) dessert, but John likes to eat his ice cream first.

11. Liza would like to borrow (your, you're) new pen.

12. Mom says (its, it's) time to go now.

13. Be careful that you don't (break, brake) your leg sliding down that hill.

14. Radash (passed, past) her physical with flying colors

15. Jeff and Jasmine have dinner with (their, they're) kids nearly every night.

16. Do you know (whose, who's) singing the solo at the concert?

Each pair of sentences contains a pair of homographs. Write the meaning for each homograph.

17. a. Mac likes to go **bass** fishing.

_____

b. Josh plays **bass** in a rock band.

_____

18. a. If you wait a **minute** or two, the cat will come to you.

_____

b. The materials my fly-fishing cousin uses to tie flies are so **minute** I can hardly hold them.

_____

19. a. Do you know Hank's **address?**

_____

b. The president of the Civic Club will **address** the group at the Monday meeting.

_____

20. a. Melanie gave Daniel a really nice **present** for Father's Day.

_____

b. Senator Patel, I'd like to **present** my brother, Jamal.

_____

16 Identifying Author's Purpose

Good writing always has a purpose. An **author's purpose** is his or her reason or goal for writing. Identifying an author's purpose helps a reader understand and evaluate a piece of writing. It also helps the reader respond appropriately. For example, if a humor writer describing a trip to Nebraska says the average temperature there is fifty degrees below zero, don't bother writing him a letter to point out that the average temperature is much higher than that. The author knows that; he was exaggerating to make a humorous, entertaining point.

There are many possible purposes for writing, but the most common are the following:

- to entertain
- to inform
- to describe
- to explain or instruct
- to persuade or express an opinion
- to evoke a mood

Many pieces of writing serve more than one purpose. For example, an amusing essay designed mainly to entertain may have a serious message, too. An article persuading you to vote may also inform you of the time and location of voting places.

Read the passage below. What is its main purpose? What is its secondary purpose?

> ### WHO WAS CHARLOTTE GILMAN?
>
> One of the most important writers in American history is too little known today. Charlotte Perkins Gilman lived from 1860 to 1935, and she devoted her life to writing and thinking about how to make the world a better place. One of her best stories is "Herland," about an ideal world. We need to reclaim this great writer and her work.

Did you recognize that the main purpose of this passage is to persuade? The author wants to convince readers that Gilman is an important writer and encourage them to read her work. The secondary purpose is to inform readers of facts about Gilman, like when she lived and the name of one of her short stories.

An **author's purpose** is his or her reason for writing. Common purposes are to entertain, inform, describe, explain or instruct, persuade, or evoke a mood.

Related Skills: 8, 9, 17. and 41

GED Readiness

Read each passage. Then circle the correct answers.

WHO TALKS MORE—MEN OR WOMEN?

Women are believed to talk too much. Yet study after study finds that it is men who talk more—at meetings, in mixed-group discussions, and in classrooms where girls or young women sit next to boys or young men. For example, communication researchers Barbara and Gene Eakins tape-recorded and studied seven university faculty meetings. They found that, with one exception, men spoke more often and, without exception, spoke for a longer time. The men's turns ranged from 10.66 to 17.07 seconds, while the women's turns ranged from 3 to 10 seconds. In other words, the women's longest turns were still shorter than the men's shortest turns.

—Excerpted from *You Just Don't Understand: Women and Men in Conversation* by Deborah Tannen

1 What is the main purpose of this passage?

1. to entertain
2. to inform
3. to explain or instruct
4. to evoke a mood

2 How do you know what the main purpose is?

1. The author describes her own personal experience.
2. The author reveals her anger at men who talk too much.
3. The author finds men's conversational styles amusing.
4. The author presents facts and statistics.

3 What is the passage's secondary purpose?

1. to persuade readers that women don't talk more than men
2. to inform readers that scientists study talk patterns
3. to describe a particular faculty meeting
4. to entertain readers with visions of chatty men

HOW DO YOU CHOOSE THE RIGHT ONE?

My parents didn't seem to have much advice to share on the topic of love. They did, however, view each and every potential love candidate of mine as though they were scrutinizing a police artist's sketch of a suspect. "Officer, I don't think that's him," their frozen faces would say. . . .

Once I no longer had my parents' authority to answer to, my own approach to love and relationships became simple: When I met a guy I kind of liked, I would follow him toward a cup of coffee. And if that seemed to go pretty well, I would live with him for three years.

—Excerpted from *Merrill Markoe's Guide to Love* by Merrill Markoe

4 What is the main purpose of this passage?

1. to entertain
2. to inform
3. to describe
4. to persuade

5 How do you know what the main purpose is?

1. The author gives good advice about love.
2. The author exaggerates to make situations funny.
3. The author provides facts and statistics.
4. The author wants to persuade readers to move in with someone on the first date.

ARE SCENTS IMPORTANT?

As Luis walked into the kitchen, the scents of desserts in progress wafted through the air. He smelled vanilla and cinnamon and caramel. Strongest of all was the aroma of chocolate. He closed his eyes and sniffed, and he was transported back to his mother's kitchen on Sunday afternoons.

6 What is the main purpose of this passage?

1. to persuade
2. to express an opinion
3. to inform
4. to describe

Identifying Author's Point of View

Some factual writing is purely informational. The author is neutral. He or she does not state or imply an opinion, or **point of view**, about the topic. However, in much writing, especially writing intended to persuade, authors reveal their points of view.

Sometimes that point of view is stated **explicitly**. A restaurant critic might describe a meal as "heavenly," or a reviewer might say a movie is "horrible." Other times the viewpoint is **implicit**, and readers must infer the author's opinion. For example, the restaurant critic might say, "It was the kind of evening you remember forever" to imply that she enjoyed herself. The reviewer might say the movie was "two hours out of my life I'll never get back" to imply that he didn't like it and suggest that you probably wouldn't either.

Read the following passages about bats.

> ### HOW DOES THE AUTHOR FEEL ABOUT BATS?
>
> There are 44 species of bats in the United States and nearly 1,000 in the world. Most bats are tiny, weighing less than two ounces. They live largely on insects. In fact, one bat can eat 600 mosquitoes in an hour. Bats rest during the day and hunt insects at night. They are flying mammals. They either hibernate or migrate for the winter.

This first passage is neutral. It provides information about bats without telling you how the author feels about them. The author does not have a point of view.

> ### HOW DOES THE AUTHOR FEEL ABOUT BATS?
>
> Above me, free-tailed bats circle the flames like moths. Moths frighten me. I hate their addiction to light. But bats delight in darkness with their eyes wide open. What do they hear that I am missing? Gifted in the location of echoes, they listen twice to all that is spoken in the desert. They are dark angels who register our longings.
>
> —Excerpted from *Desert Quartet* by Terry Tempest Williams

This passage has a positive point of view. The author contrasts her positive feelings about bats with her negative feelings about moths. She uses words with positive connotations, like *delight*, *gifted*, and *angels* to describe bats. The author's point of view is that bats are fascinating.

An **author's point of view** is the opinion he or she states or implies about the topic.

An **explicit** point of view is one that the author clearly states.

An **implicit** point of view is one that readers must infer from what the author's words suggest.

Related Skills: 5, 7, 8, and 9

GED Readiness

Read each passage. Then circle the correct answer for each question.

HOW DOES THE AUTHOR FEEL ABOUT CRAIG FERGUSON?

A fairly recent entry in the late-night talk shows is Craig Ferguson, a transplanted Scotsman. Ferguson is less well known than the competitor in his time slot, Conan O'Brien, but look for that to change. He's getting high-profile guests, he has great comedic timing, and unlike most hosts, he seems genuinely interested in what his guests have to say. If you have to get up early to go to work, his deep voice with its soft Scottish burr is just the thing to send you to sleep—if you can stop laughing long enough. Ferguson gets an A.

1 What attitude does the author express toward Craig Ferguson?

  ① neutral
  ② implicitly positive
  ③ explicitly positive
  ④ implicitly negative

2 The author uses words that make Ferguson sound

  ① inexperienced
  ② entertaining
  ③ bored
  ④ boring

HOW DOES THE AUTHOR FEEL ABOUT HIS LAND?

We want to keep this single wooded slope of land in the West undeveloped and uncut. We want to pass it on like a well-read book, not the leavings of someone's meal. . . .

Sandra and I know we do not own these 35 acres. The Oregon ash trees by the river, in whose limbs I have seen flocks of 100 Audubon's warblers, belong also to the families in Guatemala in whose forests these birds winter. The bereavement I feel at the diminishment of life around me is also a bereavement felt by men and women and children I don't know, living in cities I've never visited.

—Excerpted from "Caring for the Woods" by Barry Lopez

3 Which words express the author's attitude toward cutting down forests?

  ① a well-read book
  ② ash trees, warblers
  ③ bereavement, leavings
  ④ cities I've never visited

4 The author implies that

  ① logging is like littering
  ② he and his wife rent their house
  ③ Guatemalans visit him often
  ④ he longs to travel to cities

Rewrite each passage twice. First use words and phrases that reveal a positive point of view. Then use words and phrases that reveal a negative point of view.

Usher's new CD is _____ and _____. When I hear him sing, I feel _____.

5 Positive: _____

_____

_____

6 Negative: _____

_____

_____

Hockey is a sport that _____ me. It's _____, and the fans are _____.

7 Positive: _____

_____

_____

8 Negative: _____

_____

_____

18 Identifying Author's Style

One enjoyable aspect of reading both fiction and nonfiction is appreciating the **author's style**, or way of using language. Style is also called **voice**. Every writer has his or her own unique way of saying things.

There are many elements that make up a writer's style.

- **Diction** is word choice. Good writers use exact words, including specific nouns (*spaniel,* not *dog*) and vivid verbs (*trotted,* not *walked*) to evoke mental pictures and moods. Some writers like to use long words, while others stick to short words whenever possible. Some use informal, conversational language; others prefer formal language.
- **Syntax** is sentence structure. Some writers specialize in long, complicated sentences. Others prefer short, direct sentences. Some avoid modifiers (adverbs and adjectives); others sprinkle them all over their sentences. Some writers use inverted sentence order ("In the mirror glimmered the light.").
- **Imagery and descriptive details** are sensory words that appeal to any of the five senses. They help readers imagine what the writer is describing.
- **Figurative language** communicates ideas beyond the words' literal meaning. They include the figures of speech simile, metaphor, and personification.
  - A **simile** is a comparison using *like* or *as:* "Snow on the pine trees is *like* frosting on a cake."
  - A **metaphor** is a comparison that doesn't use *like* or *as:* "Snow on the pine trees *is* frosting on a cake."
  - **Personification** gives human qualities to animals, ideas, or objects: "My car was complaining all the way to the shop."
- **Dialogue** is conversation on the page: "Where have you been?" Jeff demanded. "Guess," said Greg.
- **Interruptions** are created with punctuation like dashes, colons, or parentheses. They can slow down the action, build suspense, or suggest uncertainty.
- **Tone** is a writer's attitude toward a subject, as expressed by diction, imagery, and formal or informal language. Tone conveys a mood. It may be serious, humorous, angry, foreboding, or any other mood.

Notice the differences in style in the following excerpts.

> The hotel was run-down. Edward paid cash to the bored clerk. He carried his suitcase down the hall. He unlocked the door and put the suitcase on one bed. Then he sat carefully on the other bed. There was dust on every surface.

Author's style (also called **voice**) is an author's unique way of using language. An author's style is made up of his or her use of diction, syntax, imagery, figurative language, dialogue, interruptions, and tone.

Related Skills: 4, 5, 17, 24, 26, and 32

> Hand in hand, Radha and Paul strolled slowly over to the huge lilac bush. Radha closed her eyes as she sniffed the purple blossoms. "They're overwhelming," she whispered. "Lilacs are the elixir of life."
>
> "Spring is here—finally," said Paul as he gently pushed her hair back from her face. "Mother Nature is awake."

The first excerpt is written in a straightforward, direct style. The sentences are short and simple with few modifiers and no figures of speech. The author's style is straightforward and objective.

The second excerpt uses descriptive language with a metaphor ("Lilacs are the elixir of life.") and personification ("Mother Nature is awake."). The sentences tend to be long and complex. The author also uses dialogue. The author's style is descriptive and emotional.

Read the passage below and answer each question.

HOW DOES THE AUTHOR DESCRIBE HER LIFE?

I love to walk a bridge and feel that split second when I am neither here nor there, when I am between going and coming, when I am God's being in transit, suspended between ground and ground. You could say it's because I'm an engineer's daughter and curious about solid structures. I've always been fascinated by the fit of a joint, the balance in trestles, the strength of a plinth. Or you could say it's because I'm a musician's daughter, who knows something about the architecture of instruments. I've pulled string over a bridge on a violin, stretched it tight, anticipated sound.

It could be, perhaps, because I am neither engineer nor musician. Because I'm neither gringa nor Latina. Because I'm not any one thing. The reality is I am a mongrel. I live on bridges; I've earned my place on them, stand comfortably when I'm on one, content with betwixt and between.

—Excerpted from *American Chica* by Marie Arana

What main metaphor is used?

① Bridges are close to God.
② A violin is a bridge.
③ The author is a bridge.
④ An engineer is a musician.

The author uses

① descriptive details
② dialogue
③ short sentences
④ many modifiers

The main metaphor is ③: the author is a bridge between two cultures (between engineer and musician; between gringa and Latina). She uses ① descriptive details: "between coming and going," "the fit of a joint," "pulled string over a bridge on a violin."

GED Readiness

Read each passage below. Circle the answer to each question.

DOES NICK UNDERSTAND WHAT IS HAPPENING?

Nick's father ordered some water to be put on the stove, and while it was heating he spoke to Nick.

"This lady is going to have a baby, Nick," he said.

"I know," said Nick.

"You don't know," said his father. "Listen to me. What she is going through is called being in labor. The baby wants to be born and she wants it to be born. All her muscles are trying to get the baby born. That is what is happening when she screams."

"I see," said Nick.

Just then the woman cried out.

"Oh, Daddy, can't you give her something to make her stop screaming?" asked Nick.

"No. I haven't any anaesthetic," his father said. "But her screams are not important. I don't hear them because they are not important."

—Excerpted from *In Our Time*
by Ernest Hemingway

❶ What is the tone of this passage?

  ① foreboding
  ② impatient
  ③ sad
  ④ happy

❷ What type of language does it use?

  ① long words
  ② short words
  ③ figures of speech
  ④ vivid verbs

❸ The author uses dialogue here to

  ① show off his vocabulary
  ② provide sensory details
  ③ have the characters give long speeches
  ④ reveal Nick's and his father's characters

WHAT IS THE TRAVELER DOING IN NORTHRIDGE?

It was clear that the sleigh from Weymore had not come; and the shivering young traveler from Boston, who had counted on jumping into it when he left the train at Northridge Junction, found himself standing alone on the open platform, exposed to the full assault of nightfall and winter.

The blast that swept him came off New Hampshire snowfields and ice-hung forests. It seemed to have traversed interminable leagues of frozen silence, filling them with the same cold roar and sharpening its edge against the same bitter black-and-white landscape. Dark, searching and swordlike, it alternately muffled and harried its victim, like a bullfighter now whirling his cloak and now planting his darts. This analogy brought home to the young man the fact that he himself had no cloak, and that the overcoat in which he had faced the relatively temperate air of Boston seemed no thicker than a sheet of paper on the bleak heights of Northridge.

—Excerpted from "The Triumph of Night"
by Edith Wharton

❹ What is the tone of this passage? What emotion is the author expressing?

  ① excited
  ② uncomfortable
  ③ relaxed
  ④ hopeful

❺ Which sentence structure does the author use?

  ① long and complex
  ② short and simple
  ③ filled with interruptions
  ④ inverted

❻ Reread paragraph 2. To what does the author compare the cold blast?

  ① ice-hung forests
  ② the black-and-white landscape
  ③ a bullfighter
  ④ a sheet of paper

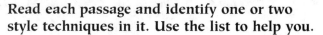

Read the description of each author. Then read each passage. Write the label for the author who most likely wrote the passage.

Author A is known for descriptive language using sensory details and modifiers. She also uses interruptions.

Author B has a writing style of short, simple sentences consisting mostly of short words.

Author C relies mostly on dialogue, with only the occasional sentence of description or narration.

WHAT ARE BRUCE AND PAT DISCUSSING?

"Bruce, can you take the kids to school tomorrow?" Pat put down her hairbrush and turned to her husband.

"I have to be at work by 8 o'clock."

"So do they, and your job is five minutes from the school. You can drop them off on your way."

"Why can't you do it?" Bruce asked.

"I have a job interview at 8:30, and it's way over on the South Side," Pat explained

"That'll be a long way to commute."

"I know, but it's a computer graphics job. It's what I've always wanted. And it'll mean more money. I already priced a plasma TV."

Bruce smiled and climbed into bed.

7 _____

WHERE IS TOMAS?

At the sound of birdsong, Tomas jumped. When they had arrived on the new planet last night, it had been dark. Today the sun was pouring down golden light as brightly as it might have at home (though it wasn't the sun he was used to). Tomas looked around him at the lush plant life, which seemed to grow as he watched. There must be forty shades of green. He scrutinized the readings on his astronaut's suit; all levels were within normal Earth range, so he removed his helmet. He smelled fresh air and—could it be honeysuckle? He was tempted to remove his gloves and touch the foliage, which seemed to come in as many textures as colors.

8 _____

Read each passage and identify one or two style techniques in it. Use the list to help you.

long sentences   modifiers   figurative language

short sentences   imagery   interruptions

HOW DOES JONI FEEL ABOUT HER GRANDFATHER?

Joni peered into the room where her grandfather spent his days. She didn't know which was more disgusting, the smell of his cigars or the smoke that stung her eyes and made the room even dimmer. She could just barely see the threadbare gray rug, the sofa whose red flower pattern looked like splashes of blood, and the coffee table piled high with books. Her grandfather was sitting on the couch with his head to one side, snoring.

9 Style: _____

WHAT IS THE AUTHOR'S OPINION OF E-MAIL?

E-mail can be worse for your brain than marijuana. In a recent study with more than 1,000 participants, e-mail users suffered a 10 percent drop in IQ scores (more than twice the decline experienced by marijuana users). The problem is the distraction factor: many people can't resist checking their e-mail often and answering it immediately. These constant changes in direction—due to their addiction to technology—slow down their brains, making it hard for them to concentrate on one thing.

10 Style: _____

WHAT IS THE SPEAKER DOING?

Hand me that screwdriver, please. Now hold the bracket in place. I'll attach it to the wall. There. Now we'll do the same with the other bracket. The shelf goes on top of them. Make sure it's even. It looks good, doesn't it? Each of these shelves will support the weight of twenty hardcover books (or twice as many paperbacks).

11 Style: _____

19

Identifying Genres

A **genre** is a category of writing, based on content, form, and style. There are four major genres: fiction, nonfiction, poetry, and drama.

- **Fiction** is made-up stories. It tells about events that happen to imaginary characters, using dialogue and narration. Among the many subcategories of fiction are science fiction, mysteries, realistic fiction, historical fiction, and tall tales.
- **Nonfiction** is true stories or information. It comes in two main types:
  - **Literary nonfiction** uses fiction techniques, like dialogue and lyrical language, to tell a true story. It includes autobiographies, biographies, and essays.
  - **Informational nonfiction** is useful information. It includes newspaper articles, how-to pieces, and reports.
- **Poetry** explores feelings and experiences in verse form, using language that is rich in imagery and figures of speech. A poem may or may not rhyme, but it always has a rhythm.
- **Drama** is a play performed on stage; the actors speak and act as fictional characters.

Read the passage and answer the questions below.

> ### WHAT IS THE INTERSTELLAR RECORD?
>
> In 1977, when the *Voyagers* were launched, one of these spacecraft carried the Interstellar Record, a hoped-for link between earth and space that is filled with the sounds and images of the world around us. It carries parts of our lives all the way out to the great Forever. It is destined to travel out of our vast solar system, out to the far, unexplored regions of space in hopes that somewhere, millions of years from now, someone will find it like a note sealed in a bottle carrying our history across the black ocean of space.
>
> —Excerpted from "The Voyagers" by Linda Hogan

A **genre** is a category of writing. The four major genres are fiction, nonfiction, poetry, and drama.

The passage above

1. uses lyrical language to tell a true story
2. is written in verse
3. is about a made-up character
4. tells readers how to launch a spacecraft

The genre of the passage is

1. drama
2. informational nonfiction
3. literary nonfiction
4. fiction

The passage uses lyrical language ①, such as "like a note sealed in a bottle carrying our history across the black ocean of space." The genre is literary nonfiction ③.

GED Readiness

Write *fiction, nonfiction, poetry,* or *drama* to show what genre of writing each phrase describes.

1 _____ a novel about life on planet Zantherus

2 _____ a movie script

3 _____ a chemistry textbook

4 _____ nursery rhymes

5 _____ an account by a politician of her life

6 _____ a Broadway play

7 _____ a short story about a man who can't get over his past

8 _____ a novel about solving a murder

9 _____ the words to a top-40 song

10 _____ an account of a movie star's life, written by someone else

11 _____ an essay about the writer's thoughts on her cat and animals in general

12 _____ a newspaper article about yesterday's vote in the Senate

Read each passage. Then circle the genre to which the passage belongs.

HOW ARE THE GEM AND ROSE ALIKE?

13 Many a gem of purest ray serene
the dark, unfathomed caves of ocean bear.
Many a rose was born to blush unseen
and waste its sweetness on the desert air.

—Excerpted from "Elegy Written in a Country Churchyard" by Thomas Gray

① drama
② essay
③ fiction
④ poetry

WHAT IS EXPRESSIONISM?

14 Vincent van Gogh sold few of his paintings in his lifetime but is hugely successful today. *The Starry Night,* which he painted while in a mental hospital, is one of the earliest examples of Expressionism. The painting shows a sky ablaze with pulsating stars. It's like no sky he ever saw; instead, it portrays how he felt.

① drama
② biography
③ fiction
④ literary nonfiction

WHY IS FERN ANGRY?

15 FERN: I told you never to come here again.
GEORGE: I had to see you. You left so fast, you didn't give me a chance to explain—
FERN: Explain what? That you're a two-timing weasel?
GEORGE: Well, you kind of knew that from the start, remember?
[She attempts to push him out the door.]
GEORGE *[stands his ground]:* And you might not want to toss around the word "two-timing" so lightly.

① drama
② realistic fiction
③ mystery fiction
④ informational nonfiction

HOW CAN YOU SAVE MONEY?

16 If you're trying to save money, the most important thing you can do is pay off your credit card in full every month. If you pay only the minimum, everything you charge is a purchase you're financing, at an interest rate that may be as high as 21 percent. If your current credit card balance is $1,000, and you pay only the minimum, you could wind up paying $1,100 in interest charges.

① drama
② poetry
③ literary nonfiction
④ informational nonfiction

20

Recognizing Basic Elements of Fiction

Fiction tells about events that happen to imaginary characters.

Prose is literature written in paragraph form. Prose may include **narrative** (a description of what happens in a story) and **dialogue** (written conversation).

A **novel** is a book-length story involving several important characters, many lesser characters, and events in their lives. If the title of a work is in italic type (*Madame Bovary*), it is a novel.

A **short story** focuses on only one or two main characters and one main event or action. If the title is in quotation marks ("A Worn Path"), it's a short story.

As you learned in Skill 19, **fiction** tells about events that happen to imaginary characters, though it can be based on real events and even on real people. For example, most characters in *The Red Badge of Courage* by Stephen Crane are fictional, but the novel takes place during the Civil War, which really happened.

Fiction is written in **prose**, or paragraph form (as opposed to poetry or drama). It uses both **narrative** (a description of what happens) and **dialogue** (written conversation) to reveal characters and move the story forward. Both novels and short stories are fiction.

A **novel** is a long (book-length) story involving several important characters, many lesser characters, and events in their lives. A skillful novelist brings together characters with their unique personalities, adventures, and struggles and combines them into one main plot and several subplots. Famous novels include *Grapes of Wrath* and *Harry Potter and the Sorcerer's Stone*.

A **short story** is much shorter than a novel. It usually focuses on only one or two main characters and one main event or action. By narrowing the focus, the short story writer achieves a single effect. A short story is meant to be read in one sitting.

All the different types of fiction have certain elements in common: **characters**, **plot** (including **conflict**), **point of view**, **setting**, **mood**, and **theme**. Some also use **symbolism**. As the jigsaw puzzle below shows, all the elements of fiction are closely interrelated. They constantly interact with and influence each other.

The **author's style**, which includes language and tone, ties all the elements together. It affects and is affected by them. Authors use figurative language and descriptive details to engage readers' senses and help them picture the story. (Style was discussed in Skill 18.)

BASIC ELEMENTS OF FICTION

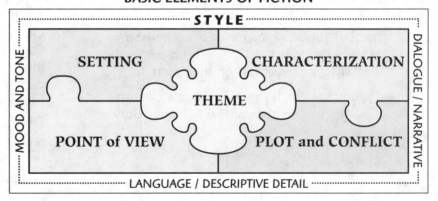

Related Skills: 16, 18, 19, and 21–27

All works of fiction include the following elements:

Characters are the people who participate in the action of a novel or short story. Good writers create believable characters you can feel strongly about. **Characterization** is how the author creates fictional people who seem lifelike. The author may describe the characters' physical appearance and their actions, show their speech patterns, reveal their unspoken thoughts, and reveal what other characters (including the narrator) say about them.

Plot is what happens. It's the chain of related events that take place in a story. Most plots include the following stages: exposition, rising action, climax, falling action, and resolution. In most plots, the events are set in motion by **conflicts**, or struggles between or within characters.

The **narrator** is the person who tells the story. **Point of view** means the perspective from which the story is told. In **first-person** point of view, the narrator is a character who participates in the story, referred to as *I*. There are two types of third-person point of view. In **third-person limited** point of view, the narrator reveals the thoughts of only one character, referring to that character as *he* or *she*. In **third-person omniscient** (all-knowing) point of view, a narrator outside the action knows everything about the story's events and reveals the thoughts of many characters.

The **setting** is the time and place in which the action occurs. The author uses the setting along with his or her choice of words to create the **mood**, or the feeling of the piece of writing. **Tone** is the author's attitude toward the story.

A **theme** is the underlying message in a work of literature. The theme may be an insight into life, a viewpoint about a social issue, a new view of an old problem, or a look into human nature.

One way writers communicate theme is through the use of symbols. A **symbol** is a person, object, place, or activity that stands for something beyond itself. For example, hearts symbolize love, and doves symbolize peace. Other symbols may be unique to a particular story.

Skills 21–27 will explore each of these elements in more detail.

Elements of fiction include
characters (people in the story)
plot (chain of events in the story)
point of view (perspective from which the story is told)
setting (time and place of the story)
tone (author's attitude)
mood (feeling of the writing)
theme (underlying message of the story)

GED Readiness

Read the following sentences and decide which element of fiction they reveal.

1 Gaunt, bruised, and shaken, he stumbled back to his village. (from "The Vision Quest" by Lame Deer)

(1) symbol
(2) character
(3) narrator
(4) theme

2 Deep, deep the road went down between the high green-colored banks. (from "A Worn Path" by Eudora Welty)

(1) setting
(2) character
(3) point of view
(4) tone

3 On July 15, her forty-fifth birthday, Amparo washed her bathtub and sprayed it with rosewater. (from "The Flat of the Land" by Diana Garcia)

(1) point of view
(2) plot
(3) tone
(4) theme

4 I came home to read to my mother, to read out loud, to read long into the dark if I must, to read all night. (from "The Leap" by Louise Erdrich)

(1) theme
(2) conflict
(3) setting
(4) character

5 He dropped a walnut on the hardwood floor and brought his heel grinding down on it. (from "The Most Dangerous Game" by Richard Connell)

(1) setting
(2) character
(3) point of view
(4) tone

6 Clear and sharp in the field of vision, the mountain peaks seemed only half a mile away, but whatever was catching the sunset was still too small to be resolved. (from "The Sentinel" by Arthur C. Clarke)

(1) setting
(2) character
(3) point of view
(4) tone

7 From time to time the boars pressed against the tree, pushing it and making it creak, eager to smash it quickly. (from "The Boar Hunt" by Jose Vasconcelos)

(1) conflict
(2) character
(3) point of view
(4) tone

8 "There she was, a speck of yellow under an umbrella that looked like a slice of orange peel." (from "Through the Tunnel" by Doris Lessing)

(1) setting
(2) character
(3) figurative language
(4) conflict

Read the description of each piece of fiction. Then write _N_ if it is a _novel_ or _S_ if it is a _short story_.

9 _____ This lengthy saga tells the exciting story of a female pirate off the coast of Ireland in the 1600s.

10 _____ This little jewel of a story captures one decisive moment in the life of photographer George Smith.

11 _____ This story covers ten years in the lives of five girls who meet in middle school. Their fates intertwine in unexpected ways.

Read the passage. Then circle the correct answers.

WHY WAS THE KNIFE UNDER THE REFRIGERATOR?

I found a knife under the refrigerator while the woman I love and I were cleaning our house. It was a small paring knife that we lost many years ago and had since forgotten about. I showed the knife to the woman I love and she said, "Oh. Where did you find it?" After I told her, she put the knife on the table and then went into the next room and continued to clean. While I cleaned the kitchen floor, I remembered something that happened four years before that explained how the knife had gotten under the refrigerator.

We had eaten a large dinner and had drunk many glasses of wine. We turned all the lights out, took our clothing off, and went to bed. We thought we would make love, but something happened and we had an argument. We had never experienced such a thing. We both became extremely angry. I said some very hurtful things to the woman I love. She kicked at me in bed and I got out and went into the kitchen. I fumbled for a chair and sat down. I wanted to rest my arms on the table and then rest my head in my arms, but I felt the dirty dishes on the table and they were in the way. I became incensed. I swept everything that was on the table onto the floor. The noise was tremendous, but then the room was very quiet and I suddenly felt sad. I thought I had destroyed everything. I began to cry. The woman I love came into the kitchen and asked if I was all right. I said, "Yes." She turned the light on and we looked at the kitchen floor. Nothing much was broken, but the floor was very messy. We both laughed and then went back to bed and made love. The next morning we cleaned up the mess, but obviously overlooked the knife.

I was about to ask the woman I love if she remembered that incident when she came in from the next room and without saying a word, picked up the knife from the table and slid it back under the refrigerator.

—"The Paring Knife" by Michael Oppenheimer

12. This passage is a
   1. work of nonfiction
   2. novel
   3. short story
   4. symbol

13. The point of view of this passage is
   1. first person
   2. third-person limited
   3. third-person omniscient
   4. none of the above

14. "Oh. Where did you find it?" is an example of
   1. narrative
   2. exposition
   3. dialogue
   4. figurative language

15. The conflict in this work is the characters' fight
   1. over doing the dishes
   2. with their landlord
   3. about drinking too much
   4. four years earlier

16. What is the setting of this story?
   1. a restaurant in a big city
   2. a diner in a small town
   3. a present-day kitchen
   4. a kitchen fifty years ago

17. What phrase best sums up the theme of this story?
   1. What's lost can never be found.
   2. Love can endure much.
   3. Anger pays off.
   4. Communicating is hard.

18. The knife is a symbol for
   1. the couple's love
   2. the breakable nature of dishes
   3. what's wrong with the refrigerator
   4. the way love hurts people

21 Understanding Characterization

All works of fiction include people, called **characters**, who participate in the action of a novel or short story. Good writers create characters who are made up but believable, people you feel as strongly about as you would about people you know in real life.

Character traits are the qualities of mind or habits of behavior shown by a character. Traits may be physical (for example, Michael is tall and graceful) or aspects of personality (Donald is pushy and obnoxious).

Writers reveal character traits through **characterization**. Authors use these four basic methods to develop a character:

- Describe the character's physical appearance and environment.
- Show how the character speaks, thinks, feels, and acts.
- Reveal what other characters say, think, or feel about the character.
- Have the narrator comment on the character.

Sometimes character traits are spelled out directly, but usually readers must infer them from a character's words, thoughts, actions, appearance, interactions, conflicts, and motivations. Read the passage below. Then study the chart on the next page to see how the author has given information about Emma.

> **Characters** are the people who participate in the action of a novel or short story.

> **Characterization** is how the author reveals character traits and creates fictional people who seem lifelike.

HOW DOES CHARLES FEEL ABOUT EMMA?

Charles's trousers were too tight at the waist. And then "The shoe straps will interfere with my dancing," he said.

"You? Dance?" Emma cried.

"Of course!"

"But you're crazy! Everybody would laugh. You mustn't. It's not suitable for a doctor, anyway."

Charles said no more. He walked up and down waiting for Emma to be ready.

He saw her from behind in a mirror, between two sconces. Her dark eyes seemed darker than ever. Her hair, drawn down smoothly on both sides and slightly fluffed out over the ears, shone with a blue luster; in her chignon a rose quivered on its flexible stem, with artificial dewdrops at the leaf-tips. Her gown was pale saffron, trimmed with three bunches of pompon roses and green sprays.

Charles came up to kiss her on the shoulder. "Don't!" she cried. "You're rumpling me!"

—Excerpted from *Madame Bovary* by Gustave Flaubert

Related Skills: 1, 2, 3, 4, 20, 22, and 39

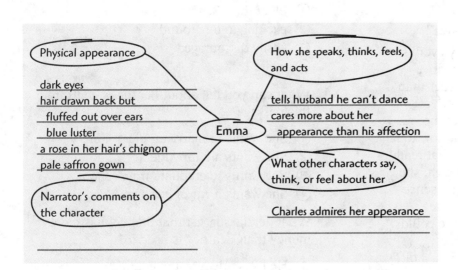

The most important character in a literary work is the **main character**. A short story usually has only one main character, but a novel may have several. Less prominent characters are called **minor characters**. The story does not focus on them; they help support the plot and reveal more about the main character.

The main character in a literary work is called the **protagonist**. He or she is involved in the story's central conflict and is usually the character readers most identify with. The **antagonist** is in opposition to the protagonist. The antagonist is not always another character. It may be a force of nature, an aspect of society, or even an internal force within the protagonist.

Round characters are complex and highly developed. They are three-dimensional. They have assorted strengths and weaknesses and a full range of emotions. They grow and change in the course of the story, which makes them *dynamic*. **Flat characters** are not highly developed. They are one-dimensional. They exist mainly to advance the plot, and they show only the traits they need to do so. They rarely change and grow during the story, so they are *static*.

Once you understand *who* a character is, you'll want to figure out *why* he acts a certain way and *how* he changes. **Motivation** is the reason behind a character's behavior. Motivation may be stated or implied. A character's motivation and the actions he or she takes often reveal character traits. For example, in the passage on page 64, Charles kisses his wife's shoulder because he admires and loves her. She cries, "Don't!" because she cares more about her appearance than about him.

The **protagonist** is the main character in a literary work. The **antagonist** is in opposition to the protagonist. It may be another character, a force of nature, a aspect of society, or even an internal force within the protagonist.

Motivation is the reason (stated or implied) behind a character's behavior.

GED Readiness

Read the following passage. Then circle the correct answers.

HOW DOES SAMUEL TREAT BEATRICE?

Samuel would still show up hopefully every so often to ask her to accompany him on a drive through the country. He was so much older than all her other suitors. And dry? Country drives; Lord! She went out with him a few times; he was so persistent and she couldn't figure out how to tell him no. He didn't seem to get her hints that really she should be studying. Truth to tell though, she started to find his quiet, undemanding presence soothing. His eggshell-white BMW took the graveled country roads so quietly that she could hear the kiskadee birds in the mango trees, chanting their query: "Dit, dit, qu'est-ce qu'il dit?"

One day, Samuel bought her a gift.

"These are for you and your family," he said shyly, handing her a wrinkled paper bag. "I know your mother likes them." Inside were three plump eggplants from his kitchen garden, raised by his own hands. Beatrice took the humble gift out of the bag. The skins of the eggplants had a taut, blue sheen to them. Later she would realize that that was when she'd begun to love Samuel. He was stable, solid, responsible. He would make Mummy and her happy.

Beatrice gave in more to Samuel's diffident wooing. He was cultured and well-spoken. He had been abroad, talked of exotic sports: ice hockey, downhill skiing. He took her to fancy restaurants she'd only heard of, that her other young, unestablished boyfriends would never have been able to afford, and would probably only have embarrassed her if they had taken her. Samuel had polish.

—Excerpted from "The Glass Bottle Trick"
by Nalo Hopkinson

❶ How many characters are discussed in this passage?

  ① one
  ② two
  ③ three
  ④ four

❷ You can tell from the description that Samuel is

  ① older than Beatrice
  ② exciting to be around
  ③ easily discouraged
  ④ white

❸ What can you tell about Beatrice's goals from this passage?

  ① She wants to marry an older man.
  ② She wants a happy life.
  ③ She wants to graduate from school.
  ④ She wants a car of her own.

❹ What details suggest that Samuel has more money than Beatrice is used to?

  ① He likes drives in the country.
  ② He grows his own vegetables.
  ③ He drives a BMW and takes her to fancy restaurants.
  ④ He follows ice hockey and skiing.

❺ What makes Beatrice begin to love Samuel?

  ① He takes her to expensive restaurants and impresses her.
  ② He takes her for country drives and shows her he's boring.
  ③ He gives her a humble gift that shows he's stable and responsible.
  ④ He gets along well with her mother.

❻ What does the reference to ice hockey and skiing as "exotic" suggest about where Beatrice lives?

  ① It's a town where people work too hard to have time for sports.
  ② It's a country where sports are considered for children only.
  ③ It's a country where people speak French.
  ④ It's a warm climate without snow and ice.

❼ Which word best describes Samuel so far?

  ① predictable
  ② fun-loving
  ③ resentful
  ④ inconsiderate

Read the following passage. Then circle the correct answers. The speaker is the narrator, Jane Eyre.

WHAT DOES JANE EYRE THINK OF JOHN REED?

"What do you want?" I asked, with awkward diffidence.

"Say, 'What do you want, Master Reed?' " was the answer. "I want you to come here." And seating himself in an armchair, he intimated by a gesture that I was to approach and stand before him.

John Reed was a schoolboy of fourteen years old; four years older than I, for I was but ten: large and stout for his age, with a dingy and unwholesome skin, thick lineaments [features] in a spacious visage [face], heavy limbs and large extremities. He gorged himself habitually at table, which made him bilious [sick], and gave him a dim and bleared eye and flabby cheeks. He ought now to have been at school; but his mama had taken him home for a month or two, "on account of his delicate health." Mr. Miles, the master, affirmed that he would do very well if he had fewer cakes and sweetmeats sent him from home; but the mother's heart turned from an opinion so harsh, and inclined rather to the more refined idea that John's sallowness [sickly skin color] was owing to over-application [studying too hard] and, perhaps, to pining after home [homesickness].

John had not much affection for his mother and sisters, and an antipathy [hatred] for me. He bullied and punished me, not two or three times in the week, nor once or twice in the day, but continually: every nerve I had feared him, and every morsel of flesh on my bones shrank when he came near. There were moments when I was bewildered by the terror he inspired, because I had no appeal whatever against either his menaces or his inflictions; the servants did not like to offend their young master by taking my part against him, and Mrs. Reed was blind and deaf on the subject; she never saw him strike or heard him abuse me, though he did both now and then in her very presence, more frequently, however, behind her back.

—Excerpted from *Jane Eyre* by Charlotte Brontë

8 How does Jane feel about John Reed?

① She respects him.
② She fears him.
③ She worries about him.
④ She likes him.

9 What is Jane's motivation for avoiding John?

① She doesn't want to upset him.
② She fears he will steal her lunch.
③ She knows he will hit her.
④ She fears making his mother angry.

10 Which words best describe John Reed?

① a delicate boy
② a good student
③ a boy working to learn self-control
④ a big bully

11 How does the author show that Mrs. Reed's perceptions about her son are inaccurate?

① The author gives the schoolmaster's contradictory opinion.
② The author describes Mrs. Reed's unreliable nature.
③ The author has the servants say that Mrs. Reed is wrong.
④ The author has John say that his mother is wrong.

12 Why does Mrs. Reed think John is homesick?

① He told her so.
② She can read her son's mind.
③ His skin is sallow.
④ She thinks he misses his sisters.

13 Who is the antagonist in the excerpt?

① Jane Eyre
② John Reed
③ John's mother
④ John's schoolmaster

Identifying Plot and Conflict

Plot is the action of a story. It's the sequence of related events that take place. A writer structures and organizes events to suit the purpose of the story he or she wants to tell.

In most plots, the events are set in motion by **conflicts**, which in fiction mean problems the characters must solve. A conflict may be external or internal.

- An **external conflict** is one in which the character struggles against some outside force: (1) another person, (2) society or a group of people (like a polluting company or an invading army), or (3) an aspect of the environment (like a life-threatening storm).
- An **internal conflict** is one in which the character struggles against himself or herself.

Most plots include five stages:

- **Exposition** introduces the story's characters, setting, and conflict. It supplies background and sets the tone.
- **Rising action** is when suspense builds and the plot thickens. The main character tries to resolve the conflict.
- The **climax** is the turning point in the plot and the emotional high point of the story. It leads to change in the main character. In some stories, this is the resolution as well, and the story ends after this third stage.
- **Falling action** shows what happens after the climax and is usually a logical result of it.
- The **resolution** reveals the story's final outcome. It resolves the conflict and ties up the loose ends.

To see how these stages work, look at the plot stages of a story you probably learned as a child, "Little Red Riding Hood."

> **Plot** is the sequence of related events that take place in a story. The five stages of a plot are exposition, rising action, climax, falling action, and resolution.

> **Conflicts** are problems the characters must solve. A conflict may be internal or external.

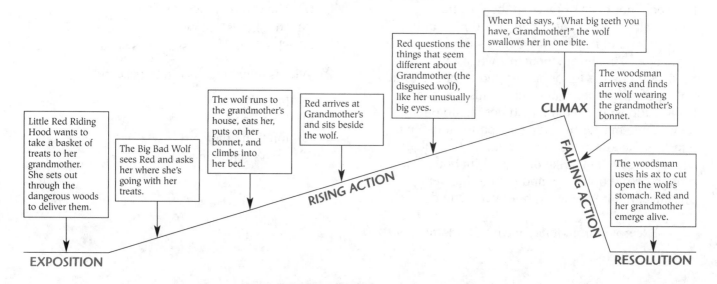

Little Red Riding Hood wants to take a basket of treats to her grandmother. She sets out through the dangerous woods to deliver them.

The Big Bad Wolf sees Red and asks her where she's going with her treats.

The wolf runs to the grandmother's house, eats her, puts on her bonnet, and climbs into her bed.

Red arrives at Grandmother's and sits beside the wolf.

Red questions the things that seem different about Grandmother (the disguised wolf), like her unusually big eyes.

When Red says, "What big teeth you have, Grandmother!" the wolf swallows her in one bite.

The woodsman arrives and finds the wolf wearing the grandmother's bonnet.

The woodsman uses his ax to cut open the wolf's stomach. Red and her grandmother emerge alive.

EXPOSITION

RISING ACTION

CLIMAX

FALLING ACTION

RESOLUTION

Related Skills: 2, 3, 11, 12, 21, 23–28, 38

Read these three excerpts from "The Dream of an Hour" by Kate Chopin. Can you identify which plot stage each excerpt shows?

> Knowing that Mrs. Mallard was afflicted with a heart trouble, great care was taken to break to her as gently as possible the news of her husband's death.

The first excerpt is the exposition stage. It tells us the main character (Mrs. Mallard) and the main plot complications (her husband has just been killed, and she has a weak heart). This opening paragraph is followed by more exposition and then rising action in which the protagonist grieves deeply her husband's death. After she has cried and then stared at the wall for a long time, she slowly begins to feel something new.

> When she abandoned herself a little whispered word escaped her slightly parted lips. She said it over and over under her breath: "free, free, free!" The vacant stare and the look of terror that had followed it went from her eyes. They stayed keen and bright. Her pulses beat fast, and the coursing blood warmed and relaxed every inch of her body.
>
> She knew that she would weep again when she saw the kind, tender hands folded in death; the face that had never looked save with love upon her, fixed and gray and dead. But she saw beyond that bitter moment a long procession of years to come that would belong to her absolutely.

The second excerpt is the climax. It is the turning point when she realizes that she will eventually be free and happier alone than with her well-meaning but somewhat suffocating husband. She spends the next several paragraphs planning her future.

> Someone was opening the front door with a latchkey. It was Brently Mallard [the husband] who entered, a little travel-stained, composedly carrying his grip-sack [suitcase] and umbrella. He had been far from the scene of the accident, and did not even know there had been one. He stood amazed at Josephine's piercing cry; at Richards' quick motion to screen him from the view of his wife.
>
> But Richards was too late.
>
> When the doctors came they said she had died of heart disease—of joy that kills.

The third excerpt is the resolution. The shock of learning that her husband is alive overwhelms Mrs. Mallard's weak heart. In the final line, the doctors are wrong. It isn't joy that kills her; it's the disappointment that she's still trapped.

GED Readiness

Read the following short story. Then circle the correct answers.

Framton Nuttel is visiting in the country as a cure for his nervous condition.

WHO IS MRS. SAPPLETON WAITING FOR?

1 "My aunt will be down presently, Mr. Nuttel," said a very self-possessed young lady of fifteen. "Do you know many of the people round here?"

2 "Hardly a soul," said Framton.

3 "Then you know practically nothing about my aunt?" pursued the self-possessed young lady.

4 "Only her name and address," admitted the caller. He was wondering whether Mrs. Sappleton was in the married or widowed state. An indefinable something about the room seemed to suggest masculine habitation.

5 "Her great tragedy happened just three years ago," said the child.

6 "Her tragedy?" asked Framton; somehow in this restful country spot tragedies seemed out of place.

7 "You may wonder why we keep that window wide open on an October afternoon," said the niece, indicating a large French window that opened onto a lawn.

8 "It is quite warm for the time of the year," said Framton; "but has that window got anything to do with the tragedy?"

9 "Out through that window, three years ago to a day, her husband and her two young brothers went off for their day's shooting. They never came back. In crossing the moor to their favorite snipe-shooting ground they were all three engulfed in a treacherous piece of bog. Their bodies were never recovered." Here the child's voice lost its self-possessed note and became falteringly human. "Poor aunt always thinks that they will come back some day, they and the little brown spaniel that was lost with them, and walk in at this window just as they used to do. That is why the window is kept open every evening until it is quite dusk. Do you know, sometimes on still, quiet evenings like this, I almost get a creepy feeling that they will all walk in through that window—"

10 She broke off with a little shudder. It was a relief to Framton when the aunt bustled into the

11 room with a whirl of apologies for being late.

12 "I hope Vera has been amusing you?" she said.

13 "She has been very interesting," said Framton.

14 "I hope you don't mind the open window," said Mrs. Sappleton briskly; "my husband and brothers will be home directly from shooting, and they always come in this way. They've been out for snipe in the marshes today."

15 She rattled on cheerfully about the shooting and the scarcity of birds, and the prospects for duck in the winter. To Framton, it was all purely horrible. He made a desperate but only partially successful effort to turn the talk on to a less ghastly topic; he was conscious that his hostess was giving him only a fragment of her attention, and her eyes were constantly straying past him to the open window and the lawn beyond. She suddenly heightened into alert attention—but not to what Framton was saying.

16 "Here they are at last!" she cried. "Just in time for tea, and don't they look as if they were muddy up to the eyes!"

17 Framton shivered slightly and turned towards the niece with a look intended to convey sympathetic comprehension. The child was staring out through the open window with dazed horror in her eyes. In a chill shock of nameless fear Framton swung round in his seat and looked in the same direction.

18 In the deepening twilight three figures were walking across the lawn towards the window; they all carried guns under their arms. A tired brown spaniel kept close at their heels. Noiselessly they neared the house.

19 Framton grabbed wildly at his stick and hat; the hall-door, the gravel drive, and the front gate were dimly noted stages in his headlong retreat. A cyclist coming along the road had to run into the hedge to avoid imminent collision.

20 "Here we are, my dear," said the [husband]. "Who was that who bolted out as we came up?"

21 "A most extraordinary man, a Mr. Nuttel," said Mrs. Sappleton, "could only talk about his illnesses, and dashed off without a word of good-bye or apology when you arrived. One would think he had seen a ghost."

"I expect it was the spaniel," said the niece

calmly; "he told me he had a horror of dogs. He was once hunted into a cemetery somewhere on the banks of the Ganges by a pack of pariah dogs, and had to spend the night in a newly dug grave with the creatures snarling and grinning and foaming just above

22 him. Enough to make anyone lose their nerve."

Romance [a made-up adventure story] at short notice was her specialty.

—Excerpted from "The Open Window" by Saki

1 What stage of the plot is paragraphs 1–4?

① exposition
② rising action
③ climax
④ resolution

2 Framton's conflict in paragraphs 16–18 is with

① the niece
② the returning hunters
③ the dog
④ himself

3 What plot complication occurs in paragraphs 13–14?

① Mrs. Sappleton explains the importance of fresh air.
② Mrs. Sappleton tells Framton she's expecting her husband's ghost.
③ Framton begins to suspect Mrs. Sappleton is crazy.
④ Framton realizes he may see ghosts.

4 The climax of the plot occurs in

① paragraph 9
② paragraph 14
③ paragraph 17
④ paragraph 21

5 How does the story change direction right after the climax?

① Mrs. Sappleton arrives.
② Framton tries to change the subject.
③ Framton runs away in terror.
④ The niece is revealed as being over-imaginative.

6 The resolution suggests that

① ghosts are real
② Framton is late for another appointment
③ Framton had a bad experience with dogs
④ the niece often makes up scary stories

Read the following passage and answer the questions that follow.

WHY WAS SANTA HANDING OUT COOKIES?

There was nothing whatever jolly about this dwarfish Santa. He neither spoke nor laughed, but showed a faint sneer as he repeatedly pointed to the big placard hung about his neck. In large black letters it read:

PLEASE HELP!
DEADLY ANTHRAX!

Curious, I moved closer to see who sponsored such a graceless oddball, and wondering, too, about the grayish powder, presumably raw sugar, he sprinkled on each cookie he was handing out to those who put money in his cup. Then my stomach contracted like a clenched fist. Between the two giant phrases, in very tiny print, was one more word: SPREAD.

—Excerpted from "A Quartet of Mini-Fantasies" by Arthur Porges

7 Compare the length of exposition in this story with the story on page 72?

_____

8 Who is the first character introduced?

_____

9 Who is Santa's conflict with?

_____

10 What is the climax of this story?

_____

23

Understanding Point of View

The **narrator** is the person who tells the story. Readers see the setting, the characters, and the plot through her or his eyes. The narrator determines the **point of view**, which is the perspective from which the story is told. There are three basic points of view: first person, third-person limited, and third-person omniscient.

First Person Point of View

- The narrator is a character in the story.
- The narrator refers to herself or himself as *I* and *me*.
- The narrator does not know other characters' thoughts.
- The narrator speaks directly to readers, presenting his or her own thoughts, feelings, and interpretations.
- Readers tend to feel close to a first-person narrator because the story is told as he or she experienced it, saw it, heard it, and understood it.

Third-person Limited Point of View

- The narrator is an outside observer, not a story character.
- The narrator focuses on the thoughts and feelings of one person (usually the main character).
- The narrator refers to all the characters as *he* or *she*.
- Because readers learn only one character's thoughts, they don't get the big picture, but they do identify with that character.

Third-person Omniscient Point of View

- The narrator is an outside observer, not a story character.
- The narrator knows (and tells readers) the thoughts and feelings of all characters.
- The narrator refers to all the characters as *he* or *she*.
- When an omniscient narrator tells the story, readers become "all-knowing" too.

What point of view is used in this passage?

> #### WHAT IS THIS PLANET?
>
> On the third day of the new year the newspaper readers of two hemispheres were made aware for the first time of the real importance of this unusual apparition in the heavens. "A Planetary Collision," one London paper headed the news.
>
> "It is brighter!" cried the people, clustering in the streets. But in the dim observatories the watchers held their breath and peered at one another. *"It is nearer,"* they said. *"Nearer!"*
>
> —Excerpted from "The Star" by H. G. Wells

You can tell from the pronouns *(they* and *their)* that this passage is in the third-person point of view. It's not the viewpoint of any one character, so it's omniscient.

The **narrator** is the person who tells the story.

Point of view is the perspective from which the story is told. The three main points of view are first person, third-person limited, and third-person omniscient.

Related Skills: 2, 3, 7, 8, 18, 21, and 29

GED Readiness

Read each passage and answer the questions.

WHAT IS MR. MARTIN PLANNING?

It was just a week to the day since Mr. Martin had decided to rub out Mrs. Ulgine Barrows. The term "rub out" pleased him because it suggested nothing more than the correction of an error—in this case an error of Mr. Fitweiler [his boss]. Mr. Martin had spent each night of the past week working out his plan and examining it. As he walked home now he went over it again. For the hundredth time he resented the element of imprecision, the margin of guesswork that entered into the business. The project as he had worked it out was casual and bold, the risks were considerable. Something might go wrong anywhere along the line. And therein lay the cunning of his scheme. No one would ever see in it the cautious, painstaking hand of Erwin Martin, head of the filing department at F & S, of whom Mr. Fitweiler had once said, "Man is fallible but Martin isn't."

—Excerpted from "The Catbird Seat" by James Thurber

1 What point of view does this passage have?

① first person
② third-person limited
③ third-person omniscient
④ none of the above

2 Through which character's viewpoint is the story told?

① Mr. Martin
② Mrs. Barrows
③ Mr. Fitweiler
④ an anonymous outside observer

3 A disadvantage of this viewpoint is that

① the narrator doesn't understand
② it's unusual
③ readers don't get the big picture
④ the narrator is an outside observer, not a character

HOW DO THE NARRATOR AND HER MOTHER GET ALONG?

The more years I spend living on the other side of the country, the better my mother and I seem to get along. It is partly an act of compromise on both our parts: I don't get angry every time my mother buys me a pleated Ann Taylor skirt, and my mother doesn't get angry if I don't wear it. We had one bad fight several years ago Christmas Eve, when my mother got up in the middle of the night, snuck into my room and took a few tucks around the waist of a full hand-painted cotton skirt I loved, and then washed it in warm water so it shrank further.

"Why can't you just accept me the way I am?" I wailed, before I remembered that I was in the house where people didn't have negative emotions.

"It's only because I adore you, baby," my mother said, and I knew not only that this was true, but also that I adored my mother back, that we were two people who needed to be adored, and the fact that we adored each other was one of life's tiny miracles. We were saving two other people an awful lot of work.

—Excerpted from "Waltzing the Cat" by Pam Houston

4 What point of view does this passage have?

_____

5 How can you recognize the point of view?

_____

6 What is a disadvantage of this point of view?

_____

7 How would this scene be different if the mother were the narrator?

_____

24 Recognizing Dialogue and Narrative

Fiction uses both narrative and dialogue to reveal characters and move the story forward. Good stories achieve a balance, overall, between narrative and dialogue.

The **narrative** of a story tells what happened and relates a series of events in time sequence. Narrative is the backbone of any story. Narrative is the narrator explaining the story.

A compelling narrative relies on good **pacing**; the writer describes only those actions and events that contribute to the story. For example, if you were on vacation in New York City for a week, you would probably spend a great deal of time getting from one place to another, standing in line, and doing everyday things like getting dressed and eating meals. But if you told friends about your vacation, you'd leave out most of those unimportant details. You'd focus on the things that made a big impression on you: the Broadway play, the Yankees game, the Statue of Liberty, the dinner at a special restaurant. You would pace your narrative for maximum dramatic effect.

Dialogue is written conversation enclosed in quotation marks. Good dialogue sounds like real people talking to each other. For most characters, that means informal language, contractions (*she's* instead of *she is*), and sentence fragments. Young characters often use slang. There may occasionally be a character who is old-fashioned enough to speak precisely, such as Mr. Burns on *The Simpsons*. To test how realistic dialogue is, read it out loud.

Dialogue brings characters to life by revealing their personalities and showing what they are thinking and feeling as they react to other people. Dialogue also helps advance the plot.

Example:

> ### WHERE ARE BOB AND NANCY?
>
> Bob grabbed Nancy's hand and pulled her aboard the subway train.
> "Do you know where we're going?" she demanded.
> "Sure," he said casually. "We're on our way downtown. We'll get off at 34th Street."
> "Umm, excuse me," said a young man in wire-rimmed glasses. "I don't mean to eavesdrop, but this train is going to Brooklyn."
> "Oh, great," Nancy muttered. "We're hopelessly lost, but at least we're making good time." She pulled her hand away from Bob's.

You learned from this dialogue that Bob is pushy, Nancy is angry with him, and they're lost on a New York subway. Notice that a new paragraph begins with each speaker. Sometimes a speaker is not identified in the paragraph, but you can figure it out by watching whose turn it is to speak.

Narrative is the backbone of any story. It relates a series of important events in time sequence. The narrator explains the story through the narrative.

Dialogue is realistic-sounding written conversation enclosed in quotation marks. It reveals characters and advances the plot.

Related Skills: 2, 3, 11, 20–23, 25–28, and 37

GED Readiness

Read the following passage. Then circle the correct answers.

The main character, Elaine, is an artist who has returned to her hometown for the first time in years and is being interviewed at an art gallery by Andrea, a reporter from the local newspaper.

WHAT ARE ANDREA AND ELAINE DOING?

1   We sit across from each other at Charna's desk and Andrea sets down her camera and fiddles with her tape recorder. Andrea writes for a newspaper. "This is for the Living section," she says. I know what that means, it used to be the Women's Pages. It's funny that they now call it Living, as if only women are alive and the other things, such as the Sports, are for the dead.

2   "Living, eh?" I say. "I'm the mother of two. I bake cookies." All true. Andrea gives me a dirty look and flicks on her machine.

3   "How do you handle fame?" she says.

4   "This isn't fame," I say. "Fame is Elizabeth Taylor's cleavage. This stuff is just a media pimple."

5   She grins at that. "Well, could you maybe say something about your generation of artists—your generation of women artists—and their aspirations and goals?"

6   "Painters, you mean," I say. "What generation is that?"

7   "The seventies, I suppose," she says. "That's when the women's—that's when you started getting attention."

8   "The seventies isn't my generation," I say.

9   She smiles. "Well," she says, "what is?"

10   "The forties."

11   "The forties?" This is archaeology as far as she's concerned. "But you couldn't have been . . ."

12   "That was when I grew up," I say.

13   "Oh right," she says, "You mean it was *formative*. Can you talk about the ways, how it reflects in your work?"

14   "The colors," I say. "A lot of my colors are forties colors." I'm softening up. At least she doesn't say *like* and *you know* all the time. "The war. There are people who remember the war and people who don't. There's a cut-off point, there's a difference."

—Excerpted from *Cat's Eye* by Margaret Atwood

---

1 "This is for the Living section" is

  ① narrative
  ② exposition
  ③ pacing
  ④ dialogue

2 How are paragraphs 3 through 6 alike in structure?

  ① They are all dialogue.
  ② They are all narrative.
  ③ They give dialogue by Elaine followed by Andrea's reaction as narrative.
  ④ They advance the plot by telling readers what Elaine plans to do next.

3 "The forties" in paragraph 10 is

  ① narrative
  ② formal
  ③ a contraction
  ④ a sentence fragment

4 Who is speaking in paragraph 11?

  ① Elizabeth Taylor
  ② Andrea
  ③ Elaine
  ④ an omniscient narrator

5 Who is thinking in paragraph 11?

  ① Charna
  ② Andrea
  ③ Elaine
  ④ an omniscient narrator

6 What does "This is archaeology as far as she's concerned" mean in paragraph 11?

_____

7 How does Elaine's attitude toward the reporter change during the interview? How does the author convey this information?

_____

Identifying Setting, Mood, and Tone

Reading becomes more interesting when you use the details the author gives to paint a mental picture of the story as it unfolds. The **setting** is when and where the events occur. It includes not just the physical time and place but also the beliefs, attitudes, and values of that particular time and place.

The **time** frames the action by explaining when the events happened—the time of day, the season, or the historical period. A story may be set in the past, present, or future. The **place** can be a specific geographic region, type of landscape (mountains, forest, lake, building), and/or weather where the action occurs.

A story may be set in a real place or a place the author made up. For example, *Stars Wars* takes place "long, long ago in a galaxy far, far away." *The Adventures of Huckleberry Finn* takes place on and near the Mississippi River in the 1850s.

In some stories, the setting is so important that it's virtually a character in its own right.

Example:

> WHAT IS THE SETTING?
>
> Miles down, below the deep, dense zone of darkness, the ocean again illuminates itself. A golden light radiates from gigantic sponges, yellow and resplendent as suns.
>
> Numberless plants and cold-blooded creatures live within this layer of light, buried eternally in the brightness of a glacial summer.
>
> A profusion of green and red anemones blossom in the white sandy lawn, amid schools of transparent jellyfish, dangling like umbrellas, which have not yet set out in quest of their wandering destiny through the seas.
>
> Hard white corals entwine like bushes, through which glide dark velvet fish, opening and closing like flowers.
>
> —Excerpted from "The Unknown" by Maria Luisa Bombal

Setting may be stated briefly and directly, often at the beginning of a story or when a new scene begins.

Examples:

> Out of a dark and soft-seated limousine I am ushered into a bright room filled with many people.
>
> —Excerpted from "Everyday Use" by Alice Walker

> It was December—a bright frozen day in the early morning.
>
> —Excerpted from "A Worn Path" by Eudora Welty

Setting is when and where the events of a literary work occur—not just the physical time and place but also the beliefs, attitudes, and values of that time and place.

Related Skills: 2, 3, 20–24, 26–28, and 35

Setting may be implied instead of stated. What can you infer about the setting of the next passage? What words give you clues?

WHAT DOES THE RIDER WANT?

The man in the gray cloak looked down from the height of his gray steed. "I must have your help, wizard," he said.

Kedrigern looked up at him, his expression noncommittal. "What's the problem? Spell? Enchantment? Curse?"

"A matter of honor," said the rider. His voice had the timbre of an instrument best suited to roaring. At the moment, however, it was lowered as if against eavesdroppers, though none were likely. Only Kedrigern, the rider, and an amiable-looking youth whom Kedrigern took to be his squire were present on the road before the wizard's cottage.

—Excerpted from "The Tournament at Surreptitia" by John Morressy

The place is probably the countryside (a cottage with no one else around). The time is the Middle Ages, since the rider is a knight with a squire. In this culture, magic must be real, since Kedrigern is a wizard.

The setting of a story may bring about conflicts or problems, and it can influence how those problems are solved. It may shape characters' personalities and reveal them.

A story's setting often helps to create the **mood**, or **atmosphere**, of the story. The mood usually suggests specific emotions, such as anxiety or elation.

Most stories have more than one setting, and each setting may convey a different mood. Imagine a group of climbers coming down from Mount Everest in a terrible snowstorm. The setting is cold and white. The mood is bleak and fearful. Then the climbers arrive at a base camp where there are fires burning, cozy tents, and hot soup. The mood changes to one of relief, even triumph.

Tone is the author's attitude toward the story and its elements. Like tone of voice in spoken language, tone evokes an emotional response in the reader. Tone can be conveyed by words and details that express certain emotions. It can be summed up with a word or phrase (excitement, anger, fear, happiness).

Reread the passage above about Kedrigern. What is its tone? What clues in the passage tell you?

The tone in the passage above is suspenseful and threatening. The suspense comes from wondering what help the rider needs and whether Kedrigern will give it. The threat comes from the rider, who seems the type to force the wizard to help him.

> **Mood** is the atmosphere or feeling of a story. Mood suggests the emotions the story creates.

> **Tone** is the author's attitude toward the story and its elements. Tone is conveyed by the author's choice of words and details that evoke an emotional response.

GED Readiness

Read each passage and answer the questions.

WHERE DOES THE STORY TAKE PLACE?

Clayt went to the window, and began to rub the dust away with his palm. "The land has the look of winter yet," he said, peering out. "That's why you can talk so easily about giving up this land. Three weeks from now those words would stick in your throats. You've forgotten, haven't you, what it's like here in late spring? So beautiful it takes your breath away. The lilac bushes reach almost to the second-floor windows by now, and they'll be covered with flowers, making the breeze smell like perfume. The maples will be leafed out on the hills. You can see ridge after ridge from here—all the way to North Carolina. The stream will be ready for trout fishing, and the blackberries will be gearing up for summer. And at twilight fawns come out to play under the trees in the meadow. You couldn't give it up if you remembered."

—Excerpted from *The Rosewood Casket*
by Sharyn McCrumb

1 During what season does this passage take place?

  ① early summer
  ② early autumn
  ③ late winter
  ④ late spring

2 What season is Clayt describing?

  ① summer
  ② autumn
  ③ winter
  ④ spring

3 Where does the scene take place?

  ① in the southern countryside
  ② in a city apartment
  ③ in a factory town
  ④ in rural Texas

4 What insight does the setting give about Clayt's character?

  ① It shows that he takes the land for granted.
  ② It shows that he loves the land.
  ③ It shows that he's not very observant.
  ④ It shows that he's afraid of confrontation.

5 What is the tone of the passage?

  ① angry and sarcastic
  ② happy and hopeful
  ③ tired and hopeless
  ④ admiring and nostalgic

6 How does the setting influence the conflict?

  ① Its beauty makes Clayt determined to hang onto the land.
  ② The trout stream is a possible source of income.
  ③ The hills and ridges make farming difficult.
  ④ Its winter drabness makes Clayt want to sell the land.

WHERE IS ASHIMA?

For Ashima, migrating to the suburbs feels more drastic, more distressing than the move from Calcutta [India] to Cambridge [Massachusetts] had been. She wishes Ashoke had accepted the position at Northeastern so that they could have stayed in the city. She is stunned that in this town there are no sidewalks to speak of, no streetlights, no public transportation, no stores for miles at a time. She has no interest in learning how to drive the new Toyota Corolla it is now necessary for them to own. Though no longer pregnant, she continues, at times, to mix Rice Krispies and peanuts and onions in a bowl. For being a foreigner, Ashima is beginning to realize, is a sort of lifelong pregnancy—a perpetual wait, a constant burden, a continuous feeling out of sorts.

—Excerpted from *The Namesake* by Jhumpa Lahiri

7 The place and time of this passage are

_____

8 Hints about the place include

_____

9 Hints about the time include

_____

10 The mood is

_____

HOW DOES THE SPEAKER FEEL ABOUT LONDON?

"I may as well tell you," he said, speaking in a highly confidential manner, "that this city has not the hundredth part of its former splendor! I have been gravely disappointed since my return. Once upon a time, to look upon London was to look upon a forest of towers and pinnacles and spires. The many-colored flags and banners that flew from each and every one dazzled the eye! Upon every side one saw stone carvings as delicate as fingerbones and as intricate as flowing water! There were houses ornamented with stone dragons, griffins and lions, symbolizing the wisdom, courage and ferocity of the occupants, while in the gardens of those same houses might be found flesh-and-blood dragons, griffins and lions, locked in strong cages. Their roars, which could be clearly heard in the street, terrified the faint-of-heart. In every church a blessed saint lay, performing miracles hourly at the behest [urging] of the populace. Each saint was confined within an ivory casket, which was secreted in a jewel-studded coffin, which in turn was displayed in a magnificent shrine of gold and silver that shone night and day with the light of a thousand wax candles!"

—Excerpted from *Jonathan Strange & Mr. Norrell*
by Susanna Clarke

11 What location is described?

① a forest
② London
③ a zoo
④ a graveyard filled with coffins

12 What is the speaker's attitude toward the present-day city?

① He loves it.
② He is disappointed with it.
③ He feels at home there.
④ He has nothing to compare it with.

13 What is the mood of the description of London as it used to be?

① proud
② ashamed
③ uncertain
④ condescending

14 What is the narrator's tone?

① confused
② sneering
③ despairing
④ disappointed

15 What detail tells you that the place the narrator remembers is not a place anyone alive today would know?

① Many buildings and spires reached high into the sky.
② Dragons and griffins lived in cages in the gardens.
③ The stone carvings were as intricate as flowing water.
④ All the shrines were made of precious metals.

16 List three details the author provides that help you picture the churches.

_____

_____

26

Recognizing Descriptive Details

Authors use **descriptive details** to engage readers' senses and help them picture the story as it unfolds. Descriptive details include:

- sensory details
- figurative language
- vivid verbs
- specific nouns
- effective modifiers

Sensory details are words and phrases that appeal to one or more of the five senses: sight, hearing, touch, taste, and smell. Sensory details evoke readers' emotions and help them experience the story as if they were there. Sensory details are also called **imagery** because they create images in readers' minds. How many sensory details does the passage below use?

> Miguel trudged down the street, pausing only to wipe sweat off his face. The hazy sun reflected off the glass skyscrapers and hurt his eyes. The pavement burned right through his shoes. He tasted the grit that filled the air from all the cars passing by. At the corner, he smelled food garbage that had been left out too long. Beach music played from a café's speakers.

Sight	Hearing	Touch	Taste	Smell
Miguel trudged	cars passing by	wipe sweat off his face	the grit that filled the air	food garbage
hazy sun reflected off glass skyscrapers	beach music played	pavement burned through his shoes		
cars passing by				

Figurative language creates images beyond the words' literal meanings. It includes similes, metaphors, personification, exaggeration, and understatement.

- A **simile** is a comparison using *like* or *as:* "Listening to Thelonious Monk is *like* diving into a cool lake."
- A **metaphor** is a comparison that doesn't use *like* or *as:* "Listening to Thelonious Monk *is* diving into a cool lake."
- **Personification** gives human qualities to animals, ideas, or objects: *"Mother Nature is angry* today."
- **Exaggeration** overstates something for emphasis or comic effect: "If I've told you once, I've told you a *million times.*"
- **Understatement** makes something seem less important than it is, often for comic effect: "Joan was *slightly annoyed* when Ed took their life savings and bought a boat."

Descriptive details engage readers' senses and help them picture the story as it unfolds.

Sensory details (also called **imagery**) are words and phrases that appeal to one or more of the five senses.

Figurative language expresses a truth beyond the words' literal meaning. It includes similes, metaphors, personification, exaggeration, and understatement.

Related Skills: 17, 20–25, and 34

Vivid verbs are precise. They give readers a more accurate sense of characters and their behavior. They also describe setting and action so clearly that readers can picture them.

Examples:

The overbearing man *bellowed* at his wife.

The rain *pattered* gently on the old tin roof.

The spoiled athlete *flounced* out of the locker room when a reporter asked him why he had *fumbled* the game-losing pass.

Specific nouns help paint word pictures. Good writers use exactly the right words, including specific nouns (*border collie,* not just *dog; red maple,* not just *tree*) to evoke mental pictures and moods.

Example:

The *weightlifter* and the *accountant* made an odd couple, but he didn't mind that she could bench press him.

Effective modifiers add to the description of a place or an event. Precise adjectives and adverbs accurately convey details about where, when, how, how big, and so on. They can reveal important details about characters.

Example:

The *well-dressed* young man sang *jauntily* as he skipped down the *narrow cobblestone* street.

How could you improve the sentence below?

Emma Stone was riding her bike along the lake one morning when a man on a scooter came up behind her, rode in front of her, and put on his brakes.

If you replace the nouns with more specific nouns, the verbs with vivid verbs, and add modifiers, you could have this:

Emma Stone was *pedaling* her *red ten-speed bicycle slowly* along *Lake Michigan* when a man on a *rusty scooter speeded* up behind her, *darted* in front of her, and *slammed* on his brakes.

Vivid verbs give precise descriptions of characters' behavior, the action, and the setting.

Specific nouns are particular, not vague (*border collie,* not *dog*).

Effective modifiers add to the description of a place or an event.

GED Readiness

Read each passage and answer the questions.

WHERE ARE CHARLIE AND GRANDPA JOE?

1 Charlie Bucket found himself standing in a long corridor that stretched away in front of him as far as he could see. The corridor was so wide that a car could easily have been driven along it. The walls were pale pink, the lighting was soft and pleasant.

2 "How lovely and warm!" whispered Charlie.

3 "I know. And what a marvelous smell!" answered Grandpa Joe, taking a long deep sniff. All the most wonderful smells in the world seemed to be mixed up in the air around them—the smell of roasting coffee and burnt sugar and melting chocolate and mint and violets and crushed hazelnuts and apple blossom and caramel and lemon peel. . . .

4 And far away in the distance, from the heart of the great factory, came a muffled roar of energy as though some monstrous gigantic machine were spinning its wheels at breakneck speed.

—Excerpted from *Charlie and the Chocolate Factory*
by Roald Dahl

❶ What feeling do the descriptive details in paragraph 1 evoke?

① fear
② comfort
③ anxiety
④ excitement

❷ What sense does paragraph 3 appeal to?

① hearing
② touch
③ taste
④ smell

❸ What sense does paragraph 4 appeal to?

① hearing
② touch
③ taste
④ sight

❹ What words in paragraph 4 are sensory?

① far away
② great factory
③ muffled roar
④ gigantic machine

Dr. Perholt is at a conference in Turkey when she buys a strange glass bottle. When she cleans it, the genie in the bottle emerges.

WHAT IS IN THE BOTTLE?

She turned on the mixer-tap in the basin, made the water warm, blood-heat, and held the bottle under the jet, turning it round and round. The glass became blue, threaded with

5 opaque white canes, cobalt-blue, darkly bright, gleaming and wonderful. She turned it and turned it, rubbing the tenacious dust-spots with thumbs and fingers, and suddenly it gave a kind of warm leap in her hand, like a frog, like

10 a still-beating heart in the hands of a surgeon. She gripped and clasped and steadied, and her own heart took a fierce, fast beat of apprehension, imagining blue glass splinters everywhere. But all that happened was that the

15 stopper, with a faint glassy grinding, suddenly flew out of the neck of the flask and fell, tinkling but unbroken, into the basin. And out of the bottle in her hands came a swarming, an exhalation, a fast-moving dark stain which

20 made a high-pitched buzzing sound and smelled of woodsmoke, of cinnamon, of sulfur, of something that might have been incense, of something that was not leather, but was? The dark cloud gathered and turned and flew in a

25 great paisley or comma out of the bathroom. I am seeing things, thought Dr. Perholt, following, and found she could not follow, for the bathroom door was blocked by what she slowly made out to be an enormous foot, a foot

30 with five toes as high as she was, surmounted by yellow horny toenails, a foot encased in skin that was olive-colored, laced with gold, like snakeskin, not scaly but somehow mailed [armored].

—Excerpted from "The Djinn in the Nightingale's
Eye" by A. S. Byatt

5 What figure of speech does the author use in lines 9–10?

_____

6 List three vivid verbs in the passage.

_____

7 List three specific nouns that evoke an image.

_____

8 What feeling do lines 28–33 evoke?

_____

HOW DOES THE AUTHOR FEEL ABOUT AYEMENEM?

1   May in Ayemenem is a hot, brooding month. The days are long and humid. The river shrinks and black crows gorge on bright mangoes in still, dustgreen trees. Red bananas ripen. Jackfruits burst. Dissolute bluebottles [flies] hum vacuously [stupidly] in the fruity air. Then they sun themselves against clear windowpanes and die, fatly baffled in the sun.

2   The nights are clear, but suffused [filled] with sloth and sullen expectation.

3   But by early June the southwest monsoon breaks and there are three months of wind and water with short spells of sharp, glittering sunshine that thrilled children snatch to play with. The countryside turns an immodest green. Boundaries blur as tapioca fences take root and bloom. Brick walls turn mossgreen. Pepper vines snake up electric poles. Wild creepers burst through laterite [red rock] banks and spill across the flooded roads. Boats ply in the bazaars. And small fish appear in the puddles that fill the PWD potholes on the highways.

4   It was raining when Rahel came back to Ayemenem. Slanting silver ropes slammed into loose earth, plowing it up like gunfire. The old house on the hill wore its steep, gabled roof pulled over its ears like a low hat.

—Excerpted from _The God of Small Things_
by Arundhati Roy

9 What feeling does paragraph 1 evoke?

① scarcity
② abundance
③ hurry
④ sadness

10 What do paragraphs 1 and 3 have in common?

① Both are about plant growth.
② Both describe rain.
③ Both take place in autumn.
④ Neither one paints a word picture.

11 In paragraph 4, "slanting silver ropes" is

① a simile
② a metaphor
③ personification
④ exaggeration

12 In paragraph 4, the words _wore_ and _pulled over its ears_ create what figure of speech?

① a simile
② a metaphor
③ personification
④ exaggeration

13 List four vivid verbs in paragraph 1.

_____

14 List four specific nouns in paragraph 3.

_____

15 List four adjectives in paragraph 4.

_____

16 Contrast the weather imagery in paragraph 1 with that in paragraph 3.

_____

17 What feeling does paragraph 3 evoke?

_____

Discovering Theme and Symbols

A **theme** is the main idea, the underlying message in a work of literature. The theme may be an insight into life, a perception about human nature, or a viewpoint about a social issue. The theme is not the subject of a story; it is the story's meaning. For example, a story may be about the subject of prejudice, and its theme may be "People who hate others hurt themselves most of all." A story, especially a novel-length story, may have several themes.

A **universal theme** is one that holds true across nearly all time periods and cultures. Most universal themes inspire strong feelings. Common universal themes include the following:

- War has no winners.
- Life is not fair.
- Suffering builds character.
- Love makes life worth living.
- You don't know what you have until it's gone.

Sometimes the theme of a story is stated directly. More often it's an **implied theme**, which readers must infer by considering all the elements of the story and asking what message it conveys. Such themes are revealed gradually through the characters, plot, setting, imagery, and other literary elements. As you read a story, notice how the following fictional elements suggest the theme:

- characters' observations (especially those of the main character) about life and human behavior
- the narrator's observations about life and human behavior
- the nature of the conflicts and how they are resolved
- the significance of important events
- the setting's influence on characters and their actions
- striking images and character descriptions
- the language the author chooses to tell the story

In the story we analyzed in Skill 22, "Little Red Riding Hood," the theme is implied. It was originally told to warn teenage girls to be suspicious of men, but that could be generalized to this universal theme: Be suspicious of people (and things) that don't look the way they normally do. This is the theme of many stories, including the chapter of *The Iliad* where the Greeks give the Trojans a giant wooden horse in which Greek warriors are concealed.

One way writers communicate themes is by using symbols. A **symbol** is a person, object, place, or activity that stands for something beyond itself. For example, hearts symbolize love, and lions symbolize strength. Other symbols may be unique to a particular story. A symbol may have more than one meaning, or its meaning may change from the beginning to the end of a story.

> A **theme** is the main idea, the underlying message in a work of literature. A theme may be **universal** and is usually **implied**.

> A **symbol** is a person, object, place, or activity that stands for something beyond itself.

Read the following short story and identify the theme and any symbols used. Ask yourself, "What lesson about life did I learn from this story? What lesson did a character learn?"

WHY IS YOLANDA AFRAID OF SNOW?

As the only immigrant in my class, I was put in a special seat in the first row by the window, apart from the other children so that Sister Zoe could tutor me without disturbing them. Slowly, she enunciated the new words I was to repeat: *laundromat, cornflakes, subway, snow.*

Soon I picked up enough English to understand holocaust was in the air. Sister Zoe explained to a wide-eyed classroom what was happening in Cuba. Russian missiles were being assembled, trained supposedly on New York City. President Kennedy, looking worried too, was on the television at home, explaining we might have to go to war against the Communists. At school, we had air-raid drills: an ominous bell would go off and we'd file into the hall, fall to the floor, cover our heads with our coats, and imagine our hair falling out, the bones in our arms going soft. At home, Mami and my sisters and I said a rosary for world peace. I heard new vocabulary: *nuclear bomb, radioactive fallout, bomb shelter.* Sister Zoe explained how it would happen. She drew a picture of a mushroom on the blackboard and dotted a flurry of chalkmarks for the dusty fallout that would kill us all.

The months grew cold, November, December. It was dark when I got up in the morning, frosty when I followed my breath to school. One morning as I sat at my desk daydreaming out the window, I saw dots in the air like the ones Sister Zoe had drawn—random, at first, then lots and lots. I shrieked, "Bomb! Bomb!" Sister Zoe jerked around, her full black skirt ballooning as she hurried to my side. A few girls began to cry.

But then Sister Zoe's shocked look faded. "Why, Yolanda dear, that's snow!" She laughed. "Snow."

"Snow," I repeated. I looked out the window warily. All my life I had heard about the white crystals that fell out of American skies in the winter. From my desk I watched the fine powder dust the sidewalk and parked cars below. Each flake was different, Sister Zoe said, like a person, irreplaceable and beautiful.

—Excerpted from "Snow" by Julia Alvarez

The key to this story's meaning is the last sentence. Yolanda learns that snowflakes are harmless and beautiful. So the theme might be that new things are not always dangerous.

Snowflakes are also the main symbol in the story. At first they symbolize death and destruction. Later, they symbolize people, each one different, irreplaceable, and beautiful.

Read the story and circle the answers.

WHAT HAPPENED TO THE GORILLAS?

1   Thirty-two sixth graders from Holmes Elementary lined the rails that protected the glass of the Gorilla Room from fingerprints. Two of them were eating their lunches. Sixteen had removed some item from their lunch bags and were throwing them instead of eating them: their teacher paid no attention. Five were whispering about a sixth who fiddled with the locked knob on the workroom door as if she didn't hear. Five were discussing the fabulous Michael K.'s eighty-two-point game last night, and three were looking at the gorillas. Anders approached one of these three. It was part of his job. He was better at the other parts.

2   "We have a mixture of lowland and mountain gorillas," he told the boy in the baseball cap. The boy did not respond. That suited Anders fine. "I know which is which," he continued, "because they're my gorillas. Now, some experts argue the noses are different or the mountain gorilla's hair is longer, but I've studied this matter and never seen that."

3   There were thirteen gorillas inside the exhibit. Five sat on rocks at the back. One baby played with a tire swing, batting it with her feet and turning an occasional somersault through the center. One stared in contemplative [thinking] concentration at nothing. Four alternated through a variety of grooming arrangements. One nibbled on the peeled end of a stick. One surveyed all the others. It was a dignified scene. *Sullen. Reserved. Moody. Shy.* These were some of the words commonly applied over the years to gorillas. They had none of the joie de vivre [joy in living] of chimps. Gorillas were not clowns. It took a dignified, reserved person to appreciate them. Perhaps it took a little loneliness. And Anders had that.

4   The boy pointed over the rail. "That one looks really mean." Anders did not have to follow the finger to know which gorilla the boy meant.

5   A lowland gorilla. Gargantua the Great. "Paul du Chaillu was probably the first white man to see gorillas," Anders told the boy. "He tracked them and shot them and came back to France and told stories about their ferocity [brutality]. Made him look brave. Made his books sell. Barnum did the same thing with his circus gorillas. He knew people would pay more to be scared than to be moved." Beyond the glass, Gargantua swiveled his huge head. The teeth were permanently exposed, but the eyes, directed obliquely left [at an acute angle], said something else. Anders was proud of those eyes.

6   "That gorilla there, well, an angry sailor poured nitric acid on him. The sailor'd lost his job and wanted to get even with the importer. The acid damaged the muscles on the gorilla's face, so he always looks like he's snarling. It's the only expression he can make."

7   A storm of peanut shells hit the glass. Anders identified the culprit and took him by the arm. Anders did not raise his voice. "I was telling a story about the big gorilla in the corner," he said to the second boy. "This will interest you. He was raised by Mrs. Lintz, an Englishwoman, and he lived in her house in Brooklyn until he got too big. He may look fierce, but he was always terrified of thunder. One night there was a thunderstorm. Mrs. Lintz woke up to find a four-hundred-pound gorilla huddled on the foot of her bed, sobbing."

8   There were perhaps six children paying attention to Anders now. Somewhere an elephant trumpeted. "They don't look at us," one boy complained, and a girl in a plaid shirt asked if they had names.

9   "Actually, we have three gorillas who were raised as pets by Englishwomen," Anders said. "John Daniel. And Toto, too, the fat one there looking for fleas. And Gargantua, whose real name is Buddy. Gorillas don't look at anyone directly and they don't like to be stared at themselves. Very unsuited to zoo life. The first gorillas brought to this country died within weeks. The gorillas who lived in private homes with mothers instead of keepers did better."

10   Toto yawned. "Toto was bought as a bride for Buddy," Anders said. "She was raised in Cuba, where she had her own pet. A cat."

11   Anders had ten children listening now. Did any of them have cats? Anders doubted it.

12   "John Daniel was purchased from Harrod's [a British department store] by Major Rupert Penny of the Royal Air Force as a present for his aunt. Mrs. Cunningham consulted no experts but used her own judgment in devising his diet, which included fruit, vegetables, and raw hamburger. And roses. He loved to eat roses, but only if they were fresh. He wouldn't eat a faded rose."

13   Too subtle for sixth graders. Anders was down to an audience of four. "So interesting," the teacher said brightly, although Anders did not think he had been listening. Probably he had been there with a different class last year and perhaps the year before that. Probably he had heard it before. Probably he had never listened. "Can you all thank Mr. Anders for showing us his gorillas?" the teacher suggested, and then without pausing for thanks, "We won't see the giraffes if we don't press on."

14   No one else was scheduled until three. Anders opened the workroom to get his own lunch and a book. He was studying Koko now, a gorilla raised by a Stanford graduate student and taught to sign. He planned to eat inside with his gorillas, but Miss Elliot arrived instead. "Have lunch with me," she said. "I made cookies. It's a beautiful day."

15   Miss Elliot often came at lunchtime. She had no real interest in Anders, or so Anders thought. Her own upbringing as the baby of a large, loving family had left her with a certain amount of affection to spare. She regarded Anders as a project. No healthy young man could be allowed to molder among the exhibits. Get him out. Give him a bit of medicinal companionship. Miss Elliot wore a uniform with an elephant on the sleeve and below that the black circle. Miss Elliot showed the elephants, but they weren't her elephants and Anders doubted she even understood the distinction.

16   If he refused her offer, he would face her brand of implacable [unyielding], perky determination. He found it unendurable. So he nodded instead and put the book back beside his tools and his sketches. He joined her at the exit, opening the door.

17   Miss Elliot shook her head. "You always forget," she said. Her tone was indulgent but firm. She reached back past him, brushing across the black circle on his sleeve, and threw the switch that turned the gorillas off. They ate lunch on the grass outside the Hall of Extinction. The cookies were stale. The flowers were in bloom.

—"Faded Roses" by Karen Joy Fowler

1 What does the story reveal about gorillas?

① They don't like stale cookies.
② They've died out.
③ They have bad tempers.
④ They're very strong.

2 What clues tell you what happened to them?

① Miss Elliot throws the switch to turn the gorillas off.
② Both animal keepers wear black circles.
③ The exhibit is in the Hall of Extinction.
④ all of the above

3 The story's title, "Faded Roses," symbolizes that

① gorillas don't like to eat faded roses
② Anders is getting old without a life
③ the gorillas seem faded to the children
④ this world is fading as its creatures vanish

4 What is the theme of the story?

① Kids are hard to entertain.
② Life is not fair.
③ You can lose much by not paying attention.
④ People need other people.

5 What does the fact that cats are so scarce (paragraph 11) suggest?

_____

_____

6 Why doesn't Anders like to turn off the gorilla exhibit?

_____

_____

28 Understanding Extended Synthesis

As you read, you draw conclusions by adding your own experience and background knowledge to the information presented. You *synthesize* the different elements. **Synthesis** is a reasoning process that puts together several bits of information to reach a new understanding.

When you integrate new information from outside the passage with what you learn from the passage, you're performing **extended synthesis**. Solving synthesis questions is like solving a puzzle. All of the pieces, when put together, give you the full picture.

The additional information you'll be given might be

- about the author's life (from diaries or biographies)
- about the author's other novels or short stories
- events that occur or characters who appear at some other time in the story
- historical background of the literary work
- critical commentary or reviews of the work

Read the passage below and the extra information given below it.

> **Synthesis** is a reasoning process that adds information together to reach a new understanding.

> **Extended synthesis** is adding new information from outside the passage to what you learn from the passage to come to a better understanding of what you are reading.

WHAT IS MRS. PROUDIE LIKE?

Triumph sat throned upon [Mrs.Proudie's] brow; and all the joys of dominion hovered about her curls. Her lord [Dr. Proudie, the bishop] had that morning contested with her a great point. He had received an invitation to spend a couple of days with the archbishop. His soul longed for the gratification. Not a word, however, in his grace's note alluded to the fact of his being a married man; and, if he went at all, he must go alone.

The bishop [Dr. Proudie], with some beating about the bush, made the lady [Mrs. Proudie] understand that he very much wished to go. The lady, without any beating about the bush, made the bishop understand that she wouldn't hear of it. It would be useless here to repeat the arguments that were used on each side, and needless to record the result. Those who are married will understand very well how the battle was lost and won; and those who are single will never understand it till they learn the lesson which experience alone can give.

—Excerpted from *Barchester Towers* by Anthony Trollope

Later in the novel, Dr. Proudie's employee, Mr. Slope, wants to have a friend of his promoted. Mrs. Proudie has a different favorite candidate.

Related Skills: 1–5, 10, 18, 20–27

Based on this information and the excerpt, what will likely happen?

   ① Dr. Proudie will hire the man Mr. Slope recommends.
   ② Mrs. Proudie will beg Mr. Slope not to influence her husband.
   ③ Mrs. Proudie will give in gracefully.
   ④ Dr. Proudie will hire the man Mrs. Proudie recommends.

In the passage, Mrs. Proudie wins an argument with her husband (she won't let him take a trip alone) and suggests that she usually gets her way ("without any beating about the bush"). The added information describes a new conflict in which her husband will make a decision. When you integrate those two pieces of information, you can conclude that ④ Mrs. Proudie will influence Dr. Proudie to hire the man she wants.

Here's another passage and extra information.

HOW DOES CLARISSA DALLOWAY FEEL?

A young man had killed himself. And they talked of it at [Clarissa's] party—the Bradshaws talked of death. He had killed himself—but how? Always her body went through it first, when she was told, suddenly, of an accident; her dress flamed, her body burnt. He had thrown himself from a window. Up had flashed the ground; through him, blundering, bruising, went the rusty spikes. There he lay with a thud, thud, thud in his brain, and then a suffocation of blackness. So she saw it. But why had he done it?

—Excerpted from *Mrs. Dalloway* by Virginia Woolf

The author, Virginia Woolf, committed suicide herself by drowning some years after writing this book.

Based on this biographical information and the passage, what is probably the author's purpose for writing the passage?

   ① to disturb readers with vivid details about death
   ② to help readers feel, as clearly as she could, what it must feel like to die
   ③ to introduce the mystery of why the man killed himself
   ④ to show how rude the Bradshaws were for bringing up such a sad subject at a party

The passage describes the character's habit of imagining vividly how a dying person must feel. The additional information tells us that the author eventually killed herself, which suggests that she probably thought a great deal over the years about what dying would feel like. When you integrate those two pieces of information, you realize that the author wants ② to describe the feeling of dying.

GED Readiness

Read the following passages. Then circle the correct answers.

The main character, Jim, is at a training school for sailors. Here he's daydreaming about how he'll act in a crisis.

HOW DOES JIM SEE HIMSELF?

On the lower deck in the babel [confusion] of two hundred voices [Jim] would forget himself, and beforehand live in his mind the sea-life of light literature. He saw himself saving people from sinking ships, cutting away masts in a hurricane, swimming through a surf with a line; or as a lonely castaway, barefooted and half naked, walking on uncovered reefs in search of shellfish to stave off starvation. He confronted savages on tropical shores, quelled mutinies on the high seas, and in a small boat upon the ocean kept up the hearts of despairing men—always an example of devotion to duty, and as unflinching as a hero in a book.

—Excerpted from *Lord Jim* by Joseph Conrad

1 Later in the novel, Jim's ship begins to sink. The cowardly officers take the few lifeboats, leaving the passengers to drown. At the last moment, Jim jumps into a lifeboat, too.

Given the behavior Jim expected of himself, how will he feel about rescuing himself instead of the passengers?

① relieved
② guilty
③ concerned
④ heroic

2 The author went to sea himself at age 17. What detail from the passage did he most likely experience firsthand?

① the babel of two hundred voices
② cutting away masts in a hurricane
③ life as a lonely castaway
④ quelling mutinies on the high seas

IS THE "REST CURE" HELPING THE NARRATOR?

If a physician of high standing, and one's own husband, assures friends and relatives that there is really nothing the matter with one but temporary nervous depression—a slight hysterical tendency—what is one to do?

My brother is also a physician, and also of high standing, and he says the same thing.

So I take phosphates or phosphites—whichever it is—and tonics, and air and exercise, and journeys, and am absolutely forbidden to "work" until I am well again.

Personally, I disagree with their ideas.

Personally, I believe that congenial work, with excitement and change, would do me good.

But what is one to do?

I did write for a while in spite of them; but it *does* exhaust me a good deal—having to be so sly about it, or else meet with heavy opposition.

—Excerpted from "The Yellow Wallpaper"
by Charlotte Perkins Gilman

3 With nothing else to think about, the narrator becomes convinced that there are women trapped in the wallpaper of her room. She pulls the paper off in an attempt to free them.

What effect does the rest cure enforced by her husband have on the narrator?

① It makes her feel better physically.
② It makes her feel better mentally.
③ It makes her more hysterical.
④ It gives her time to think about decorating.

4 The author herself underwent a rest cure. She sent this story to the doctor who had made her stop writing. He modified his cure to permit patients some mental stimulation.

What does the doctor's response suggest about the effect of the rest cure on Gilman?

① It made her more productive afterward.
② It was just the relaxation she needed.
③ It brought her closer to the doctor.
④ It was a very unpleasant experience.

Read the following passages. Then circle the correct answers.

WHO IS GANDALF?

Gandalf! If you had heard only a quarter of what I have heard about him, and I have only heard very little of all there is to hear, you would be prepared for any sort of remarkable tale. Tales and adventures sprouted up all over the place wherever he went, in the most extraordinary fashion. He had not been down that way under The Hill for ages and ages, not since his friend the Old Took died, in fact, and the hobbits had almost forgotten what he looked like. He had been away over The Hill and across The Water on businesses of his own since they were all small hobbit-boys and hobbit-girls.

All that the unsuspecting Bilbo saw that morning was an old man with a staff. He had a tall pointed blue hat, a long grey cloak, a silver scarf over which a white beard hung down below his waist, and immense black boots.

"Good Morning!" said Bilbo, and he meant it. The sun was shining, and the grass was very green. But Gandalf looked at him from under long bushy eyebrows that stuck out further than the brim of his shady hat.

"What do you mean?" he said.

—Excerpted from *The Hobbit* by J. R. R. Tolkien

5 Tolkien began writing *The Hobbit* around 1930. Nearly twenty years earlier, at age 19, he had been on vacation in Switzerland when he bought a postcard of a painting called *Der Berggeist (The Mountain Spirit)*. It showed an old man with a white beard, a long cloak, and a wide-brimmed hat.

From this purchase and the passage, what can you conclude about Tolkien?

① He should have become a painter instead of a writer.
② He had the character of Gandalf in his mind for a long time.
③ He had no sense of humor.
④ He saw animals in Switzerland that gave him the idea for hobbits.

6 Later in the novel, Gandalf risks both his life and Bilbo's. What can you conclude about the progress of their relationship?

① Gandalf never trusts Bilbo.
② Bilbo takes Gandalf for granted.
③ They avoid each other after Bilbo nearly dies.
④ They become close friends.

The Left Hand of Darkness *takes place on a planet called Gethen, where people are androgynous (neither male nor female) most of the time. At certain times they enter* kemmer, *a period of sexual awakening.*

WHAT'S IT LIKE TO SWITCH GENDERS?

When the individual finds a partner in *kemmer,* hormonal secretion is further stimulated (most importantly by touch—secretion? scent?) until in one partner either a male or female hormonal dominance is established. . . . The mother of several children may be the father of several more.

—Excerpted from The *Left Hand of Darkness* by Ursula K. Le Guin

7 Later in the novel, a character says,

"Gethenians, though highly competitive (as proved by the elaborate social channels provided for competition, for prestige, etc.) seem not to be very aggressive; at least they apparently have never yet had what one would call a war. They kill one another readily by ones and twos; seldom by tens and twenties; never by hundreds or thousands. Why?"

What does this comment suggest about people who are not androgynous?

① Most women are not very competitive.
② Most wars are started by men.
③ Neither men nor women fear death.
④ Few murderers can stop after killing one person.

Learning How to Read a Poem

The skills you have learned for reading fiction are useful as you read poetry. In Skills 29–35, you will learn new skills and identify traits that are unique to poetry.

Poetry is a form of literary expression that (unlike prose) breaks lines of text in different places to contribute to its meaning and/or its sound. Poetry has **rhythm** (a beat), but it doesn't always **rhyme**. Poetry often uses **stanzas** (verses), imaginative language, and **figures of speech** to convey emotions and ideas.

Poetry is the most condensed and the most interactive form of literature. A good poet boils down an emotion or an experience to its essence. Then he or she describes it so that when you read it, you don't just understand the words; you share the feeling. You may have to work a little harder to read poems, but they reward the effort.

① First, read the title. Think about what the title means to you and what you expect the poem to be about.

② Read the poem straight through to get the general idea and the **mood.** This first time, don't stop for words you don't know or confusing punctuation. Once you see the poem as a whole, these things may make more sense.

③ Identify the **speaker.** Like a narrator in fiction, the speaker in a poem is not always the person writing the poem. The speaker can be a fictional character, an animal, or even a thing.

④ Now read the poem again. This time, go slowly. Look up unfamiliar words in a dictionary. Notice where sentences begin and end. If words are in a peculiar order, try to puzzle out what the sentence means. Apply what you've come to understand about the poem to the parts you find more difficult.

⑤ Notice the language used and any unusual **diction, comparisons, imagery,** and **figures of speech.** Are there any objects or events in the poem that might serve as **symbols?** What feelings and ideas do they make you think of?

⑥ Read the poem out loud. Listen to the sound of the words and the **rhythm** of the language. Do some words **rhyme?** Are they in a pattern? Pause to breathe where there's a period or other end mark, not at the end of every line. Notice how lines are grouped together and whether any are repeated. What is the poet stressing by repeating certain words and lines?

⑦ Use all of this information to figure out the poem's literal meaning. Then **make inferences** and **draw conclusions** until you feel you understand its layers.

> **Poetry** is a form of literary expression that breaks lines of text in different places to contribute to its meaning and/or its sound. A poem is written in groups of lines, called **stanzas.** Poetry has **rhythm,** but it doesn't always **rhyme.**

⑧ **Paraphrase** in your own words what the poem is saying or **summarize** it briefly. This will help you figure out both its subject (what it's about) and its **theme** (its underlying message about life).

You can take notes or underline and circle parts of the poem at any stage as you analyze it. Try reading and analyzing the poem below.

> ### WHAT IS THE MAN'S PROBLEM?
> #### Not Waving but Drowning
> Nobody heard him, the dead man,
> But still he lay moaning:
> 3 I was much further out than you thought
> 4 And not waving but drowning.
>
> Poor chap, he always loved larking
> And now he's dead
> It must have been too cold for him his heart gave way,
> They said.
>
> 9 Oh, no no no, it was too cold always
> (Still the dead one lay moaning)
> 11 I was much too far out all my life
> 12 And not waving but drowning.
> —by Stevie Smith

[handwritten margin notes:]
- Ask: Has there been a time when things went wrong b/c their words/Gestures were misunderstood.
- then read
- write script
- What is relationship to speaker
- What image do you see.

On your second, slower reading, what does the title make you expect? Someone gesturing desperately for help but being misunderstood? Notice that there are three speakers in this poem:

- the narrator, who tells the story
- the dead man, who says lines 3–4 in the first stanza and lines 9 and 11–12 in the third stanza
- "they", who speak the second stanza. The dead man tries to speak to "they," but only the narrator and the reader hear him.

Are there any words you don't know? Does it help to know that *larking* means "joking around"?

Note how the title is repeated at the ends of stanzas 1 and 3. The image of the man far out from shore gives you the literal meaning of what happens in the poem: A man drowns. Combined with line 11, it also gives you the theme: Life is full of failures to communicate; we can't understand each other no matter how hard we try. The man has been drowning (misunderstood) all his life.

GED Readiness

Read the following excerpt from a poem. Then circle the correct answers.

HOW DOES THE SPEAKER FEEL?

The Day Is Done

1   The day is done, and the darkness
        Falls from the wings of Night,
    As a feather is wafted downward
4   From an eagle in his flight.

5   I see the lights of the village
        Gleam through the rain and the mist,
    And a feeling of sadness comes o'er me
        That my soul cannot resist.

    A feeling of sadness and longing,
10   That is not akin to pain,
    And resembles sorrow only
        As the mist resembles the rain.

13 Come, read to me some poem,
        Some simple and heartfelt lay,
    That shall soothe this restless feeling,
16   And banish the thoughts of day.

    Not from the grand old Masters,
        Not from the bards sublime
    Whose distant footsteps echo
20   Through the corridors of Time

    For, like strains of martial music,
        Their mighty thoughts suggest
    Life's endless toil and endeavor;
        And to-night I long for rest.

25 Read from some humbler poet,
        Whose songs gushed from his heart,
    As showers from the clouds of summer
        Or tears from the eyelids start.

        —by Henry Wadsworth Longfellow

1 Who are the characters in this poem?

① the eagle and the speaker
② the eagle and the person who will read aloud
③ the speaker and the person who will read aloud
④ the speaker, the Masters, and the bards

2 What is the speaker's mood?

① calm
② sad
③ energetic
④ pained

3 How many stanzas does this excerpt include?

① two
② three
③ five
④ seven

4 How many lines are there in each stanza?

① two
② four
③ six
④ eight

5 Which pair of words rhymes?

① *flight* and *Night*
② *darkness* and *downward*
③ *pain* and *lay*
④ *poet* and *heart*

6 "Come, read to me some poem," is a

① line
② stanza
③ sentence
④ figure of speech

7 When the poet uses a simile in lines 1–4, he says the darkness falls like

① an eagle
② night
③ a feather
④ flight

8 When you combine the title with lines 13–16, what can you infer that the speaker wants?

① to go out and party
② to relax after a long day
③ to get some work done
④ to be alone

Read the following poem excerpt. Then circle the correct answers.

HOW DOES THE STUDENT AMAZE HIS TEACHER?

Poetry Workshop at the Homeless Shelter
So I'm the white teacher reading
some Etheridge Knight poems to the four
residents who showed: *For Black Poets*
Who Think of Suicide—thinking
5   these guys have seen it all and want
something hard-core, when a black man
named Tyrone raises his hand:
These poems offend me.
They do? I say. Yes. I was raised
10 *not to curse, and I don't see why*
a poem has to use those words.

What poems do you like?
Langston Hughes.
Yeah, someone else says, Jean Toomer, man.
15 Tyrone says, *Let's talk about calculating a poem.*
Pardon me, I say—
You know, cipherin a poem—
Why don't you show me?
Tyrone draws this two-dimensional
20 image of this three-dimensional grid, based
on numerology, he says, in which each letter
of the alphabet corresponds to a number.

Look, it's like you start
with a 13, 25, then go to 8, 5, 1, 18, 20—
25 *that's the start of my first line:*
"My heart opens to the new world"—See?
I am stunned by it all—strange genius
or just strange? *How long*
29 *have you been writing this way?*
30 *All my life, but nobody understands it.*
I got boxes in my room filled with calculations,
I got plays and soap operas, and one day
I'll sell them.

—by Jan Beatty

9 Who are the two main characters?

① Langston Hughes and Jean Toomer
② Etheridge Knight and Tyrone
③ the poetry teacher and Tyrone
④ Etheridge Knight and the poetry teacher

10 Who is the narrator (whose spoken words and thoughts are both given)?

① Etheridge Knight
② Langston Hughes
③ Tyrone
④ the teacher

11 What surprises the teacher in stanza 1?

① the fact that only four residents showed up
② Tyrone's objection to swearing
③ the fact that some residents are black
④ Tyrone's willingness to raise his hand

12 Which is an example of rhyme in stanza 1?

① *white* and *Knight*
② *poems* and *poets*
③ *thinking* and *these*
④ *curse* and *words*

13 Who says, "Why don't you show me?" in stanza 2?

① the teacher
② Tyrone
③ Langston Hughes
④ Jean Toomer

14 Line 29 breaks where it does

① so that lines 29 and 30 will be the same length
② because the teacher's words end there
③ because line breaks occur at the end of sentences
④ so that its last word rhymes with the last word in line 30

15 Why is the teacher amazed by the first line of Tyrone's poem?

① She believes in numerology.
② She didn't think a homeless man could write.
③ She finds the words emotionally moving.
④ She can't believe his poems haven't been published.

Identifying Subject and Theme

The **subject** of a poem is what it's about. No subject is off limits: a drowning man, nightfall, a snake, the girl next door, a crime. A poem can take as its subject anything under the sun (and beyond). Think about how varied the subjects of your favorite songs are.

A good poem (or song) appeals to both your mind and your emotions. The subject is just one of many contributors to the complete effect. British poet T. S. Eliot said that the subject of a poem is like the bit of meat a burglar brings to distract a guard dog "while the poem does its work" upon the reader through form, rhythm, rhyme, imagery, and all the other elements you'll learn about in Skills 31–35.

The subject leads naturally to the **theme**, a poem's underlying message about life or human nature. If you read a dozen poems whose subject is love, every one could have a different theme. One poem's message might be that "love conquers all." Another's might be "love is an illusion." A poem may have several themes.

As you read the poem below, think about its subject. What message about that subject is the poet trying to convey? Review the steps of "Learning How to Read a Poem" (Skill 29) as you read.

> The **subject** of a poem is what it's about. No subject is off limits.

> The **theme** of a poem is its underlying message about life or human nature.

HOW DOES THE MOTHER FEEL?

Milk-Bubble Ruins

In the long, indolent mornings of fifth-grade
spring vacation, our son sits with the
tag-ends of his breakfast, and blows bubbles in his milk
with a blue straw, and I sit and watch him.
The foam rises furiously
in a dome over the rim of his cup,
we gaze into the edifice of fluid,
its multiple chambers. He puffs and they pile up,
they burst, they subside, he breathes out slowly, and the
multicellular clouds rise,
he inserts the straw into a single globe
and blows a little, and it swells. Ten years ago,
he lay along my arm, drinking.
Now, in late March, he shows me
the white light
pop and dissolve as he
conjures and breaks each small room of milk.

—by Sharon Olds

"Milk-Bubble Ruins" is effective for two main reasons: The theme is universal and the subject is simply a boy drinking milk and blowing bubbles with his straw.

The theme has to do with how fast time flies. The mother remembers him as a baby. ("Ten years ago, / he lay along my arm, drinking.") The white light pops and dissolves as the years of his life flash before his mother. He's the active person in the poem. He "breaks each small room of milk" in the same way that he's breaking out of the confines of childhood and approaching adolescence. This is a poem about a boy's coming of age and his mother's struggle to let go of the "ruins" of his childhood, which she treasures.

Try another example.

HOW DOES THE POET FEEL ABOUT HIS FATHER?

Those Winter Sundays

Sundays too my father got up early
and put his clothes on in the blueblack cold,
then with cracked hands that ached
from labor in the weekday weather made
5 banked fires blaze. No one ever thanked him.

I'd wake and hear the cold splintering, breaking.
When the rooms were warm, he'd call,
and slowly I would rise and dress,
9 fearing the chronic angers of that house,

10 Speaking indifferently to him,
who had driven out the cold
and polished my good shoes as well.
What did I know, what did I know
of love's austere and lonely offices?

—by Robert Hayden

The subject is the speaker's childhood, when his father got up first every morning ("Sundays too") in the bitter cold and warmed the house before anyone else crawled out of bed. Looking back, the speaker realizes how much his father sacrificed for him and how little he appreciated it, so one theme might be that we don't know what we have until it's gone. Another theme could be actions speak louder than words. (Line 9 suggests the father yelled a lot.)

GED Readiness

Read the following poems. Then circle the correct answers.

WHO IS THE POEM ABOUT?

Nobody

I'm nobody! Who are you?
Are you nobody, too?
Then there's a pair of us—don't tell!
They'd banish us, you know.

5 How dreary to be somebody!
How public, like a frog
To tell your name the livelong day
To an admiring bog!

              —by Emily Dickinson

1 Who is the poem about?

  ① a person who hates feeling like a nobody
  ② a person who enjoys feeling like a nobody
  ③ a celebrity
  ④ a frog

2 What is the theme?

  ① Our society doesn't respect "nobodies."
  ② When two nobodies get together, they become somebody.
  ③ Frogs are born performers.
  ④ People don't need praise from others.

3 It's important to the speaker to be

  ① private
  ② admired
  ③ in a crowd
  ④ outdoors

4 What does the second stanza resemble in today's world?

  ① new studies showing how important bogs and other wetlands are to the environment
  ② new studies showing mutations in many species of frog
  ③ tabloid coverage of movie stars
  ④ cartoons featuring animals

HOW DOES THE SPEAKER FEEL ABOUT THE ASTRONOMER?

When I Heard the Learn'd Astronomer

When I heard the learn'd astronomer
When the proofs, the figures, were ranged in columns before me,
When I was shown the charts and diagrams, to add, divide, and measure them,
When I sitting heard the astronomer where he lectured with much applause in the lecture-room,
5 How soon unaccountable I became tired and sick,
Till rising and gliding out I wander'd off by myself,
In the mystical moist night-air, and from time to time
    Looked up in perfect silence at the stars.

              —by Walt Whitman

5 What is the subject of the poem?

  ① An astronomer gives a lecture about the stars, complete with proofs and charts.
  ② A man studies proofs, figures, charts, and diagrams.
  ③ A student gets sick and leaves the room.
  ④ A man listening to an astronomer's lecture gets bored and goes outside.

6 How does the speaker feel about the astronomer?

  ① He thinks the astronomer is not very good.
  ② He thinks the astronomer is excellent.
  ③ He thinks the astronomer has forgotten the mystery of the night sky.
  ④ He thinks the astronomer has chosen the wrong profession.

7 Which statement best reflects the theme?

  ① Nothing can substitute for direct personal experience.
  ② Science must collect a great deal of evidence before making a claim.
  ③ It's not hard to fool an audience.
  ④ There's no accounting for taste.

Read the following poem. Then circle the correct answers.

WHAT DOES THE SPEAKER BELIEVE ABOUT LIFE?

The Black Snake

When the black snake
flashed onto the morning road,
and the truck could not swerve—
death, that is how it happens.

5 Now he lies looped and useless
6 as an old bicycle tire.
I stop the car
and carry him into the bushes.

He is as cool and gleaming
10 as a braided whip, he is as beautiful and quiet
as a dead brother.
I leave him under the leaves

and drive on, thinking
about *death*: its suddenness,
15 its terrible weight,
its certain coming. Yet under

17 reason burns a brighter fire, which the bones
18 have always preferred.
It is the story of endless good fortune.
20 It says to oblivion:* not me!

It is the light at the center of every cell.
22 It is what sent the snake coiling and flowing
    forward
happily all spring through the green leaves
    before
24 he came to the road.

—by Mary Oliver

*being forgotten

8 What is the subject of the poem?

① A snake crosses a road.
② A truck runs over a snake.
③ A dead snake looks like a bicycle tire.
④ The speaker thinks about death.

9 How does the poet succeed in bringing the subject to life?

① She uses a simile in lines 5–6.
② She describes the snake so vividly he seems real.
③ She has the speaker think about reason versus instinct.
④ She has the speaker treat the snake with respect.

10 Where is the theme discussed?

① stanzas 1–2
② stanzas 2–3
③ stanzas 4–5
④ stanzas 5–6

11 Which statement best sums up the theme?

① Life is more powerful than death.
② Death awaits us all in the end.
③ Even snakes are beautiful if you look closely.
④ A short, happy life is better than a long, unhappy one.

12 How does the speaker feel about the snake being run over?

① She's relieved the truck isn't damaged.
② She's glad there's one less snake in the world.
③ She regrets that its life is destroyed.
④ She feels angry that it got in the way.

13 What does the poet mean when she says, "which the bones have always preferred" (lines 17–18)?

_____

_____

14 Why do lines 22–24 flow without punctuation?

_____

_____

Appreciating the Shape of Poetry

The shape of a poem, also called its **form**, is the way it looks on the page. Form includes the number of lines in each stanza and how long the lines are. The stanzas in a poem, like verses in a song, are separated by a line of space.

For example, this poem has two stanzas for structural reasons. Can you figure out why?

> **WHAT HAPPENED TO THE SPEAKER?**
>
> **A Shropshire Lad**
> **XIII**
>
> When I was one-and-twenty
> I heard a wise man say,
> "Give crowns and pounds and guineas
> But not your heart away;
> 5 Give pearls away and rubies
> But keep your fancy free."
> But I was one-and-twenty,
> No use to talk to me.
>
> When I was one-and-twenty
> 10 I heard him say again,
> "The heart out of the bosom
> Was never given in vain;
> 'Tis paid with sighs a plenty
> And sold for endless rue.*"
> 15 And I am two-and-twenty,
> And oh, 'tis true, 'tis true.
>
> —by A. E. Housman
>
> *regret

Housman wrote this poem in two stanzas to contrast the speaker at two stages in life. In the first stanza, he's twenty-one and naïve, and he dismisses the advice. In the second, he's twenty-two and his heart has been broken, and he agrees with the advice.

Sometimes stanzas in poetry function like paragraphs in prose; they signal that a new idea is being introduced. Other times, however, stanzas are broken not just in the middle of an idea but in the middle of a sentence, to indicate flow and continuity. Lines and stanzas are broken in different places to contribute to a poem's meaning and/or its sound. Poems that don't follow a set pattern are in **free verse**.

 Related Skills: 29–30 and 32–35

The following poem looks much more uneven than the Housman poem, but it still has a carefully designed structure. How many stanzas does it have? Why are the lines uneven lengths and indented different amounts from the left margin?

WHAT DOES THE SPEAKER PLAN TO DO?

Right Here
Right here
on this
      clean
white page

5 I'll scatter some words,
     watch them grow,
    I'll plant
a meadow.

   I'll dig a pond right here.
10 Dig down deep until
    the water
    and the words
     run clear.

  I'll build me a barn.
15   Lay the lines out straight and
raise the roof!

      Write
here.

—by Alice Schertle

"Right Here" has five stanzas separated by lines of space. The lines and stanzas are broken in different places to contribute to the poem's meaning and to its sound. In stanza 2, the words are scattered like flower seeds. In stanza 3, the last three lines mimic a pond being dug deep. In stanza 4, "Lay the lines out straight" is itself straight, the longest line in the whole poem. "Raise the roof" caps stanza 4 like a roof. The final stanza is a play on words: "Write here" (right here).

Sometimes a poet shapes a poem to look like the subject it's about. These are called **concrete poems**. For example, a poem about a cat may be written so that the words form an outline shape of a cat.

GED Readiness

Read the poem and answer the questions.

HOW IS THE MOTHER A HERO?

The Age of Reason

"When can we have cake?" she wants to know.
And patiently we explain: when dinner's
   finished.
Someone wants seconds; and wouldn't she like
   to try,
while she's waiting, a healthful lettuce leaf?
5   The birthday girl can't hide her grief—

worse, everybody laughs. That makes her sink
two rabbity, gapped teeth, acquired this year,
into a quivering lip, which puts an end
9 to tears but not the tedium she'll take
10   in life before she's given cake:

"When I turned seven, now" her grandpa says,
"the priest told me I'd reached the age of
   reason.
That means you're old enough to tell what's
   right
from wrong. Make decisions on your own."
15   Her big eyes brighten. "So you mean

I can decide to open presents first?"
Laughter again (she joins it) as the reward
of devil's food is brought in on a tray.
"You know why we were taught that?" asks my
   father.
20   "No." I light a candle, then another

in a chain. "—So we wouldn't burn in Hell."
A balloon pops in the other room; distracted,
she innocently misses talk of nuns'
severities I never knew at seven.
25   By then, we were Unitarian

and marched off weekly, dutifully, to hear
nothing in particular. "Ready!"
I call, and we huddle close to sing
something akin, you'd have to say, to prayer.
30   Good God, her hair—

one beribboned pigtail has swung low
as she leans to trade the year in for a wish;
before she blows it out, the camera's flash
captures a mother's hand, all hope, no blame,
35   saving her from the flame.
                              —by Mary Jo Salter

1 How many stanzas does the poem have?

① one
② three
③ five
④ seven

2 How many lines are in each stanza?

① two
② four
③ five
④ seven

3 How does the last line in each stanza differ from the other lines in the stanza?

① It always ends a sentence.
② It's always indented at the left margin.
③ It's always about the birthday girl.
④ It always contains six words.

4 Why are the last lines of every stanza not full sentences?

① They don't have subjects and verbs.
② They show the birthday girl's impatience with dinner.
③ They're followed by a line of space.
④ They keep the reader moving forward fast into the next stanza.

5 What do the forms of stanzas 1 and 6 have in common?

① Both end with a dash.
② Both are free form.
③ Each is one long sentence.
④ Neither has dialogue.

6 Why is the mother a hero? Which lines show her behaving heroically?

_____

_____

7 What do lines 9–10 predict about the birthday girl's future?

_____

Read the following poems. Then circle the correct answers.

WHAT DO HORSES THINK?

Horses Graze
Cows graze.
Horses graze.
They
4 eat
   eat
6 eat.
   Their graceful heads
   are bowed
   bowed
10 bowed
   in majestic oblivion.
   [lines 12-31] . . .
32 In Sweden,
   China,
   Afrika,
35 in India or Maine,
   the animals are sane;
37 they know and know and know
   there's ground below
   and sky
40 up high.

—by Gwendolyn Brooks

8 Why are lines 4–6 so short?

① Each line is like one bite of grass.
② The poet was trying to fill the page.
③ They mimic a horse's trot.
④ They remind you of a too-thin, hungry horse.

9 Why are India and Maine run together in line 35 instead of separate like lines 32–34?

① to speed up the pace of the poem
② to remind readers that it's a small world
③ because the line starts with "in"
④ to balance and rhyme with line 36

10 The word *know* is repeated in line 37 to

① be a play on the word "no"
② emphasize the horses' sanity
③ contrast horses with dumb cows
④ suggest that the horses are wrong

WHAT IDEAS DOES THIS POEM GIVE YOU?
A Seeing Poem

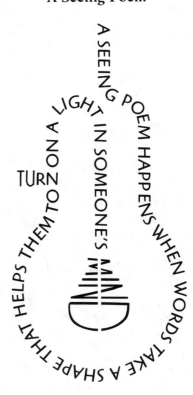

—by Robert Froman

11 What kind of poem is this?

① free verse
② concrete
③ two stanza
④ rhymed

12 What metaphor does its shape evoke?

① a burned-out mind
② a bright idea
③ a fragile, breakable thought
④ a dim glow

13 Why did the poet capitalize all the letters?

① to show that all the letters have the same importance
② to show that all the words have the same importance
③ to fit the words better visually to the lightbulb shape
④ to achieve the effect of shouting

32

Understanding Rhythm and Meter

One of the first things you notice about a poem is its rhythm. **Rhythm** is the beat of a poem, the pattern of sound created by the rise and fall of syllables and words. Rhythm occurs not just in poetry and song but in spoken language. Rhythm is all around you: in the tick of your watch, the pace of your walk, even the beating of your heart.

Rhythm can be either *regular* or *irregular.* In a poem with a regular rhythm, there is a regular pattern of stressed and unstressed syllables called **meter.** Read aloud the lines below and listen to the rise and fall of the syllables.

> Tyger, tyger, burning bright
> in the forests of the night.
>
> —Excerpted from "The Tyger" by William Blake

The poem has a regular meter. It starts with an accented syllable *(Ty-).* That syllable is followed by an unaccented syllable *(-ger).* This meter continues throughout the poem.

Rhythm serves several purposes. It's contagious, as you know if you've ever tapped your foot while listening to music. It can involve and excite readers. It can also hypnotize readers, encouraging their minds to drift and leaving them open to the poem's message.

Beyond meter, another aspect of rhythm is **repetition,** which is the use of a word, a phrase, or even an entire line or stanza again and again in a poem. Poets use repetition to call attention to an important idea and to increase the unity in a work.

Try reading the Shakespearean sonnet on page 105 out loud. The meter in this poem is two unstressed syllables *(Let me)* followed by a stressed syllable *(not).* This rhythm continues throughout the poem. (Note that *fixed* in line 5 is pronounced with two syllables: *fix´ ed.)*

One reason Shakespeare chose such a regular meter is that it suits his subject, which is an unalterable type of love. This meter also stresses the key words in the poem, such as *not, minds, alters, bends,* and *fixed.* The last two lines reinforce the message: If I'm wrong about this, I'm no writer and no one has ever loved.

Rhythm is the beat of a poem, the pattern of sound created by the arrangement of stressed (emphasized) and unstressed syllables in a line. Rhythm can be either regular or irregular.

In a poem with a regular rhythm, **meter** is a regular pattern of stressed and unstressed syllables.

Repetition is the use of a word, a phrase, or even an entire line or stanza again and again in a poem. Repetition calls attention to important ideas and increases the unity in a work.

DOES THE POET BELIEVE IN LOVE?

Sonnet 116

Let me not to the marriage of true minds
Admit impediments. Love is not love
Which alters when it alteration finds,
Or bends with the remover to remove:
5 O, no! it is an ever-fixed mark
That looks on tempests and is never shaken;
It is the star to every wandering bark,*
Whose worth's unknown, although his height be taken.
Love's not Time's fool, though rosy lips and cheeks
10 Within his bending sickle's compass* come:
Love alters not with his brief hours and weeks,
But bears it out even to the edge of doom.
　　If this be error and upon me proved,
　　I never writ, nor no man ever loved.

　　　　　　　　　　　—by William Shakespeare

*boat (line 7) *reach (line 10)

Some poems have an irregular rhythm. Note the stressed and unstressed syllables in the excerpt below. They're irregular (they don't alternate evenly), but they have a purpose. What effect do they have on how you feel as you read?

HOW DID THE MOTHER FEEL?

Now That I Am Forever with Child

How the days went
while you were blooming within me
I remember   each upon each
the swelling changed planes of my body

5 how you first fluttered   then jumped
and I thought it was my heart.

　　　　　　　　　　　—by Audre Lorde

Notice how the most important words (like *you, bloom, swell, changed,* and *heart)* are stressed. The uneven meter of line 5 reflects its meaning: "fluttered   then jumped."

GED Readiness

Read the following poems. Then circle the correct answers.

WHAT DOES THE SPEAKER LIKE ABOUT THE NIGHT?

Dream Variations

To fling my arms wide
In some place of the sun,
To whirl and to dance
Till the white day is done.
5 Then rest at cool evening
Beneath a tall tree
While night comes on gently,
8   Dark like me—
That is my dream!

10 To fling my arms wide
In the face of the sun,
Dance! Whirl! Whirl!
Till the quick day is done.
Rest at pale evening . . .
15 A tall, slim tree . . .
Night coming tenderly,
17   Black like me.

—by Langston Hughes

❶ How does the poet feel about the day?

① He is depressed by how short the day is.
② He is excited by the day and feels like dancing.
③ He doesn't like the white hot sun.
④ He wants to spend the day under a shady tree.

❷ Which of the following does NOT describe how the poet feels about night?

① Night is gentle and tender.
② Night is black like the poet.
③ Night is restful.
④ Night is dark and frightening.

❸ What about lines 8 and 17 helps to emphasize their meaning?

① repetition
② irregular rhythm
③ the rise and fall of syllables
④ capitalization

HOW DOES THE SPEAKER REALLY FEEL ABOUT POETRY?

I Hate Poetry

I hate poetry
the way a junky hates the fix
he can't afford
and will have to hustle for
5 and often enough
won't even get a rush from,
just keep off the horrors
for another hour.
I hate poetry
10 the way a married couple
who don't believe in divorce
hate each other.
I hate poetry
the way Alcoholics Anonymous
15 hates liquor
and has meetings about it.
I hate poetry
the way an atheist hates God
and shakes his fist
20 at the empty hole in the sky.
And the more poetry I hear
the more I hate it
and the more I write it.
Here I am.

—by Julia Vinograd

❹ The rhythm of this poem is

① metrical
② repetitive
③ regular
④ irregular

❺ What word is stressed every time it appears?

① I
② hate
③ more
④ it

❻ The repetition of the title serves to

① make readers agree with it
② state the poem's theme
③ make the poem more musical
④ emphasize the narrowness of the poem's lines

Read the poems. Then answer the questions that follow.

IS IT EASY TO LOSE THINGS?

One Art

1 The art of losing isn't hard to master;
so many things seem filled with the intent
to be lost that their loss is no disaster.

Lose something every day. Accept the fluster
of lost door keys, the hour badly spent.
6 The art of losing isn't hard to master.

Then practice losing farther, losing faster:
places, and names, and where it was you meant
to travel. None of these will bring disaster.

I lost my mother's watch. And look! My last, or
Next-to-last, of three loved houses went.
12 The art of losing isn't hard to master.

I lost two cities, lovely ones. And, vaster,
Some realms I owned, two rivers, a continent.
I miss them, but it wasn't a disaster.

—Even losing you (the joking voice, a gesture
I love) I shan't have lied. It's evident
18 the art of losing's not too hard to master
though it may look like (*Write* it!) like disaster.

—by Elizabeth Bishop

❼ What poetic technique is shown in lines 1, 6, 12, and 18?

_____

❽ What does the title suggest about how losing door keys compares with losing a lover?

_____

❾ Does this poem have a regular or an irregular rhythm?

_____

WHAT ARE ALIVE POEMS?

Remember

Remember the sky that you were born under,
know each of the stars' stories.
Remember the moon, know who she is,
Remember the sun's birth at dawn, that is the
5 strongest point of time. Remember sundown
and the giving away to night.
Remember your birth, how your mother
struggled
to give you form and breath. You are evidence of
her life, and her mother's, and hers.
Remember your father. He is your life, also.
11 Remember the earth whose skin you are:
red earth, black earth, yellow earth, white earth,
brown earth, we are earth.
Remember the plants, trees, animal life who all
have their
15 tribes, their families, their histories, too. Talk to
them,
listen to them. They are alive poems.
Remember the wind. Remember her voice. She
knows the
origin of this universe.
Remember you are all people and all people
are you.
20 Remember you are this universe and this
universe is you.
Remember all is in motion, is growing, is you.
Remember language comes from this.
Remember the dance language is, that life is.
Remember.

—by Joy Harjo

❿ What kind of rhythm does this poem have, regular or irregular? How do you know?

_____

⓫ What repetition is used throughout the poem?

_____

⓬ Name one stressed word in line 11.

_____

Listening to the Sound of Poetry

The most striking thing about the sound of poetry is **rhyme**, the repetition of the same stressed vowel sound and succeeding sounds in two or more words.

- **End rhymes** occur at the ends of lines.
- **Internal rhymes** occur within lines.
- **Slant rhymes** are words that almost but don't quite rhyme (like *sneezes* and *trees*, or *world* and *girl*).

The **rhyme scheme** is the pattern formed by the end rhyme. To show it, different letters of the alphabet are assigned to each new rhyme. In lines 1 and 3 of the poem below, *cloud* and *crowd* rhyme, so they're both marked *a*. *Hills* and *daffodils* rhyme, so they're marked *b*. *Trees* and *breeze* rhyme and are marked *c*.

I Wandered Lonely as a Cloud	
I wandered lonely as a cloud	*a*
That floats on high o'er vales and hills	*b*
Till all at once I saw a crowd,	*a*
A host of golden daffodils.	*b*
Beside the lake, beneath the trees	*c*
Fluttering and dancing in the breeze.	*c*

—by William Wordsworth

Besides rhyme, several other sound devices help poets express meaning and emotions. The most important are

- **alliteration**, the repetition of consonant sounds at the beginnings of words ("**S**ee the **s**ights of the **c**ity.")
- **consonance**, the repetition of consonant sounds within words or at the ends of words ("a stro**k**e of lu**ck**")
- **assonance**, the repetition of vowel sounds within non-rhyming words ("t**i**me out of m**i**nd")
- **onomatopoeia**, words that suggest or imitate the sounds they describe (like *buzz* or *clank*)

Sound devices are based entirely on how words sound, not how they're spelled. For example, *rhyme* and *time* rhyme, but *tough* and *through* do not. *See* and *city* are alliterative even though one starts with *s* and the other with *c*. Most tongue twisters use alliteration and assonance: *Peter Piper picked a peck of pickled peppers.*

Free verse is poetry that has no fixed pattern of meter or rhyme. Free verse often uses sound devices and a relaxed rhythm like that of everyday conversation. It usually has irregular line lengths.

Rhyme is the repetition of the same stressed vowel and consonant sounds in two or more words. Rhymes may occur at the ends of lines or within lines. Slant rhymes almost but don't quite rhyme.

The **rhyme scheme** is the pattern formed by the end rhyme. To show it, different letters of the alphabet are assigned to each new rhyme.

Sound devices frequently used by poets include **alliteration, consonance, assonance**, and **onomatopoeia**.

Free verse is poetry that has no fixed pattern of meter or rhyme. It may use sound devices, the rhythm of everyday speech, and irregular line lengths.

Related Skills: 17, 29-32, and 33-35

In bad poetry, sound devices can distract readers from the poem's meaning. In good poetry, they reinforce the meaning. Certain sounds, like *fl-* and short *i*, suggest a light mood *(flicker, ripple)*. A long *o* or *oo* sound often suggests sadness *(groan, gloom)*. The more vowel sounds a line has, the more musical it sounds. Sound devices can also affect the speed at which lines are read, which contributes to their meaning.

Look at a poem that uses many sound devices.

WHAT DOES THE SPEAKER VALUE MOST?

My City

1	When I come down to sleep death's endless night,	a
2	The threshold of the unknown dark to cross,	b
3	What to me then will be the keenest loss,	b
	When this bright world blurs on my fading sight?	a
	Will it be that no more I shall see the trees	c
6	Or smell the flowers or hear the singing birds	d
7	Or watch the flashing streams or patient herds?	d
	No, I am sure it will be none of these.	c
9	But, ah! Manhattan's sights and sounds, her smells,	e
10	Her crowds, her throbbing force, the thrill that comes	f
	From being of her a part, her subtle spells,	e
	Her shining towers, her avenues, her slums—	f
	O God! the stark, unutterable pity,	g
	To be dead, and never again behold my city!	g

—by James Weldon Johnson

First, note that the rhyme scheme is different in the two different stanzas. In stanza 1, it's *a, b, b, a, c, d, d, c. Night* and *sight* (a) rhyme, as do *cross* and *loss* (b), *trees* and *these* (c), and *birds* and *herds* (d). In stanza 2, the rhyme scheme is *e, f, e, f, g, g: smells* and *spells* (e), *comes* and *slums* (f), and *pity* and *city* (g).

Do you see any examples of alliteration? There are *down* and *death* in line 1 and *sights* and *sounds* in line 9, among others. *Me, be,* and *keenest* in line 3 have assonance. For consonance, there are *dark* and *keenest* (lines 2–3), *singing* and *flashing* (lines 6–7), and *smells* and *thrill* (lines 9–10).

The main effect of the sound devices in stanza 1 is to slow readers down to the pace of life in the country. In stanza 2, they speed things up to the city's pace, reminding readers of what the speaker will miss when he dies.

GED Readiness

Read the following poems. Then circle the correct answers.

WHAT DOES THE SPEAKER LONG FOR?

One Perfect Rose

A single flow'r he sent me, since we met.
    All tenderly his messenger he chose;
Deep-hearted, pure, with scented dew still
    wet—
    One perfect rose.

5 I knew the language of the floweret;
    "My fragile leaves," it said, "his heart
    enclose."
Love long has taken for his amulet*
    One perfect rose.

Why is it no one ever sent me yet
10   One perfect limousine, do you suppose?
Ah no, it's always just my luck to get
    One perfect rose.

            —by Dorothy Parker

*good-luck charm

1 This poem has three stanzas of four lines each. What is the rhyme scheme of each stanza?

  ① *a, b, a, b*
  ② *a, b, b, a*
  ③ *a, b, c, d*
  ④ *a, b, c, c*

2 An example of end rhyme in the poem is

  ① *sent* and *met*
  ② *dew* and *wet*
  ③ *dew* and *knew*
  ④ *suppose* and *rose*

3 An example of alliteration is

  ① *tenderly* and *messenger*
  ② *language* and *fragile*
  ③ *single* and *since*
  ④ *do* and *you*

4 An example of assonance is

  ① *tenderly* and *messenger*
  ② *love* and *long*
  ③ *yet* and *get*
  ④ *one* and *rose*

WHAT GAME ARE THEY PLAYING?

Catch

Two boys uncoached are tossing a poem
    together,
2 Overhand, underhand, backhand, sleight of
    hand, every hand,
3 Teasing with attitudes, latitudes, interludes,
    altitudes,
High, make him fly off the ground for it, low,
    make him stoop,
5 Make him scoop it up, make him as-almost-as-
    possible miss it,
Fast, let him sting from it, now, now fool him
    slowly,
Anything, everything tricky, risky, nonchalant,
Anything under the sun to outwit the prosy,
Over the tree and the long sweet cadence down,
10 Over his head, make him scramble to pick up
    the meaning,
11 And now, like a posy, a pretty one plump in his
    hands.

            —by Robert Francis

5 Line 2 is an example of

  ① consonance
  ② slant rhyme
  ③ alliteration
  ④ onomatopoeia

6 *Attitudes* and *latitudes* (line 3) is an example of

  ① internal rhyme
  ② slant rhyme
  ③ alliteration
  ④ onomatopoeia

7 In line 11, the words *posy, pretty,* and *plump* are an example of

  ① internal rhyme
  ② alliteration
  ③ consonance
  ④ assonance

8 The reason for so many sound devices is to

  ① make the poem easy to memorize
  ② distract readers from the lack of end rhymes
  ③ reflect the playfulness of the subject
  ④ make the simple subject more complex

Read the poem. Then circle *T* for each true answer and *F* for each false one.

WHAT IS WRONG WITH THE SPEAKER?

Fahrenheit Gesundheit

Nothing is glummer
Than a cold in the summer.
A summer cold
4 Is to have and to hold.
A cough in the fall
Is nothing at all.
7 A winter snuffle
Is lost in the shuffle,
9 And April sneezes
10 Put leaves on the treeses,
But a summer cold
Is to have and to hold,
13 And there is no rescue
14 From this germ grotesque.*
You can feel it coming
In your nasal plumbing.
But there is no plumber
For a cold in the summer.
Nostrilly, tonsilly,
20 It prowls irresponsilly;
In your personal firmament*
Its abode is permanent. . . .

—by Ogden Nash

*ugly or bizarre (line 14) *world (line 21)

T F **9** The rhyme scheme of this poem is *a, a, b, b, c, c, d, d* (and so on).

T F **10** *Have* and *hold* in line 4 are an example of consonance.

T F **11** *Snuffle* in line 7 is an example of onomatopeia.

T F **12** When the author makes *trees* rhyme with *sneezes* (lines 9–10) by adding a syllable, the effect is intended to be funny.

T F **13** The author rhymed *rescue* with *grotesque* (lines 13–14) because he didn't know it is pronounced *grō tesk´*.

Read the poem. Then answer the questions that follow.

WILL THE SPEAKER FEEL SAD?

Song

When I am dead, my dearest,
2   Sing no sad songs for me;
Plant thou no roses at my head,
    Nor shady cypress tree;
5 Be the green grass above me
    With showers and dewdrops wet:
And if thou wilt,* remember,
    And if thou wilt, forget.

I shall not see the shadows,
10   I shall not feel the rain;
I shall not hear the nightingale
12   Sing on, as if in pain:
And dreaming through the twilight
    That doth* not rise nor set,
15 Haply* I may remember,
    Haply I may forget.

—by Christina Rossetti

*will (lines 7, 8)   *does (line 14)
*perhaps (lines 15, 16)

14 Which lines rhyme in the first stanza?

_____

15 In line 2, *sing, sad,* and *songs* are an example of

_____

16 In line 5, *green* and *grass* are an example of

_____

17 In line 10, *shall* and *feel* are an example of

_____

18 *Rain* and *pain* (lines 10 and 12) are an example of

_____

34 Using Imagery and Figurative Language

Poetry often uses imagery and figurative language to convey emotions and ideas.

Imagery is descriptive language that appeals to one or more of the five senses: sight, hearing, touch, taste, and smell. Imagery paints word pictures (images) in readers' minds. It awakens readers' feelings and helps them experience the poem at an emotional level. A poem rich in imagery embodies physical sensations and enables you to imagine a scene. The haiku below appeals to the senses of sight and hearing.

> The lightning flashes!
> And slashing through the darkness,
> A night-heron's screech.
>
> —by Matsuo Basho

A **central image** is one that the entire poem describes or that it comes back to again and again (as opposed to an image that's described in a line or two).

Figurative language expresses a truth beyond the words' literal meaning. It can create vivid images and add extra dimensions to language. Commonly used figures of speech include similes, metaphors, and personification.

- A **simile** is a comparison using *like* or *as*. For centuries, poets compared sunset, with its lovely colors, to beautiful images like flowers and redbirds. Then T. S. Eliot shook things up and grabbed readers' attention by comparing a sunset to the bloody innards of a surgical patient: "when the evening is spread out against the sky / like a patient etherised upon a table" (from *The Love Song of J. Alfred Prufrock*).
- A **metaphor** is a comparison that doesn't use *like* or *as*: "Their thoughts are night gulls" (from "Old People Dozing" by Denise Levertov). A metaphor can be merely implied or suggested instead of spelled out: "Mornings shaking open blue tablecloths" (from "Ama Credo" by Margaret Reckord) implies that the sky is a tablecloth.
- **Personification** gives human qualities to animals, ideas, or objects: "Tree leaves tremble. / They listen to this boy" (from "Speaking" by Simon J. Ortiz).

When a poem compares one central image to something else for several lines or even for the entire poem, it's called an **extended metaphor** or **extended simile**.

Imagery is descriptive language that appeals to the five senses. A **central image** is one that the entire poem describes or that it comes back to again and again.

Figurative language creates vivid images and adds extra dimensions to language. Commonly used figures of speech are simile, metaphor, and personification.

An **extended metaphor** or **extended simile** extends the comparison for several lines or even for the entire poem.

WHAT PICTURES DOES THIS POEM PAINT?

Pretty Words

Poets make pets of pretty, docile words:
I love smooth words, like gold–enameled fish
Which circle slowly with a silken swish,
And tender ones, like downy–feathered birds:
5 Words shy and dappled,* deep–eyed deer in herds,
Come to my hand, and playful if I wish,
Or purring softly at a silver dish,
Blue Persian kittens, fed on cream and curds.

I love bright words, words up and singing early;
10 Words that are luminous* in the dark, and sing;
Warm lazy words, white cattle under trees;
I love words opalescent,* cool, and pearly,
Like midsummer moths, and honied* words like bees,
Gilded and sticky, with a little sting.

—by Elinor Wylie

*marked with small patches of color (line 5) *shining (line 10)
*reflecting rainbows (line 12) *sweet as honey (line 13)

How does this poem paint such vivid pictures? First, it uses simile and metaphor to compare words to different kinds of animals: fish, birds, deer, kittens, cattle, moths, and bees. Note that the poem uses similes for fish ("smooth words, *like* gold-enameled fish") and birds ("tender ones [words], *like* downy-feathered birds"). But it uses metaphors for all the others (words are "shy and dappled, deep-eyed deer in herds"). Then it brings those metaphors alive with imagery, sensory details about each animal. The fish are smooth and gold-enameled. They circle and swish. The birds are tender and downy-feathered and they're up and singing early. The deer are shy, dappled, and deep-eyed. The kittens are blue Persians who purr softly and eat cream and curds from a silver dish.

Stanza 2 starts by referring back to the birds. Then it compares words to cattle: warm, lazy, white, hanging around under trees. Words as moths are opalescent, cool, and pearly. Bee words are honied, gilded, and sticky—with a sting. The poem starts out saying poets make pets of "pretty, docile" words. It goes on to give beautiful images that lift a reader's heart. Yet it ends with a sting: a reminder that words can hurt. They're not all tame animals.

The comparison of words to various animals in this poem is an extended metaphor because it goes on for the entire poem.

GED Readiness

Read the following poems. Then circle the correct answers.

WHAT IS THE POEM'S CENTRAL IMAGE?

Night Clouds

The white mares of the moon rush along the
   sky
Beating their golden hoofs upon the glass
   Heavens;
The white mares of the moon are all standing
   on their hind legs
Pawing at the green porcelain doors of the
   remote Heavens.
5 Fly, Mares!
Strain your utmost,
Scatter the milky dust of stars,
Or the tiger sun will leap upon you and destroy
   you
With one lick of his vermilion* tongue.

—by Amy Lowell

*red (line 9)

1 What is the poem's central image?

① the crescent moon
② clouds that look like white horses
③ the green porcelain doors of the Heavens
④ the rising sun

2 What are Heaven's doors made of?

① golden glass
② green porcelain
③ milky stardust
④ the red sun

3 What is chasing the white mares of the moon?

① night clouds
② the remote Heavens
③ stardust
④ the morning sun

4 The final metaphor in the poem is

① the Milky Way is made of stars
② the sun is the same color as a tiger
③ the sun is a tiger
④ the sun is vermilion

HOW DOES THE SPEAKER'S PARTNER FEEL?

Simile

1 What did we say to each other
2 that now we are as the deer
3 who walk in single file
   with heads high
   with ears forward
   with eyes watchful
7 with hooves always placed on firm ground
   in whose limbs there is latent* flight.

—by N. Scott Momaday

*postponed but ready to go

5 Who is the speaker?

① one member of a couple
② an employee
③ the poet
④ a deer

6 What is the poem's extended simile?

① Words are like deer.
② Deer are always watchful.
③ Two people are like cautious deer.
④ Deer limbs are like flight.

7 How do you know the poem uses a simile and not a metaphor?

① Line 1 says "we."
② Line 2 says "as the deer."
③ Line 3 says "single file."
④ Line 7 says "on firm ground."

8 What senses do lines 3–7 appeal to?

① hearing and balance
② hearing and smell
③ sight and taste
④ sight and touch

9 What does the speaker mean by the comparison to deer?

① People in a relationship are as happy as deer running free.
② Deer are very easily spooked.
③ Both partners are ready to run away at the slightest problem.
④ Spooked deer run away together.

Read the poem. Then circle *T* for each true answer and *F* for each false one.

WHAT DOES THE SPEAKER WANT?

The Lake Isle of Innisfree

I will arise and go now, and go to Innisfree,
And a small cabin build there, of clay and
  wattles* made:
Nine bean-rows will I have there, a hive for the
  honeybee,
4 And live alone in the bee-loud glade.

5 And I shall have some peace there, for peace
  comes dropping slow,
Dropping from the veils of the morning to
  where the cricket sings;
7 There midnight's all a glimmer, and noon a
  purple glow,
And evening full of the linnet's* wings.

I will arise and go now, for always night and
  day
10 I hear lake water lapping with low sounds
  by the shore;
While I stand on the roadway, or on the
  pavements grey,
I hear it in the deep heart's core.

—by William Butler Yeats

*branches (line 2)   *a type of bird (line 8)

T F ⑩ The image in stanza 1 is of a small
     house with a garden.

T F ⑪ Line 4 appeals primarily to the sense of
     hearing.

T F ⑫ The image in stanza 2 is of a soldier
     coming home from war.

T F ⑬ The figures of speech in line 7 are
     similes.

T F ⑭ Stanza 3 appeals primarily to the sense
     of hearing.

T F ⑮ The emotion evoked in stanza 3 is
     longing.

T F ⑯ The overall emotion the poem's imagery
     evokes is peacefulness.

Read the poem and answer the questions.

HOW DID THE SPEAKER FEEL?

Recuerdo*

We were very tired, we were very merry—
We had gone back and forth all night on the
  ferry.
It was bare and bright, and smelled like a
  stable—
But we looked into a fire, we leaned across a
  table
5 We lay on a hill-top underneath the moon;
And the whistles kept blowing, and the dawn
  came soon.

We were very tired, we were very merry—
We had gone back and forth all night on the
  ferry.
And you ate an apple, and I ate a pear,
10 From a dozen of each we had bought
  somewhere;
And the sky went wan,* and the wind came
  cold,
12 And the sun rose dripping, a bucketful of gold.

We were very tired, we were very merry—
We had gone back and forth all night on the
  ferry.
15 We hailed, "Good-morrow, mother," to a shawl-
  covered head,
And bought a morning paper, which neither of
  us read;
And she wept, "God bless you!" for the apples
  and pears,
And we gave her all our money but our subway
  fares.

—by Edna St. Vincent Millay

*returning or circling (title)   *pale (line 11)

⑰ Which senses does stanza 1 appeal to?

_____

⑱ Which new sense is appealed to in stanza 2?

_____

⑲ What is the figure of speech in line 12?

_____

Analyzing Mood and Emotions

Emotions are simply feelings. Joy, sadness, excitement, anger, pleasure, fear, love, hate—you can find all these emotions and more in poetry. In fact, the main purpose of most poems is to capture emotions in words and share them with readers so vividly that they feel those emotions too.

Mood is very important in poetry. The mood of a poem may be humorous or serious, happy or sad, or any of a hundred other feelings. The overall mood of a poem comes from the specific emotions it conveys. The mood may change from one stanza of a poem to another, especially if events or thoughts cause the speaker or main character to undergo a change in attitude.

Look at the emotions and changes of mood in this poem about nature.

> The overall **mood**, or atmosphere, of a poem comes from the specific emotions it conveys. The mood may change from one stanza to another or even within a stanza.

HOW DOES THE SPEAKER FEEL?

The Peace of Wild Things

When despair for the world grows in me
and I wake in the night at the least sound
in fear of what my life and my children's lives may be,
I go and lie down where the wood drake*
5 rests in his beauty on the water, and the great heron feeds.
I come into the peace of wild things
7 who do not tax their lives with forethought
8 of grief. I come into the presence of still water.
And I feel above me the day-blind stars
10 waiting with their light. For a time
I rest in the grace of the world, and am free.

—by Wendell Berry

*male duck

The speaker announces his emotion at the poem's start: despairing. In lines 7–8, he adds "forethought of grief." If you have ever worried about the future for yourself, your family, or the planet, you know how he feels. But then the mood shifts gradually to one of peace and freedom.

How does the poet get there—and take you with him? He slows down, with more unstressed syllables and words like *rest, peace, still water,* and *waiting.* He describes the ducks and herons and his surroundings with such precision that you too can feel his mood relax. The final line brings together rest, grace, and freedom, all of them ideas that fight despair and inspire good feelings.

Related Skills: 1–5, 17, 18, 25, 29–34

GED Readiness

Read the following poem. Then circle the correct answers.

WHAT DOES THE SPEAKER LOVE?

Amo Ergo Sum

Because I love
The ferns grow green, and green the grass, and green
The transparent sunlit trees.

Because I love
5 Larks rise up from the grass
And all the leaves are full of singing birds.

Because I love
The summer air quivers with a thousand wings,
Myriads of jewelled eyes burn in the light.

10 Because I love
The iridescent shells upon the sand
Take forms as fine and intricate as thought.

Because I love
There is an invisible way across the sky,
15 Birds travel by that way, the sun and moon
And all the stars travel that path by night.

Because I love
There is a river flowing all night long.

Because I love
20 All night the river flows into my sleep,
Ten thousand living things are sleeping in my arms,
And sleeping wake, and flowing are at rest.

—by Kathleen Raine

❶ The poem's title means "I Love, Therefore I Am." What does it suggest about the mood of the poem?

① The mood is angry.
② The mood is welcoming.
③ The mood is depressed.
④ The mood is lonely.

❷ How does the author achieve the mood?

① She repeats the word "Because" at the start of each stanza.
② She uses alliteration.
③ She uses birds as a symbol for love.
④ She lists specific things she loves.

❸ The emotions

① remain the same throughout the poem
② change from one stanza to the next
③ change from positive to negative
④ change from positive to negative and back again

❹ How does the final stanza reinforce the poem's mood?

① It's written in irregular rhythm.
② It shows that the speaker loves "ten thousand living things."
③ It uses longer and longer lines to evoke how strongly the speaker feels.
④ It repeats the word "sleep."

Read the poem and answer the questions.

WHAT DID THE SPEAKER DO?

This Is Just to Say
I have eaten
the plums
that were in
the icebox

5 and which
you were probably saving
for breakfast

8 Forgive me
9 they were delicious
so sweet
11 and so cold

—by William Carlos Williams

❺ What does the title suggest about the poem's mood?

_____

❻ What emotions does stanza 2 suggest?

_____

❼ Why does the speaker say lines 9–11? How do they change your interpretation of lines 5–8?

_____

36

Reading Drama as a Literary Form

Drama has many of the same elements as fiction, among them characterization, plot and conflict, dialogue, setting, theme, and symbolism. A good story is a good story, no matter what form it's told in. But drama differs from fiction in one major way. It's meant to be performed live on a stage. A play, or **drama**, is a story performed by actors and told mainly through the words and actions of characters. A play with a conflict that ends badly for the main character is called a **tragedy**. A play that ends happily for the main character is a **comedy**.

Plays are structured in major divisions called **acts**. Acts may be further divided into **scenes**. Each scene shows an action that takes place in one location among specific characters. The plots of most plays follow the story organization you learned in Skill 22: exposition, rising action, climax, falling action, and resolution. Here is the structure of the three-act comedy *Mary, Mary* by Jean Kerr. In this play, each act has only one scene.

ACT ONE	A Saturday morning in winter
ACT TWO	Saturday night, late
ACT THREE	Sunday morning

The written version of a play is called a **script**. The script of a movie is called a screenplay. The first page of most scripts is a **cast list**, a list of all the characters. The list may give their names, ages, occupations, physical descriptions, and personality traits, especially for main characters. Here is the cast list for *Mary, Mary*.

> A play, or **drama**, is a story performed by actors and told mainly through the words and actions of characters. A play is divided into **acts**, which may be further divided into **scenes**.

> A **script** is the written version of a play. It includes a **cast list**, or list of all the characters, and **stage directions** to describe characters' appearance and actions.

Bob McKellaway, a young independent publisher in his thirties.

Mary McKellaway, his former wife, divorced within the year and now working on her own.

Tiffany Richards, Bob's present fiancée, in her twenties, independently wealthy.

Oscar Nelson, a tax lawyer and a friend of both Bob and Mary. Fiftyish.

Dirk Winston, recently from Hollywood, and a wartime friend of Bob.

Related Skills: 2–5, 10, 20–27, and 37–39

Most plays consist almost entirely of **dialogue**, or conversation between characters. Dialogue

- advances the plot
- reveals character

Stage directions usually appear in brackets or parentheses and italic type. Stage directions describe characters' appearance and actions, as well as the sets, costumes, and lighting. They also explain the **setting** (where and when the action takes place) and mention any **props**, objects the actors are to use.

Example:

WHAT IS THE DISAGREEMENT ABOUT?

BOB: Nonsense. Why should you care about vulgar good looks when you have me? No— [*with a sigh and moving away from her*] —the truth is my ex-wife is descending upon me this afternoon.

OSCAR: It was my suggestion. I thought she might be able to shed some light on this tax matter.

TIFFANY: [*abruptly*] I'm delighted. I want to meet her. I've always wanted to meet her.

BOB: Well, you're not *going* to meet her—

TIFFANY: [*sitting down, firmly, in a chair*] Yes, I am.

[*Oscar, sensing that he'd better, slips away into the inner office with his papers and closes the door.*]

BOB: Darling, you are a sweet, reasonable girl, and I insist that you stay in character. Besides, I have those galleys to finish. [*as though to conclude the matter*] Kiss me, and stop all this nonsense.

TIFFANY: [*deliberately refusing to move*] I won't.

—Excerpted from *Mary, Mary* by Jean Kerr

The names in capital letters tell you which character is speaking (Bob, then Oscar, then Tiffany, and so on). All the words that aren't in brackets are what these characters say. The stage directions tell the actor playing Bob (and you, the reader), what Bob does when he admits to his fiancée, Tiffany, that his ex-wife will be arriving soon: He sighs and moves away from Tiffany. The next stage direction shows how Tiffany speaks: abruptly. A later stage direction gets Oscar out of the way so the engaged couple can argue in private.

GED Readiness

Read each passage and answer the questions.

HOW IS LON AND WINNIE'S MARRIAGE?

Characters
Martha, the Maid, a maid.
Lon, Winnie's husband. Thirty-five and mild.
Winnie, thirty, sweet and charming. Always.
5 **Danna,** thirty. Sharp and a little hysterical just tonight.
Joe, thirty. The All American Sweetheart of a man. Unfortunately crazy.

SCENE: *The very dark front hall of a New York*
10 *apartment. Maybe track lighting. Chic.*

[MARTHA, the maid, stands at the front door. LON enters, lighting a cigarette.]

LON: I think all the guests are here, Martha.

MARTHA: Is this the shoplifters or the smokers
15 or the sex-offenders or the drunks?

LON: I think it's the weight-watchers, but just in case it's the smokers I stepped out here to have a cigarette.

WINNIE: *[Enters from another way.]* Happy
20 anniversary, darling, I'm so thankful you're here.

LON: Happy anniversary, Winnie. My helpful little helpless wife. I thought you were in with your guests.

25 WINNIE: I just popped up for a moment to tuck in the children.

LON: Why is it that every anniversary we have to give a party for one of your charity groups?

WINNIE: I just feel our life is so perfect we
30 should help those less fortunate.

[They exit arm in arm.]

MARTHA: *[To the audience.]* Already you know we're in trouble, right?

[The doorbell rings. MARTHA reaches to open it,
35 *turns to look at audience.]*

One tip. Always bet on somebody named Winnie.

[She opens the door. DANNA staggers in a step.]

40 DANNA: Thank God someone's here! You're not Winnie. You're . . . she talks about you all the time . . . you're Abigail or Eleanor or Lady Bird . . .

—Excerpted from *Abstinence*
by Lanford Wilson

1 Lines 1–8 are the

① introduction
② cast list
③ stage directions
④ setting

2 Lines 9–10 describe this scene's

① characters
② dialogue
③ stage directions
④ setting

3 Lines 11–12 are

① the cast list
② a scene
③ stage directions
④ dialogue

4 Lines 13–18 are

① the cast list
② Lon talking to Winnie
③ stage directions
④ dialogue

5 How does Martha feel about her employers' marriage?

① She agrees with Winnie that their life is perfect.
② She thinks it's nice that they're celebrating.
③ She thinks they're in trouble.
④ She thinks Winnie is selfish.

6 What clues tell you that Winnie may be getting on Lon's nerves?

_____

HOW DOES MEDVEDENKO FEEL ABOUT MASHA?

The Seagull *is set at the estate of SORIN, a wealthy man.*

ACT I takes place in the park of SORIN's estate.
ACT II takes place on the croquet lawn.
ACT III takes place in the dining room.
ACT IV takes place in the study.

There is an interval of two years between Acts III and IV.

ACT I
A wide path, leading away from the audience to a lake in the background, is blocked by a rough stage, put up for an amateur dramatic performance. It hides the lake from view. To left and right of this stage, bushes. A few chairs and a small table.

The sun has just set. JACOB and other workmen can be heard hammering and coughing on the stage behind the drawn curtain. MASHA and MEDVEDENKO come in, left, on their way back from a walk.

MEDVEDENKO: Why do you wear black all the time?

MASHA: I'm in mourning for my life, I'm unhappy.

MEDVEDENKO: Why? *[Reflects]* I don't understand. You're healthy and your father's quite well off, even if he's not rich. I'm much worse off than you—I'm only paid twenty-three roubles a month, and what with pension deductions I don't even get that. But I don't go round like someone at a funeral. *[They sit down.]*

MASHA: Money doesn't matter, even a poor man can be happy.

MEDVEDENKO: Yes—in theory. But look how it works out. There's me, my mother, my two sisters and my young brother. But I only earn twenty-three roubles and we need food and drink, don't we? Tea and sugar? And tobacco? We can hardly make ends meet.

MASHA: *[looking back at the stage]* The play will be on soon.

MEDVEDENKO: Yes. Nina Zarechny will act in it and Constantine Treplev wrote it. They're in love and this evening they'll be spiritually united in the effort to present a unified work of art. But you and

I aren't soul-mates at all. I love you. I'm too wretched to stay at home and I walk over here every day, four miles each way, and it just doesn't mean a thing to you. And that's understandable. I have no money; there are a lot of us at home, and anyway why marry a man who doesn't get enough to eat?

MASHA: What rubbish.

—Excerpted from *The Seagull* by Anton Chekhov

7 How many acts does *The Seagull* have?

_____

8 Where does Act I take place?

_____

9 What time of day is it when the play opens?

_____

10 What characters are heard but not seen as the play opens? What are they doing?

_____

11 Who is the first scene about?

_____

12 What are the characters in Scene 1 waiting for?

_____

13 After which line of dialogue do the characters sit down?

_____

14 What are Medvedenko's two biggest concerns?

_____

15 How does Masha respond to his declaration of love?

_____

Watching a play is much like watching a movie or television show because you actually see the story unfold. Actors interpret their parts, aided by elaborate stage sets, period costumes, and sound effects. Reading a play, however, requires additional skills. You have to use your imagination to fill in everything that's missing.

You learned in Skill 36 about **stage directions**, which suggest a character's feelings, tone of voice, facial expressions, gestures, and actions. They also describe the sets, costumes, and props.

Terms like *stage right, stage left,* and *down right* tell the actors where action takes place. Since the actors face the audience, stage right (to the actors' right) is the audience's left. *Down* refers to the part of the stage closest to the audience, so *down right* is close to the audience and to the actors' right. The *wing* is the area on either side of the stage that is not visible to the audience.

Sometimes authors rework their stories completely from a play to a novel. Cherie Bennett wrote *Anne Frank and Me* about a teen named Nicole. In the play, Nicole's father denies that the Holocaust took place. When Bennett turned the play into a novel, she had Nicole meet Holocaust disbelievers through a website instead. In the play, the conflict between father and daughter is very dramatic, but the novel warns readers of the Internet's pitfalls.

There are also smaller differences between plays and novels.

- In a novel, **dialogue** is in quotation marks. In a play, dialogue appears, without quotation marks, after the name of the character who speaks.

Example:

Novel: "Look out!" Ed shouted. "He's got a gun!"
Play: ED: [shouting] Look out! He's got a gun!

- In a novel, a **narrator**, or storyteller, describes how the characters feel and tells what they are doing. In a play, **stage directions** describe how the characters feel and tell the actors what to do.

Example:

Novel: When Chaz came home from school, he had a black eye. "It's nothing, Mom," he said.
Martha fixed an ice pack. "What happened?" she asked.
Play: CHAZ: [coming home from school with a black eye] It's nothing, Mom.
MARTHA: [fixing an ice pack] What happened?

> **Stage directions** suggest a character's feelings, tone of voice, facial expressions, gestures, and actions. They also describe the sets, costumes, lighting, and any props the actors use.

Related Skills: 2–5, 17, 20–27, 36, and 38–39

GED Readiness

Read the passage and answer the questions.

HOW WILL KEN DO AT HIS NEW JOB?

DR. RUSSELL: How's it going, Ken?

KEN: *[With a start.]* Oh! Dr. Russell. You startled me.

DR. RUSSELL: *[Chuckling.]* Scared the hell out
5 of you is what you mean. Let's say what we mean, Ken. If we're going to help others get in touch with their feelings we have to be honest about out own.

KEN: Right. *[Suddenly.]* And I'll tell you
10 something else that's crazy. My phones haven't rung. And I feel it's because they know it's me. I feel they've decided to ring for the others because they know they're better at this than I am. I mean, I know it's insane and phones are
15 electronic instruments . . .

DR. RUSSELL: That's fine, Ken. Be aware of that feeling. Of course, it's not a feeling you'll want to share with a disturbed person. But there can be a lot of resentment when you're
20 talking to someone bent on self-destruction. Recognize it. *[He claps him on the back.]* Then keep it to yourself.

KEN: *[Calling after him.]* Dr, Russell! Do you think . . . would it be possible for someone to
25 sit with me for the first couple of calls? In case I run into something over my head . . .

DR. RUSSELL: We're all in over our heads here, Ken. Just remember your Schneidman, your training, your seminars, and then follow
30 your instincts.

KEN: Just . . . just for the first call? You see . . . I've never actually dealt with another human being in trouble. I mean, the . . . simulated situations are close, but these are real people.
35 I mean . . . someone may actually live or die because of what I say on the phone.

DR. RUSSELL: If you feel that way, Ken, this is not the job for you.

KEN: *[Quickly.]* Right. I mustn't be arrogant.

40 DR. RUSSELL: Remember that what these people want most is someone to talk to, they want help, otherwise they wouldn't be calling. I'm not going to tell you that a rebuff or harsh treatment couldn't push someone over the
45 edge.
[MARTY enters from stage left.]

    —Excerpted from *Hot Line* by Elaine May

1 How does Dr. Russell's greeting make Ken feel?

  ① It pleases him.
  ② It angers him.
  ③ It surprises him.
  ④ It comforts him.

2 How might lines 21–22 be written in a novel?

  ① "Recognize it," Dr. Russell said *[clapping him on the back]*. "Then keep it to yourself."
  ② Recognize it, Dr. Russell said, clapping him on the back. Then keep it to yourself.
  ③ "Recognize it," Dr. Russell said, clapping him on the back. "Then keep it to yourself."
  ④ *Recognize it,* Dr. Russell said, clapping him on the back. *Then keep it to yourself.*

3 What is Ken's biggest fear?

  ① Dr. Russell won't think he's doing a good job.
  ② A caller may die because of what he says.
  ③ Hotline callers won't like him.
  ④ He's too arrogant to help people.

4 What can you conclude about Dr. Russell?

  ① He's not very sensitive to Ken's feelings.
  ② He's dedicated to helping all disturbed people.
  ③ He provides a rigorous training program.
  ④ He enjoys a good practical joke.

5 How does Marty arrive on stage?

  ① He's on stage when the curtain rises.
  ② He enters from the audience's left.
  ③ He walks into the wing.
  ④ He enters from stage left.

Identifying Plot and Conflict

Drama uses action to tell a story. This action, or **plot**, is the sequence of related events that take place. The plot of a play relies almost entirely on how the characters respond to situations.

As with fiction (see Skill 22), plot in drama includes five stages: exposition, rising action, climax, falling action, and resolution. William Shakespeare, who refined the structure of drama as we know it today, wrote his plays in five major divisions, called **acts**, that correspond to those five stages. Most plays today have fewer than five acts. Some have only one act. One-hour television dramas are often structured in four acts separated by commercials.

Acts may be divided into **scenes**. Each scene shows an action that takes place in one location among specific characters. Look at the structure of Shakespeare's play *A Midsummer Night's Dream*.

Act I	Scene I. Athens. The palace of THESEUS. Scene II. Athens. QUINCE's house.
Act II	Scene I. A wood near Athens. Scene II. Another part of the wood.
Act III	Scene I. The wood. TITANIA lying asleep. Scene II. Another part of the wood.
Act IV	Scene I. The same part of the wood. Scene II. Athens. QUINCE's house.
Act V	Scene I. Athens. The palace of THESEUS.

> **Plot** is the sequence of related events that take place in a play. The plot includes **conflicts**, which may be external or internal.

> A **play** is divided into one to five **acts**, which may be further divided into **scenes**. Each scene shows an action that takes place in one location among specific characters.

The events of the story are usually set in motion by **conflicts** (problems the characters must solve). A conflict may be **external** (in which the character struggles against some outside force) or **internal** (in which the character struggles against himself or herself). Most scenes reveal conflict between characters.

Example:

> HERMIA: But I beseech your grace that I may know
> The worst that may befall me in this case
> If I refuse to wed Demetrius.
>
> THESEUS: Either to die the death or to abjure [give up]
> For ever the society of men.

In this excerpt from *A Midsummer Night's Dream*, the conflict is external: between Theseus, who wants Hermia to marry Demetrius, and Hermia, who doesn't want to marry him. Hermia runs away to the woods, where she meets the characters who propel the plot.

Related Skills: 1–5, 17, 22, and 30–35

GED Readiness

Read the passage and answer the questions.

Act I   Scene 1: In and around the Hillsboro Courthouse: the courtroom square, Main Street, and the converging streets. It is an hour after dawn on a July day.

Scene 2: The courtroom. A few days later. The townspeople are packed into the sweltering courtroom.

Act II   Scene 1: The courthouse lawn. The same night.

Scene 2: The courtroom, two days later. It is bright midday, and the trial is in full swing.

Act III The courtroom, the following day.

Bert Cates is a high school biology teacher in jail for teaching his students about evolution. Henry Drummond is the lawyer defending Cates in a small town. In this passage from Act II, Scene 2, Drummond is questioning Matthew Brady, an evangelist and Bible expert.

WHAT IS BRADY'S OPINION OF THE BIBLE?

BRADY: Everything in the Bible should be accepted, exactly as it is given there.

DRUMMOND: *[Leafing through the Bible]*: Now take this place where the whale swallows Jonah. Do you figure that actually happened?

BRADY: The Bible does not say "a whale," it says "a big fish."

DRUMMOND: Matter of fact, it says "a great fish" but it's pretty much the same thing. What's your feeling about that?

BRADY: I believe in a God who can make a whale and who can make a man and make both do what He pleases!

VOICES [of courtroom audience]: Amen, amen!

DRUMMOND: *[Turning sharply to the clerk]* I want those "Amens" in the record! *[He wheels back to Brady.]* I recollect a story about Joshua, making the sun stand still. Now as a expert, you tell me that's as true as the Jonah business, right? *[Brady nods, blandly]* That's a pretty neat trick. You suppose Houdini [a magician] could do it?

BRADY: I do not question or scoff at the Lord—as do ye of little faith.

DRUMMOND: Have you ever pondered just what would naturally happen to the earth if the sun stood still?

BRADY: You can testify to that if I ever get you on the stand. *[There is laughter.]*

DRUMMOND: If they say that the sun stood still, they must've had a notion that the sun moves around the earth. Think that's the way of things? Or don't you believe the earth moves around the sun?

BRADY: I have faith in the Bible!

DRUMMOND: You don't have much faith in the solar system.

—Excerpted from *Inherit the Wind* by Jerome Lawrence and Robert E. Lee

1 What conflict is revealed in this passage?

(1) between Brady and his own beliefs
(2) between Brady and the audience
(3) between Brady's beliefs and science
(4) between Brady's beliefs and the Bible

2 What plot development is Brady trying to achieve?

(1) He wants to keep the science teacher in jail.
(2) He wants to convert Drummond to his faith.
(3) He wants to embrace all belief systems as valid.
(4) He wants to make the sun stand still.

3 Brady assumes that Drummond

(1) is a bad lawyer
(2) doesn't believe in God
(3) is an expert on astronomy
(4) knows what he's talking about

4 How many acts are in this play?

_____

5 How many scenes are in Act III?

_____

6 Where does Act II, Scene 1, take place?

_____

39 Understanding Characterization

Characters are the people who participate in the action of a drama. **Characterization** is how the playwright reveals character traits and creates believable characters. To understand characters in a drama, start with the **cast list**, which may give their names, ages, occupations, physical descriptions, and personality traits. Character is further revealed through

- physical appearance and environment
- what the character says and does
- what other characters say about her or him

When you watch a drama, you pay close attention to the characters' words (dialogue) and their nonverbal communication (tone of voice, facial expressions, gestures, costumes). When you read a drama, you glean that information from stage directions.

Based on what you observe, you make inferences about the characters' dramatic roles. Do they cause conflicts? Do they influence events? Do they make decisions that affect the outcome? You also form opinions about the characters' personalities and relationships. How do they react to events? Do their words show an understanding of another character's viewpoint?

Motivation is the reason a character acts a certain way and how he or she changes in the course of the drama. Motivation may be stated or implied. A character's motivation and the actions he or she takes in response to it often reveal character traits.

Example:

> BENEATHA: You didn't tell us what Alaiyo means . . . for all I know, you might be calling me Little Idiot or something . . .
>
> ASAGAI: Well . . . let me see . . . I do not know how just to explain it . . . The sense of a thing can be so different when it changes languages.
>
> BENEATHA: You're evading.
>
> ASAGAI: No—really it is difficult . . . *[Thinking]* It means . . . it means One for Whom Bread—Food—Is Not Enough. *[He looks at her.]* Is that all right?
>
> BENEATHA: *[Understanding, softly]* Thank you.
>
> —Excerpted from *A Raisin in the Sun* by Lorraine Hansberry

This short conversation shows you that Beneatha has a sense of humor ("Little Idiot") and that both she and Asagai have a spiritual side ("One for Whom Bread—Food—Is Not Enough.") It also reveals the depth of their love.

Characters are the people who participate in the action of a novel, short story, or drama.

Characterization is how the author reveals character traits and creates fictional people who seem lifelike.

Motivation is the reason (stated or implied) behind a character's behavior.

Related Skills: 2–5, 20–27, and 36–38

GED Readiness

Read the passage and answer the questions.

Elwood P. Dowd has a six-foot-tall rabbit named Harvey as a drinking companion. His sister, Veta, takes him to Dr. Chumley for a cure. Lofgren is the cabbie who drives them to the sanitarium.

WILL ELWOOD CHANGE?

VETA: Elwood, don't keep Dr. Chumley waiting—that's rude.

ELWOOD: Of course. *[Gives the cab driver a bill.]* Here you are—keep the change. I'm glad
5 to have met you and I'll expect you Tuesday with your brother. Will you excuse me now?

LOFGREN: Sure. *[Elwood exits. Chumley follows.]*

CAB DRIVER: A sweet guy.

10 VETA. Certainly. You could just as well have waited.

CAB DRIVER: Oh, no. Listen, lady. I've been drivin' this route fifteen years. I've brought 'em out here to get that stuff and drove 'em back
15 after they had it. It changes 'em. *[Crosses to desk.]*

VETA: Well, I certainly hope so.

CAB DRIVER: And you ain't kiddin'. On the way out here they sit back and enjoy the ride.
20 They talk to me. Sometimes we stop and watch the sunsets and look at the birds flyin'. Sometimes we stop and watch the birds when there ain't no birds and look at the sunsets when it's rainin'. We have a swell time and I
25 always get a big tip. But afterward—oh-oh— *[Starts to exit again.]*

VETA: Afterwards—oh-oh! What do you mean afterwards—oh-oh?

CAB DRIVER: They crab, crab, crab. They yell
30 at me to watch the lights, watch the brakes, watch the intersections. They scream at me to hurry. They got no faith—in me or my buggy— yet it's the same cab—the same driver—and we're going back over the very same road. It's
35 no fun—and no tips. *[Turns to door.]*

VETA: But my brother would have tipped you, anyway. He's very generous. Always has been.

CAB DRIVER: Not after this he won't be. Lady, after this, he'll be a perfectly normal human
40 being.

—Excerpted from *Harvey* by Mary Chase

1 Which of the following descriptions apply to Elwood? Choose three.

  ① rude
  ② angry
  ③ polite
  ④ friendly
  ⑤ loud
  ⑥ generous

2 Which of the following descriptions apply to Veta? Choose three.

  ① anxious
  ② regretful
  ③ rude
  ④ suspicious
  ⑤ nervous
  ⑥ upset

3 Which of the following descriptions apply to Lofgren, the cab driver? Choose three.

  ① ungrammatical
  ② friendly
  ③ frightened
  ④ drunk
  ⑤ greedy
  ⑥ savvy about human nature

4 Why does Vita have second thoughts about her brother's cure?

_____

_____

5 Does the cab driver have a positive or a negative opinion about "normal" human beings?

_____

_____

40

Identifying Types of Nonfiction

As you learned in Skill 19, a **genre** is a category of writing based on its content, form, and style. There are four major genres: fiction, nonfiction, poetry, and drama. The topics of **nonfiction** include real (not made-up) people, places, events, and social issues.

Informational nonfiction is designed to convey useful information. It includes

- business documents you might find in the workplace, like memos, contracts, and employee handbooks
- consumer documents, like apartment rental contracts and credit card agreements
- editorials in newspapers and magazines designed to persuade readers to share a political or social opinion
- speeches, like the annual State of the Union address or Martin Luther King, Jr.'s "I Have a Dream" speech
- purely factual news articles
- feature articles in magazines and newspapers on a vast array of subjects, from how to build a bookcase to what life is like for astronauts in space
- reports, such as research reports on scientific studies and consultants' analyses of how businesses can improve

Literary nonfiction uses creative style and fiction techniques, like dialogue and lyrical language, to tell a true story. It includes

- essays, which can be general or personal or a combination
- reviews of books, TV shows, restaurants, and so on
- commentary that describes and analyzes an art form
- biography, a factual record of the life of an individual (perhaps a historical figure, movie star, sports star, or politician)
- autobiography or memoir, a biography written by its subject
- diaries or journals, records of personal activities, events, travels, or reflections
- letters

Visual communication uses images to convey information or emotion or to entertain. It includes

- film and TV
- photographs
- cartoons, including both humorous and political cartoons
- tables and graphs
- maps and timelines
- paintings and sculpture

Nonfiction is about real people, places, events, and social issues.

Informational nonfiction is designed to convey useful information.

Literary nonfiction uses fiction techniques to tell a true story.

Visual communication uses images to convey information or emotion or to entertain.

GED Readiness

Read each description. Circle the word or phrase that identifies what kind of nonfiction it is.

1 a drawing that shows a sturdy net, labeled "Social Security," with a man in a suit trying to damage the net with scissors

   ① photograph
   ② political cartoon
   ③ political essay
   ④ humorous cartoon

2 an extended warranty for a television with built-in DVD player

   ① news article
   ② feature article
   ③ timeline
   ④ consumer document

3 an article describing the latest CD by the band Green Day and advising readers whether it's worth buying or not

   ① news article
   ② report
   ③ review
   ④ essay

4 the Gettysburg Address

   ① speech
   ② autobiography
   ③ commentary
   ④ map

5 a memo to all employees regarding vacation schedules

   ① journal
   ② business document
   ③ editorial
   ④ news article

6 an explanation of the ways readers can use new computer software to keep in touch with their extended families

   ① letter
   ② biography
   ③ how-to article
   ④ graph

Write *informational*, *literary*, or *visual* to show what type of nonfiction communication each phrase describes.

7 _____ an economics textbook

8 _____ a pie chart showing how the federal budget is being spent

9 _____ an essay about the author's trip to Greece and what it taught him

10 _____ a research report analyzing a clinical trial of medications for patients with heart disease

11 _____ a cell-phone contract

12 _____ a journal kept by a pioneer woman in the early 1800s

Read each passage. From the list below, choose the category to which the passage belongs.

consumer document   business document
personal essay   speech

13 As I look out at this wonderful crowd today, I feel hope for the future. Thank you all for braving such frigid temperatures to show your support for freedom of expression.

_____

14 In the months we do not read your meter, we calculate your bill based on your past electrical use. If you would like to read your own meter to avoid estimated bills, call us for meter reading cards.

_____

15 When I first visited my mother in the nursing home, I didn't know what to say or how to act. I told her I was sorry I lived so far away and promised to visit oftener. When she reached out one of her gnarled hands, I remembered those hands making birthday cakes and Halloween costumes.

_____

Analyzing Literary Nonfiction

Literary nonfiction uses fiction techniques (like dialogue, characters, conflict, plot, theme, setting, and lyrical language) to tell a true story. This genre includes biography, autobiography, diaries and journals, and essays.

Biography is a factual record of the life of an individual told in third-person point of view. A biographer describes major events in the subject's life and interprets their meaning. His or her purposes are usually to inform and entertain.

For example, this biography set in Afghanistan describes wearing a burka, the garment that covers a woman from head to foot.

> They walk on, and weave their heads around in all directions to see better. Burka women are like horses with blinkers: they can look only in one direction. Where the eye narrows, the grille stops and thick material takes its place; impossible to glance sideways. The whole head must turn; another trick by the burka inventor: a man must know what his wife is looking at.
>
> —Excerpted from *The Bookseller of Kabul* by Asne Seierstad

Biography is a factual record of the life of an individual.
Autobiography is a biography written by its subject.

Diaries and **journals** are records of personal activities, events, travels, or reflections.

An **essay** is a nonfiction work that presents the author's opinion and observations on a subject.

Autobiography tells the life story of the writer from a first-person point of view. Autobiography is written to inform and entertain and sometimes to persuade.

Diaries and **journals** are records of personal activities, events, travels, or reflections.

An **essay** presents the author's opinion and observations on a subject. The writer may use a first-person or a third-person point of view. Essays come in many subjects, themes, tones, and styles.

Example:

> Learning to be satisfied with the ordinary did not come so easily as learning to be comfortable with athletic mediocrity [average ability]. Years ago when I started to write, fresh from a regimen of great books, I hoped for big things and wanted the landmarks I built in the literary world to stand out. Somehow, though, I never got around to writing about King Lears and Hamlets. Instead I wrote about turtles, cicadas, and birds, not bald eagles either but robins and starlings. For a while I was irritated at myself for accomplishing so little, but then I quit fretting and decided I might as well be satisfied with lesser things. Once I decided this, writing became fun, and I began receiving rewards.
>
> —Excerpted from *May Days* by Samuel Pickering

GED Readiness

Read the passages and answer the questions.

WAS PRESIDENT JEFFERSON AN OPTIMIST?

About a year after these young visitors left Monticello, John Adams wrote his friend there what he described as a very frivolous letter. In this he asked if [Thomas] Jefferson would be
5 willing to live his seventy years over again. In his reply Jefferson, who was actually nearing seventy-three, said emphatically that he would. He believed this world to be a good one on the whole, "framed on a principle of benevolence,"
10 and dealing out more pleasure than pain. He recognized that there were differences of opinion on this point, differences not unrelated to temperament, and he made here one of the most famous and one of the most revealing
15 of his characterizations of himself. "My temperament is sanguine [cheerful]," he said. "I steer my bark [boat] with Hope in the head, leaving Fear astern [behind]. My hopes indeed sometimes fail; but not oftener than the
20 forebodings of the gloomy."

—Excerpted from *Jefferson: The Sage of Monticello*
by Dumas Malone

1 What type of literary nonfiction is this passage?

① biography
② autobiography
③ journal
④ letter

2 What is the main idea of the passage?

① Jefferson lived to be seventy-two.
② Jefferson enjoyed life enough to be willing to live it again.
③ Different people have different attitudes toward life.
④ People who expect the worst are sometimes surprised.

3 What can you infer that the word *benevolence* in line 9 means?

① pain
② love of life
③ kindness
④ hopefulness

HOW DOES THE AUTHOR FEEL ABOUT TANNING?

Standards of beauty in every era are things that advertise, usually falsely: "I'm rich and I don't have to work." How could you be a useful farmhand, or even an efficient clerk-typist, if you have long, painted fingernails? Four-inch heels, like the bound feet of Chinese aristocrats, suggest you don't have to do anything efficiently, except maybe put up your tootsies on an ottoman and eat bonbons. (And I'll point out here that aristocratic men wore the first high heels.) In my grandmother's day, women of all classes lived in dread of getting a tan, since that betrayed a field worker's station in life. But now that the field hand's station is occupied by the office worker, a tan, I suppose, advertises that Florida and Maui are within your reach. Fat is another peculiar cultural flip-flop; in places where food is scarce, beauty is three inches of subcutaneous [under the skin] fat deep. But here and now, jobs are sedentary [sitting] and calories are relatively cheap, while the luxury of time to work them off is very dear [expensive].

—Excerpted from *High Tide in Tucson*
by Barbara Kingsolver

4 What does the author say about standards of beauty?

① They lie.
② They advertise a person's efficiency.
③ They're the same in all times and places.
④ They always feature high heels.

5 This passage is organized in terms of

① cause and effect
② comparison and contrast
③ chronological order
④ order of importance

6 According to the author, when do societies value large women?

① when they have suntans
② when most jobs involve sitting all day
③ when people are dying of AIDS
④ when food is scarce

Interpreting Commentary and Reviews

Commentary is a form of nonfiction in which the writer comments about an art form: a book, a performance (film, theater, dance, or music), or a work of visual art (sculpture, painting, or photography).

A **review** discusses one specific work of art. It gives readers information that helps them decide whether to go to a particular show or read a certain book. By contrast, **criticism** may consider one artist's career or discuss an entire form of art (not just a specific painting but oil painting in general, or landscapes in general, or impressionism as a style). It may compare and contrast works or put them in historical context. To understand criticism, you must understand the facts about the art form and the critic's opinions.

People who write commentary and reviews are called **critics**. They evaluate an artistic work and assess its strengths and weaknesses.

In commentaries about the visual arts, the author re-creates in words the art's physical appearance. The writing style is highly descriptive. As a reader, you must be able to analyze the writer's style (including tone) to evaluate his or her opinion. When you read such a description, try to picture in your mind's eye what the art looks like. The reviewer may also interpret the emotions or the message that the art seems to convey.

When you read commentary and reviews, ask these questions:

- What facts about the work itself does the critic include?
- What does the critic say about the artist and his or her abilities and background?
- What does the critic like about the work? What does the critic dislike about the work? Look for words that communicate the critic's opinions and feelings. Remember that most reviews intend to persuade readers to share the reviewer's opinions.
- Does the critic recommend the work? Does the critic recognize the value of the art form?
- How does the critic present the message? Is the argument convincing? Why or why not?

Example:

> Last night the woman who's been called the new Queen of the Blues performed at Legends. Does Shemekia Copeland deserve the title? Frankly, no, but only because she's not singing classic blues. She sang funky R&B, with the emphasis on the funk, and she did it magnificently, with a powerhouse voice and an emotional edge.

This excerpt from a review tells readers that the reviewer liked the performance and begins to explain why.

Commentary is a form of nonfiction in which the writer comments about an art form.

A **review** discusses one specific work of art while **criticism** discusses trends or characteristics of an entire form of art.

Critics are people who write commentary and reviews evaluating artistic works.

Related Skills: 2–9, 16–18, and 26

GED Readiness

Read the passage and answer the questions.

Zora Neale Hurston was popular during the Harlem Renaissance of the 1930s for her stories set in the South and written in a rural black dialect.

WHAT MADE HURSTON'S WRITING UNIQUE?

Hurston's saving distinction was her exquisitely sensitive ear. She was sometimes out of tune, as when she tried to devise metaphors that were self-consciously literary ("there is a basin in the mind where words float around"). But when she deployed colloquial black speech and celebrated its ability to move beyond mere denotation, she was a spectacular writer, and the farthest thing from a flag waver. When, for instance, she describes a speeding train in *Jonah's Gourd Vine*, she uses a word that perfectly conveys the sound of the wheels clicking over the track joints: it "schickalacked" over the rails. A girl walks "hippily" past a porch full of gaping men. A woman is only "mouf [mouth] glad" rather than "sho nuff [sure enough] glad" when she tries to deflect with a forced smile her man's gathering anger.

—Excerpted from *Required Reading*
by David Delbanco

1 What is the main idea of this passage?

  ① Hurston wrote "out of tune."
  ② Hurston's greatest strength was her literary metaphors.
  ③ Hurston's books give readers a view of other people's lives.
  ④ Hurston captured colloquial black speech on the page.

2 What does the critic mean when he says Hurston had an "exquisitely sensitive ear"?

  ① She could hear what people were whispering fifty feet away.
  ② She was in pain from an ear infection.
  ③ She noticed how real people talked.
  ④ She was good at recognizing voices.

Read the passage. Write *F* in front of each fact and *O* in front of each opinion.

WHAT MAKES A GREAT HORSE PAINTING?

At the Walters Art Museum in Baltimore, today's kids can gaze at some of the greatest horses of all time—and learn how they developed both in the stable and on canvas. Running through June 5, "Stubbs & the Horse" features 35 drawings and 40 paintings by George Stubbs (1724–1806), long considered the world's finest equine [horse] painter. Don't know a hoof from a haunch? No problem, says Kathy Nusbaum, the museum's manager of children and family programs. The exhibit is designed for horse lover and novice alike. Stubbs tends to dramatize moments between animals rather than humans. In "Mares and Foals" (1763–65), body language—flattened ears, turned heads—reveals the dynamics of a group of equine moms. A staid coachman stands in marked contrast to the fuzzy dog happily greeting a royal black horse ("The Prince of Wales's Phaeton, With the Coachman Samuel Thomas and a Tiger-Boy," 1793).

—Excerpted from "Walters' Mane Event"
by Mary Quattlebaum, *Washington Post*

3 _____ Today's kids can gaze at some of the greatest horses of all time.

4 _____ Running through June 5, "Stubbs & the Horse" features 35 drawings and 40 paintings by George Stubbs.

5 _____ George Stubbs is the world's finest equine painter.

6 _____ Stubbs was born in 1724 and died in 1806.

7 _____ The exhibit is designed for horse lover and novice alike.

8 _____ Stubbs tends to dramatize moments between animals rather than humans.

9 _____ "Mares and Foals" was painted between 1763 and 1765.

Analyzing Informational Nonfiction

You've learned that nonfiction is about real people, events, and ideas. **Informational nonfiction** is designed to convey useful information. It includes magazine and newspaper articles, reports, and speeches. Editorials, business documents, and consumer documents will be covered in Skills 44–47.

An **article** is a short nonfiction piece in a newspaper or magazine. Its purpose is to inform and sometimes to entertain readers. In an objective manner, it presents facts, including the answers to the questions *who, what, when, where, why,* and *how.* It cites sources of statistics. If it includes opinions, they are quotes from people who are knowledgeable about the situation.

Example:

> ### PRESIDENT SEEKS BUDGET CUTS
>
> President Bush will seek deep cuts in spending for social programs in his new budget. He also wants to tighten farm subsidies.
>
> Since 2000, the federal government has gone from a surplus of $236 billion to a deficit of $413 billion, according to the Congressional Budget Office. Democrats in Congress are gearing up to fight the Bush budget. One senator says their main goals are to protect social services and cancel the tax cuts for the wealthiest Americans. Taxes have not been such a small percentage of gross domestic product since 1951.
>
> The budget is expected to go to Congress Friday. Hearings will begin next Monday.

A **report** is a written account that conveys information to a specific group. The most important quality of a report is accuracy. Examples include a scientific report on the results of testing a new drug, a company's annual financial report, and a formal record of the proceedings of a meeting.

A **speech** is spoken communication on a subject. A speech is organized much like an essay, with an interesting introduction, details that support the main idea, and a strong conclusion. A speech may have several purposes: to entertain, inform, persuade, or even inspire. You analyze a speech in the same way as an essay: look for the author's purpose, message, style, and tone. Notable speeches include Abraham Lincoln's Gettysburg Address and John F. Kennedy's inaugural address. Speeches may be made in many forums: political rallies, business meetings, awards shows, and commencement ceremonies, among others.

Informational nonfiction is writing designed to convey useful information. It includes

- **articles** from newspapers or magazines
- **reports** that convey information to a specific group
- **speeches,** or spoken communication

Related Skills: 1–6, 10–14, and 44–47

GED Readiness

Read the passages and answer the questions.

WHY WAS THE PLANE SHOT DOWN?

After a secret three-year investigation, federal prosecutors have decided to end a criminal inquiry into whether at least four Central Intelligence Agency officers lied to lawmakers and their agency superiors about a clandestine [secret] antidrug operation that ended in 2001 with the fatal downing of a plane carrying American missionaries, Justice Department officials said this week.

"The Justice Department has declined a criminal prosecution," said Bryan Sierra, a Justice Department spokesman, in response to a question about the previously undisclosed investigation. . . .

The officials said the investigation had not been directly related to the act of shooting down the plane, which was carried out by a Peruvian Air Force jet after the missionary plane was misidentified as a potential drug smuggling aircraft by a C.I.A. surveillance plane.

—Excerpted from "U.S. Drops Criminal Investigation of C.I.A. Antidrug Effort in Peru" by Douglas Jehl and David Johnston, *New York Times*

❶ Who was on trial?

_____

❷ What were the defendants charged with?

_____

❸ Who shot the plane down and why?

_____

_____

❹ Who was actually on the plane?

_____

❺ Who announced that there would be no prosecution?

_____

WHAT WAS KING'S DREAM?

I am happy to join with you today in what will go down in history as the greatest demonstration for freedom in the history of our nation.

Fivescore years ago, a great American, in whose symbolic shadow we stand today, signed the Emancipation Proclamation. This momentous decree came as a great beacon light of hope to millions of Negro slaves who had been seared in the flame of withering injustice. It came as a joyous daybreak to end the long night of their captivity.

But one hundred years later, the Negro still is not free; one hundred years later, the life of the Negro is still sadly crippled by the manacles of segregation and the chains of discrimination; one hundred years later, the Negro lives on a lonely island of poverty in the midst of a vast ocean of material prosperity; one hundred years later, the Negro is still languished [neglected] in the corners of American society and finds himself in exile in his own land.

So we've come here today to dramatize a shameful condition. In a sense we've come to our nation's capital to cash a check. When the architects of our republic wrote the magnificent words of the Constitution and the Declaration of Independence, they were signing a promissory note to which every American was to fall heir.

—Excerpted from "I Have a Dream" by Martin Luther King, Jr., delivered August 28, 1963

❻ What is King's tone in this speech?

  ① cheerful
  ② accepting
  ③ nervous
  ④ determined

❼ One purpose of the speech is to

  ① demand equal treatment now
  ② give a history lesson
  ③ say that civil rights have been achieved
  ④ warn people of an economic crash

Interpreting Editorials

An **editorial** is a short piece of nonfiction in a newspaper or magazine that is designed to persuade you to share a certain belief or take a certain action. Remember from Skill 7 that a fact is a statement that can be proved. An opinion cannot be proved and expresses feelings, beliefs, or personal judgments. An editorial expresses someone's opinion.

A publication's main editorials are usually in essay form. Other editorials may appear as columns by staff members or syndicated columnists, guest editorials by readers, letters to the editor, and political cartoons. These are often on a newspaper's **op-ed (opinion-editorial) page**.

To decide whether you should be persuaded by an editorial, ask these questions:

- Does it provide facts to back up the writer's opinions?
- Are the facts it provides accurate or distorted? Are they relevant to the issue?
- Is the writer's reasoning sound, or does it include errors and false assumptions?
- Can you identify the writer's values (principles he or she considers important)? What effect do those values have on the writer's opinions? Do you share those values?

> An **editorial** is a short piece of nonfiction that is designed to persuade. In a newspaper, editorials can be found on the **op-ed (opinion-editorial) page**.

Example:

> Dear Editor:
>
> You ran an editorial claiming that No Child Left Behind is a bad law. You said it's about drilling kids for tests, not about learning, and the tests focus on trivia instead of in-depth understanding.
>
> When I was young, drilling and rote memorization *were* learning, and we turned out all right—a lot better than parents today, who care more about being friends with their children than raising them right. If a question is on a test, it isn't trivial.
>
> Let's face it, many kids out there are just plain dumb. They need drilling to do well on tests. Teachers are just plain lazy. If they didn't want the government telling them what to teach, they should have done a better job in the first place.

The only fact this letter provides is the writer drilled as a student. That's not relevant. The writer's reasoning is unsound. He thinks all kids are dumb, all teachers are lazy, and parents don't know how to discipline. He also makes the false assumptions that any question on a test is important and that the government knows best what teachers should teach. The letter fails in its persuasive intent.

Related Skills: 1–5, 7–9, 18, 41–42, and 48

GED Readiness

Read the passages and answer the questions.

HOW DOES THE WRITER FEEL ABOUT HIGH INTEREST RATES?

Several top issuers [of credit cards] now hit consumers with rates just shy of 30%—rates that would be considered usury [illegal] in most states but aren't in South Dakota and Delaware, which have no rate ceilings and are home to some of the largest issuers.

Adding to the unfairness, consumers can get punished for insignificant slips or none at all. Issuers, who periodically review how consumers handle other bills and how much they owe, can decide that a consumer is a worse risk today than yesterday. Even if the consumer is paying that issuer on time, the company may jack up the rate. Still worse, the unexpected hike applies to old balances.

Rates nearing 30% are abusive. If the credit card companies want to distinguish themselves in the marketplace from loan sharks, they ought not to use flimsy excuses to jack up interest rates and suck their customers dry.

—Excerpted from "30% Interest? State Rules Leave Consumers Defenseless," *USA Today*

1 What is the author's main point?

① Credit card companies shouldn't be allowed to raise interest rates unfairly.
② Consumers should stop charging so many purchases on their credit cards.
③ Loan sharks charge even higher interest than card companies.
④ Card issuers review customers' ability to pay.

2 Did the editorial persuade you? Why or why not?

_____

_____

Dear Editor,

As we prepare to celebrate Earth Day, all Americans should take note of an important report on the state of the planet. The Millennium Ecosystem Assessment measures the decline in the earth's functioning. More than 1,300 scientists from 95 countries have contributed to the report.

For the earth to keep supporting us, ecosystems must be able to filter water, provide food, and pollinate crops. Yet 60 percent of those functions are being degraded by human activities. We damage the planet by polluting the air and water, deforesting millions of acres, overfishing, and other destructive practices.

It's possible to change such practices. For example, one coffee plantation in Central America was using pesticides to kill weeds, but the poisons killed off bees too. When the plantation cut back on pesticides, it saved money and the bees came back. Scientists calculated that the amount of pollinating of the coffee crop that the bees do now is worth $60,000 a year.

The Millennium Ecosystem Assessment was commissioned five years ago by the United Nations and by countries that signed environmental treaties. The conclusion is clear: We must do a better job taking care of the earth if we want it to take care of us. We can start by recycling and cutting down on purchases. We can also vote for officials, both local and national, who support the environment.

3 Name two facts this letter provides.

_____

_____

4 How does it affect your assessment of the letter to know who commissioned and who worked on the report?

_____

_____

5 Does the writer's reasoning support her conclusion (paragraph 4)? Does it include any errors or false assumptions?

_____

Understanding Workplace and Business Documents

In our information-based economy, employers need workers who can follow written documents. **Workplace and business documents** are any written materials that employees encounter at work.

- **Mission and goal statements** clarify a company's purpose for existing in the marketplace. They also spell out the company's unique benefits for customers. Employees need to understand these statements in order to contribute to the company's success.
- **Employee handbooks** give workers essential information about conditions of their employment. They explain expectations for employees' performance and behavior, training opportunities, salary and benefits, review and evaluation, disciplinary measures, grievances, and termination procedures. They may also cover work schedules, medical needs, and leaves of absence.
- **Training manuals** provide practical step-by-step guidance on how employees should perform their jobs.
- **Legal documents** advise employees of federal and national laws governing behavior in the workplace regarding safety, discrimination, and sexual harassment.
- **Program brochures** may be available for orientation, insurance, employee development, educational assistance, counseling, substance abuse prevention, and retirement.
- **Memos** may be about any conceivable workplace subject.

> **Workplace and business documents** are any written materials that employees may encounter at work. Among them are mission and goal statements, employee handbooks, training manuals, program brochures, and memos.

Example:

> To: All employees
> Re: Employee Assistance Program (EAP)
>
> If you (or a family member) are having problems with any type of addiction, the Employee Assistance Program is here for you. Common addictive disorders include alcohol or drug dependency, smoking, and compulsive eating or gambling. If you feel that any of these behaviors has gotten out of control, we can help you with information, counseling, and referrals. If your life has been affected by someone else's addiction, we can provide a support system and help you decide what to do.
>
> All EAP services are FREE and strictly confidential. Call 1-555-9876 today to talk to an EAP counselor. We can help you develop an action plan and get on the road to recovery.

The first two lines tell you who the memo is aimed at and its general subject. The first paragraph describes the behaviors EAP can help with. The second tells you how to reach a counselor and assures you the program is free and confidential.

GED Readiness

Read the passages and answer the questions.

WHAT AGENCY PROTECTS YOUR RIGHT TO A SAFE, HEALTHFUL WORKPLACE?

- You have the right to request an OSHA inspection if you believe that there are unsafe and unhealthful conditions in your workplace.
- Your employer must correct workplace hazards by the date indicated on the citation and must certify that these hazards have been reduced or eliminated.
- You have the right to copies of your medical records or records of your exposure to toxic and harmful substances or conditions.
- Your employer must post this notice in your workplace.

The Occupational Safety and Health Act of 1970 assures safe and healthful working conditions. To file a complaint, report an emergency, or seek OSHA advice, call 1-800-321-OSHA or visit www.osha.gov.

1 What agency protects your right to a safe workplace?

  ① Orderly Shelter and Home Agency
  ② Safe and Healthful Workplace Agency
  ③ Occupational Safety and Health Administration
  ④ Equal Employment Opportunity Commission

2 How are employees likely to find out about their OSHA rights?

  ① They may see a TV commercial about OSHA.
  ② They may read about them in newspapers.
  ③ Companies must mail the information to workers.
  ④ Companies must post the information in the workplace.

3 If you've been exposed to toxic substances at work, what can OSHA help you do?

  ① Get a blood test.
  ② Get copies of your medical records.
  ③ See your family doctor.
  ④ Go on a cleansing fast.

Employee Corrective Action Notice

Employee's Name _____

Notice Date _____

Job Title _____

This notice is a ☐ First   ☐ Second
               ☐ Third   ☐ Final Warning

Reason for corrective action: (Check below)

☐ Absenteeism   ☐ Lack of cooperation
☐ Quantity of work   ☐ Insubordination
☐ Quality of work   ☐ Disregard for safety
☐ Tardiness   ☐ Other causes (Explain)

Explanation and details for reason checked above:

_____

_____

I hereby state that I have received a full explanation of my failure to perform. I understand that further failure on my part will be considered due cause for disciplinary action, up to and including termination.

_____
Employee's signature

_____
Supervisor's signature

4 What is the purpose of this form?

_____

5 Is dress code violation a reason for corrective action?

_____

6 Who must sign this form?

_____

Understanding Community and Consumer Documents

Community and consumer documents are any written materials that people encounter in their personal lives—as residents of a neighborhood, as citizens of their state or country, or as purchasers of goods and services. Such documents often include **forms,** documents with blank spaces you need to fill in to provide information about yourself or your opinions. Forms often use abbreviations, which are important to understand.

Among the many types of community documents are these:

- change-of-address forms
- hospital admittance forms
- posters for block parties
- library card applications
- minutes of school board meetings
- voter registration forms

To protect themselves, consumers should read and understand the information that companies provide. Among the many types of consumer documents are these:

- apartment rental contracts
- catalog order forms
- classified ads for selling things
- credit card agreements
- cell-phone calling plans
- nutrition labels on food products
- warranties for appliances and electronic products

Community documents are any written materials that people encounter as residents of a neighborhood or citizens of their state or country.

Consumer documents are any written materials that people encounter as purchasers of goods and services.

Example:

FIX-ALL HARDWARE

605 Consumer Way, Ligonier, PA 15658

Call toll-free: (800) 555-4321 or visit www.fixallhw.com

Item #	Description	Qty.	Price	Total
831-40	Flexible flashlight	2	$14.99	$ 29.98
673-21	Cordless drill	1	$38.99	$ 38.99
200-12	Plastic switchplates	12	$ 2.49	$ 29.88
	Delivery:			$ 8.00
	TOTAL:			$106.85

☒ Check   ☐ Credit card # _____

Signature _____

Deliver to: Mitchell Jones
555 Rand Road
Elgin, IL 60125

GED Readiness

Read the form and answer the questions.

Voter Registration Application

Are you a citizen of the United States?
☐ Yes ☐ No

Will you be 18 or older by Election Day?
☐ Yes ☐ No

_____

Last Name First Name Mid Initial

_____

Street Address

_____

City County State Zip

_____

Telephone # (optional)

  / /19
_____

Birthdate

_____

Driver's License # OR Social Security #

In what party do you wish to register?
☐ Democratic ☐ Republican ☐ Green
☐ Libertarian ☐ Other

Place signature with full name below.
Please see Penalty for Falsifying Declaration.

X _____

This application must be received at least
30 days before the election. If envelope is
misplaced, mail to Voter Registration Office,
Lansing, MI 48824.

---

1 If the election is November 2, when do you need to return your application?

  ① by November 1
  ② by October 2
  ③ by September 30
  ④ by September 2

2 What are the requirements to be eligible to vote?

  ① You must be a U.S. citizen.
  ② You must be at least eighteen.
  ③ You must tell the truth on your application.
  ④ all of the above

3 What identification do you need to register?

  ① Social Security and driver's license numbers
  ② Social Security or driver's license number
  ③ credit card number
  ④ birth certificate

Read the classified ad and answer the questions.

---

2 BR apt., $1\frac{1}{2}$ baths, 3rd fl., river view, balc.
Historic bldg. w/character in Mt. Odin area.
Just painted, new A/C, pkg. gar. $900/mo., util.
incl. lst + last mos. rent.

---

4 What does "2 BR apt." stand for?

_____

5 Will the tenant have to pay heating costs?

_____

6 What does "pkg. gar." stand for?

_____

7 What do you think "historic building" really means here (keeping in mind that the ad is trying to sell you on this apartment)?

_____

8 How much will the tenant have to pay before moving in?

_____

Using Business and Consumer Letters

Letters are an essential part of communication for both businesspeople and consumers. A **business letter** is any formally written message addressed to a person or organization for business purposes. A **consumer letter** is a written message to or from a purchaser or consumer.

If you are reading a business or consumer letter, you need to understand

- what the letter writer is trying to say
- what the writer wants you to do (fill an order letter, donate money, resolve a complaint, and so on)

If you are writing a business or consumer letter, it will be taken more seriously if you follow this standard format:

A **business letter** is any written message addressed to a person or organization for business purposes.

A **consumer letter** is a written message to or from a purchaser or consumer.

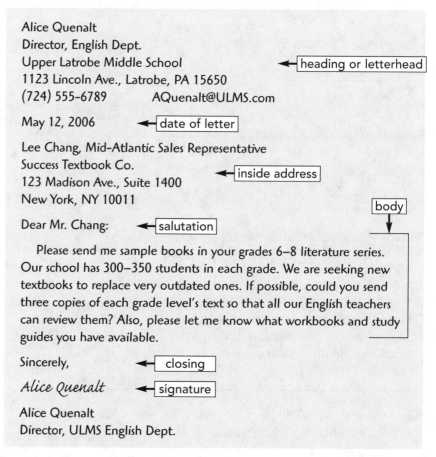

Alice Quenalt
Director, English Dept.
Upper Latrobe Middle School ← heading or letterhead
1123 Lincoln Ave., Latrobe, PA 15650
(724) 555-6789   AQuenalt@ULMS.com

May 12, 2006 ← date of letter

Lee Chang, Mid-Atlantic Sales Representative
Success Textbook Co.
123 Madison Ave., Suite 1400 ← inside address
New York, NY 10011
                                                    body

Dear Mr. Chang: ← salutation

    Please send me sample books in your grades 6–8 literature series. Our school has 300–350 students in each grade. We are seeking new textbooks to replace very outdated ones. If possible, could you send three copies of each grade level's text so that all our English teachers can review them? Also, please let me know what workbooks and study guides you have available.

Sincerely, ← closing

Alice Quenalt ← signature

Alice Quenalt
Director, ULMS English Dept.

The letter writer followed the standard format. If you were Lee Chang, how would you respond? You'd want to make the sale, so you would send the requested books with a polite cover letter and with information about ordering.

GED Readiness

Read the letters and answer the questions.

Randall Winton, Police Chief
123 Main St.
Laurel Hills, PA 16870

Dear Chief Winton:

I live in the Dogwood Acres subdivision, which (as I'm sure you know) has seen an enormous increase in crime in recent years. Drug dealers are taking over our neighborhood. Just last week, someone set fire to the house across the street, but no one has been arrested yet.

My neighbors and I fear for our children's safety, so we are starting a Neighborhood Watch to take back our streets.

May we have the support of the police department? First, we'd like an officer to speak to our group on ways we can protect our families. Second, we'd like a reassurance that when we call 911, a patrol car will arrive in ten minutes or less.

Will you help us save our neighborhood? Thank you. You can reach me at (814) 555-7294 evenings and (814) 555-1725 during the day.

Sincerely yours,

Alma T. Cisneros

Alma T. Cisneros

1 What is the letter writer's main goal?

_____

2 What tone does she take in the letter—cooperative or angry? Why?

_____

3 What is the problem she's complaining about?

_____

4 What specifically does she want from Randall Winton?

_____

_____

Leon Rodriguez, Owner
Citywide Auto Service
1022 Dempster Rd.
Evanston, IL 60202

Dear Mr. Rodriguez:

We are considering hiring Joe Chenet for a position as a welder. Enclosed is a copy of a release form signed by Mr. Chenet authorizing you to verify his work record and tell us about his performance.

Please complete the following questions and return the form to us in the enclosed postage-paid envelope. Thank you for providing this information.

Dates of employment _____

Last position held _____

Responsibilities _____

_____

Quality of work _____

Would you rehire? _____

Regards,

Indira Patel

Indira Patel, Human Resources Director

5 What is the purpose of this letter?
  (1) to find out what skills welders need
  (2) to advertise Citywide Auto Service
  (3) to check the references of a job applicant
  (4) to notify welders of a job opening

6 Who gave the letter writer permission to ask for background information?
  (1) Leon Rodriguez
  (2) Joe Chenet
  (3) Ms. Patel
  (4) the owner of Citywide Auto Service

7 What is Ms. Patel's job?

_____

_____

Interpreting Cartoons

Cartoons are a type of visual communication that uses images and humor to make a point. **Comics** usually appear on the comics pages of a newspaper and can be about anything from wordplay to family ties to wacky pets. **Editorial cartoons** usually appear on a newspaper's editorial pages and express an opinion about current events and political issues.

Because cartoons are so compressed (in terms of space and number of words), much of their message is implied. That means that to get the message, you need to infer information and opinions that are not spelled out.

To interpret a cartoon, you need to understand

- the background of the political issue or daily life shown
- the topic of this particular cartoon
- the words, whether in dialogue, captions, or labels
- the meaning of any symbols the cartoonist uses
- the opinion the cartoonist is promoting
- the characters involved

To understand the **background** of a political cartoon, it helps to read a daily newspaper and know what issues are going on in the world. If you see a cartoon that shows a big SUV labeled "Environment" going over a cliff, it will make more sense if you know that many people are worried about shortages of fossil fuels, extinction of animal and plant species, and increased deaths due to pollution (including pollution from cars and SUVs).

Cartoons usually announce their **topic** with a caption or dialogue. The cartoon on the next page is about banning books, as the dialogue and the signs show. A cartoon may be about a controversial political issue, a celebrity or a popular TV show, misunderstandings between men and women, differences of opinion between friends or family members, hassles at work (especially difficult bosses), or anything else you can think of.

Read any **dialogue** and **labels** in the cartoon first. Then read the **caption**, if there is one. The caption is often a punchline that's funnier after you've formed an opinion about what's going on.

Popular **symbols** in cartoons include Uncle Sam to represent the United States and bulging bags with dollar signs on them to designate a greedy businessperson.

The artist's **opinion** may be the opposite of the opinion a character proclaims if the character is unappealing or if the opinion is presented as foolish.

Cartoons are a type of visual communication that uses images and humor to make a point.

Comics usually appear on newspaper comics pages and can be about anything.

Editorial cartoons usually appear on a newspaper's editorial pages and express an opinion about current events.

Related Skills: 1–5, 7–10, 16–18, 21, and 27–28

In daily comic strips, your knowledge of the **characters** from reading the strip over months or years contributes to your understanding of their actions, motivations, and relationships. For example, you probably know that Garfield the cat is lazy, Spiderman is heroic, and Dilbert is one of the few sane people in his office. Political cartoons may be one episode only, so artists often rely on stereotypes (standard, simplified characters you can make assumptions about, like greedy politicians or slacker teens).

The background for the cartoon above is that sometimes people want to ban books that they perceive as obscene or racist or otherwise bad for society. The characters are a skeptical-looking reporter, the smug man she's interviewing, and the protesters in the background. The artist's opinion is the opposite of what the man is saying. How do you know that? Because he gives the man such a ludicrous goal ("Ban all books") and such a lame reason for it. If you need to rearrange the letters to make a book obscene, then the obscenity is in the eye of the beholder, not in the book itself. By ridiculing censors, the cartoonist is praising freedom of speech.

GED Readiness

Read the cartoons and answer the questions.

by Nicole Hollander

1 Who are the characters in this comic strip?

  ① a wife and husband
  ② a customer and a bartender
  ③ a mother and son
  ④ a boss and an employee

2 What does Sylvia imply is the equivalent of her listener's car?

  ① his job
  ② his drink
  ③ his TV
  ④ his girlfriend

3 What in panel 2 hints at Sylvia's point?

  ① She calls the car "her."
  ② She says the man likes to be in control.
  ③ She makes the man and his car sound like a couple.
  ④ all of the above

4 When Sylvia says, "And someday if you should meet a car you like better . . ." she is implying that

  ① he's the type of man who would leave his girlfriend for another woman
  ② he's the type of man who buys a new car every few years
  ③ he's very dependable
  ④ he's looking for a car with good mileage

5 In panel 3, "Sylvia, you pervert everything" is a

  ① line of dialogue
  ② label
  ③ caption
  ④ symbol

6 What can you infer about Sylvia's attitude toward life?

  ① She's very concerned about her health.
  ② She takes everything seriously.
  ③ She likes to enjoy herself.
  ④ She doesn't like to argue.

7 What hints does the cartoonist give to help you figure out Sylvia's attitude toward life?

  ① She's dressed in jeans.
  ② She's smoking and drinking.
  ③ She's so angry with the bartender that she stops speaking to him.
  ④ She avoids disagreeing with the bartender.

8 Based on what you infer about the bartender, which statement below would he be most likely to say?

  ① We need a woman president.
  ② I'd like to see stricter environmental protections.
  ③ The customer is always right.
  ④ I want to buy a sports car someday.

by Richard Thompson

9 What is the character above doing?

① shopping
② watching TV
③ voting
④ building a sign

10 Two of the choices are "Democrat extra crunchy" and "Fat-free Republican" to suggest that

① most Democrats are nuts and most Republicans are fat
② the differences are no more meaningful than those at the grocery store
③ the man is choosing a type of ice cream
④ food is an issue in this election

11 What does the choice "Apathetican" suggest?

① Some people don't care who wins.
② Some voters speak Latin.
③ There's a party for people who are looking for a new path.
④ The Apathetic Party can win.

12 What is the artist's opinion about political parties today?

① The more choices, the better.
② Only two parties have any chance of winning.
③ Each party has serious supporters.
④ They're all basically the same.

by Sandy Huffaker

13 What does the wheezing character represent?

① an individual with a bad cold
② a man who can't afford new clothes
③ the United States
④ Iraq

14 What background information helps you interpret this cartoon?

① Canada and the countries of Europe all have government-sponsored health insurance.
② The United States is a wealthy country.
③ The United States does not have government-sponsored health insurance.
④ all of the above

15 What is the artist's opinion?

① Government-sponsored health care is wasteful and inefficient.
② The United States needs government-sponsored health care.
③ The United States is in a bad way.
④ Europe needs the United States.

16 Why are Europe and Canada represented by strongmen?

① to show that their citizens have health insurance and are strong and healthy
② to suggest that they are larger than the United States
③ to show that lifting moneybags builds muscles
④ to remind readers that Arnold Schwarzenegger is from Europe

Interpreting Tables and Graphs

Tables and graphs often provide additional information for articles in newspapers and magazines. A **table** has information organized into horizontal rows and vertical columns that make it easy to locate and compare bits of information.

Example:

DISTRIBUTION OF THE LABOR FORCE IN THE U.S. BY AGE, 1982, 1992, 2002, AND PROJECTED 2012
(Percentage)

	Labor force			
Total, 16 and older	100.0	100.0	100.0	100.0
16 to 24	22.3	16.9	15.7	15.0
25 to 39	39.5	41.5	34.6	31.8
40 and older	38.1	41.6	50.0	52.9
65 and older	2.3	2.3	2.5	3.3
75 and older	0.4	0.4	0.6	0.6
	1982	1992	2002	2012

Group (row axis label)

Source: U.S. Bureau of Labor Statistics

Just like a passage of text, every table has a topic. The title gives the topic. In this table, each row is labeled by an age group, and the columns are labeled "Labor force."

Graphs use images to organize and convey information. Like a table, every graph has a topic, usually stated directly in its title. Always read the title and check the labels and data to understand what a graph is showing.

Example:

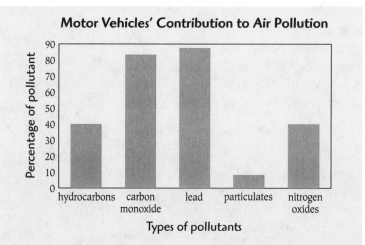

Motor Vehicles' Contribution to Air Pollution

A **table** is information organized into horizontal rows and vertical columns.

Graphs use images to organize and convey information.

- A **line graph** uses lines to connect different data points. It is best used to show changes over time.
- A **bar graph** uses bars to display information. It is best used to compare amounts.
- A **circle graph** uses segments of a circle to display information. It is best used to compare percentages.

GED Readiness

Read the graphs and answer the questions.

Chemicals in the Human Body

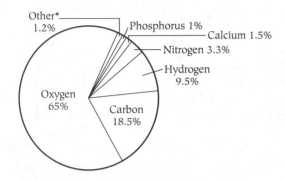

*The body contains very small amounts of 18 other chemicals.

Oil* Prices, 2005

*Light sweet crude oil
Source: U.S. Dept. of Energy

1 Which chemical makes up the greatest part of the body?

① oxygen
② carbon
③ hydrogen
④ calcium

2 Which one chemical makes up the least part of the body?

① nitrogen
② calcium
③ phosphorus
④ other

3 How much hydrogen does the body contain?

① 9.5 pounds
② 9.5 ounces
③ 9.5 percent
④ $9.50 worth

4 What do the percentages of all the chemicals in the circle graph add to?

① 65%
② 98.8%
③ 1.2%
④ 100%

5 What are the numbers on the left side?

① number of gallons
② number of barrels
③ dollars per gallon
④ dollars per barrel

6 When did the price of oil first exceed $55?

① February 2005
② March 2005
③ February 2004
④ March 2004

7 What is this graph about?

_____

8 What kind of oil is being tracked in this graph?

_____

9 Where does the information in this graph come from?

_____

10 How low did the price of oil fall in May 2005?

_____

Understanding Reference Sources

Reference sources give information or tell you where to find information about a given subject you want to research.

- **Almanacs** give quick facts about people, events, sports records, weather, and many other topics.
- **Atlases** provide maps and information about countries.
- **Dictionaries** give the definitions and pronunciations of words.
- **Thesauruses** are dictionaries that list synonyms and antonyms.
- **Encyclopedias** provide short articles about many topics.
- **Glossaries** provide terms and definitions used in a book.
- **Indexes** list subjects covered in a book and their pages.
- **Card catalogs** are computer listings of books in a library.
- **Internet search engines** direct you to online references.

A **dictionary** defines words, tells you how to pronounce them, and gives their parts of speech, different spellings, and history. Words in the dictionary are arranged in alphabetical order. At the top of each dictionary page are two **guide words**. The guide word on the left is the same as the first entry word on the page. The guide word on the right is the same as the last entry word on the page.

Example:

> **code** \ ´kōd\ *n* [ME, fr. MF, fr. L *caudex, codex* trunk of a tree, document formed orig. from wooden tablets] (14c) **1:** a systematic statement of a body of law; *esp:* one given statutory force **2:** a system of principles or rules <moral code> **3a:** a system of signals or symbols for communication **b:** a system of symbols (as letters or numbers) used to represent assigned and often secret meanings **4:** GENETIC CODE **5:** a set of instructions for a computer **code·less** \-ləs\ *adj*

An **index** is an alphabetical listing at the back of a book that tells you on what pages to find specific subjects.

Example:

Chesnutt, Charles Waddell, **47**

Chicago Commission of Race Relations, 1

child labor, 4, 16. *See also* forced labor

Chilembwe Uprising, **47**

cholera, 5

Christian religion
 in Egypt, 79
 in Ethiopia, 84
 on Madagascar, 154

Cinque, Joseph, **48–49**

Civil Rights Act of 1964, **47,** 51

Civil Rights Bill of 1866, 201, 203

Reference sources give information or tell you where to find information about a given subject you want to research.

A dictionary lists words in alphabetical order, defines them, and tells you how to pronounce them.

An **index** is an alphabetical listing in a book, magazine, or newspaper that tells you on what pages to find specific subjects.

GED Readiness

Read the dictionary entry and answer the questions.

¹**key·board** \ˈkē•bȯrd\ *n* (1819) **1:** a bank of keys on a musical instrument (as a piano) that usu. consists of seven white and five raised black keys to the octave **2:** an assemblage of systematically arranged keys by which a machine or device is operated **3:** a board on which keys for locks are hung **4:** a musical instrument that is played by means of a keyboard

²**key·board** *vt* (1961): to capture or set (as data or text) by means of a keyboard *vi:* to operate a machine (as for typesetting) by means of a keyboard — **key·board·er** *n*

1 Which definition of the noun *keyboard* makes sense in this sentence: *When her computer crashed for the third time, Barb pounded the keyboard in fury?*

  ① definition 1
  ② definition 2
  ③ definition 3
  ④ definition 4

2 Which definition of the noun *keyboard* makes sense in this sentence: *The keyboard on Howard's grand piano is out of tune?*

  ① definition 1
  ② definition 2
  ③ definition 3
  ④ definition 4

3 What part of speech is entry 2 for *keyboard?*

  ① noun
  ② verb
  ③ adverb
  ④ conjunction

4 If the guide words for a page are *keratin* and *khaki,* will *keyboard* be on that page?

_____

5 Which usage occurred earlier, *keyboard* as a noun or as a verb?

_____

Read the index entry and answer the questions.

Ginkgo tree, Age of the species, 107
Ginseng (anti-cancer drug), 223
Giraffes
  Gestation period, 244
  Life spans, 245
  Names for the young, 255
  Speed, 268
Glacier National Park, 143
Glaciers
  Effects on terrain, 64-66
  Ice Ages, 67
  United States, 67
Glands, human
  Effect of visual stimuli, 248
  Endocrine, 242
  Largest, 246
  See also individual glands (e.g., Pituitary glands)
Glass
  Bulletproof, 269
  Fiberoptic, 318
  Movie stunt glass, 104

6 If you look up *ginkgo,* what can you learn about it?

  ① where ginkgos grow
  ② how old ginkgos get
  ③ what ginkgo leaves look like
  ④ the definition

7 If you wanted to find out how fast a giraffe can run, where would you look?

  ① page 244
  ② page 245
  ③ page 255
  ④ page 268

8 How many pages are devoted to glaciers?

  ① one
  ② three
  ③ four
  ④ sixty-four

Taking the GED Test

Congratulations on completing the instruction section of this book. You are now familiar with the types of questions you will see on the GED Language Arts, Reading Test. As you ready yourself for the GED Test, you may want to think about these test-taking strategies:

- Get a good night's sleep before the test.

- Eat breakfast before the test, especially if you are taking the test in the morning.

- Arrive at the testing center a few minutes early. If you have never been to the testing center, visit it before the day of the test so that you can find it easily.

- Read the test directions carefully. Read each question carefully and be sure you understand what is being asked. Then select the answer that matches that question.

- Grid your answers carefully, ensuring that you mark each answer in the place provided for it. If you erase an answer, be sure you erase it completely.

- Have a strategy for answering questions. Read through each reading passage and questions once and then answer each question.

- If you are not sure of an answer, make an educated guess. When you leave a question unanswered, you will always lose a point, but you may gain the point if you make a correct guess.

- During the test, work quickly and accurately. If you do not know the answer to a question, try to eliminate any options that do not make sense and select the best answer from the remaining options.

- Difficult questions may precede easy ones. Because all of the questions have equal point value, make sure you have an opportunity to answer all of the easy questions. Don't spend a lot of time on a difficult question. If you find yourself spending a lot of time on a single item, stop working on that item. Write the question number on your scratch paper. Then mark the answer you think is correct, and go on to the next question. If you have time at the end of the test, return to the difficult questions and check your answers.

- If you find yourself feeling nervous or unable to focus, close your eyes for a moment or two and take a few deep breaths. Then return to the test.

About the Posttest

This Posttest is a review of the 50 skills presented in this book. It is parallel in form to the Pretest you took at the beginning of this book. It will demonstrate what you have learned from the specific skills you practiced throughout this book and will identify any areas you need to review before taking the GED Language Arts, Reading Test.

Take this test just as you would the GED Test. On the GED Test, you will have 65 minutes to read the seven passages and answer the 40 questions. On this test, take 75 minutes to read the passage and answer the 50 multiple-choice questions.

Answer every question on this Posttest. When time is up, mark the items you did not finish. Then take extra time to answer those items, too. That will give you an idea of how much faster you need to work on the actual test.

After you finish, turn to the Answer Key on page 171 to check your answers. Then use the Posttest Evaluation Chart (pages 170–171) to figure out which skills to review in the instruction section of this book. Use the pages from Contemporary's *GED Language Arts, Reading* for further review and practice.

Posttest

Questions 1 through 8 refer to the following business information.

WHAT DOES THE NEW POLICY ASK PEOPLE TO DO?

Dear Employees:

Hi-Tech Industries has never discriminated on the basis of age, race, physical ability, or sex. Now we are taking that policy a step further by encouraging all employees to use nonsexist language in their writing.

Some people say nonsexist language isn't important, but the language we use shapes the way we think. Our Harrisburg division instituted a nonsexist language policy in late 2003, and since then profits have climbed steadily. We believe that using inclusive language will increase respect among employees. If it increases profits too, all the better. We welcome feedback on this and any other Tamarack Paper Company policy.

Harrison Vaneesh

Harrison Vaneesh, Division Chief

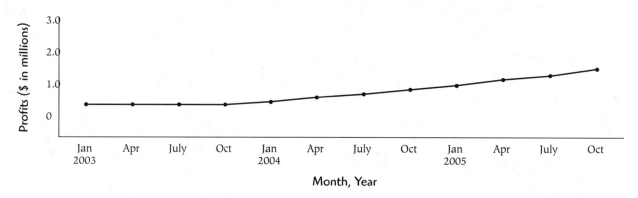

Profits of Harrisburg Division, Tamarack Paper Company

To: All employees
Re: New Policy on Inclusive Language

1. Avoid using *his, him,* or *he* to refer to people of both sexes. You can make the sentence plural or use *his or her* or *you.*

   No: Each employee is welcome to bring *his* family.
   Yes: All employees are welcome to bring *their* families.
   Yes: Each employee is welcome to bring *his* or *her* family.
   Yes: You are all welcome to bring *your* families.

2. Don't use the term *Mrs.* unless you're absolutely sure it's that person's preference. If you don't know the person's name, don't assume it's a man.

   No: Dear *Mrs.* Smith:
   Yes: Dear *Ms.* Smith:
   No: Dear *Sir:*
   Yes: Dear *Subscription Manager:*

3. Don't use sex-specific job titles or feminine endings like *-ess* and *-enne.*

   No: The new *chairman* will start Monday.
   Yes: The new *chair* will start Monday.
   No: She filed a *workman's* compensation claim.
   Yes: She filed a *worker's* compensation claim.
   No: We watched a *comedienne* last night.
   Yes: We watched a *comedian* last night.

1. Why is the company starting a policy of inclusive language?

   1. to create controversy
   2. to acknowledge that most of its employees are women
   3. to avoid discriminating
   4. to make men feel insecure

2. Which direction were the Harrisburg division's profits heading in April 2005?

   1. rising
   2. falling
   3. steady
   4. fluctuating up and down

3. What job title do the guidelines recommend for someone who runs a committee?

   1. chairman
   2. chairwoman
   3. chairperson
   4. chair

4. What is the purpose of Harrison Vaneesh's letter?

   1. to increase his company's profits
   2. to inform employees of a policy change
   3. to defend his decision against unhappy employees
   4. to warn employees who may be fired

5. If a Tamarack Paper Company customer sent in an order form signed "Joan Smyth," how should an employee address her in the reply letter's salutation?

   1. Dear Mrs. Smyth:
   2. Dear Ms. Smyth:
   3. Dear Mr. Smyth:
   4. Dear Customer:

6. Based on the letter and the graph, what effect can you conclude that Harrison Vaneesh hopes the nonsexist language policy will have on the company?

   1. It will raise profits.
   2. It will increase respect among employees.
   3. It will shape the way employees think.
   4. all of the above

7. What types of nonfiction does this piece combine?

   1. biography, journal, and letter
   2. essay and cartoon
   3. speech and graph
   4. letter, graph, and memo

8. The sample sentences in the memo are organized by

   1. chronological order
   2. cause and effect
   3. comparison and contrast
   4. order of importance

Questions 9 through 17 refer to the following excerpt from a poem.

HOW DOES THE SPEAKER FEEL ABOUT ANIMALS?

Auguries of Innocence

To see a World in a Grain of Sand
And a Heaven in a Wild Flower
Hold Infinity in the palm of your hand
And Eternity in an hour.

5 A Robin Red breast in a Cage
Puts all Heaven in a Rage.
A dove house fill'd with doves & Pigeons
Shudders Hell thro' all its regions.
A dog starv'd at his Master's Gate
10 Predicts the ruin of the State.
A Horse misus'd upon the Road
Calls to Heaven for Human blood.
Each outcry from the hunted Hare [rabbit]
A fibre from the Brain does tear.

by William Blake

9 How does the speaker feel about animals?

① He wants to keep them in cages.
② He wants to protect them.
③ He wants to hunt them for food.
④ He believes they predict the future.

10 The subject of lines 5–14 is

① robins, doves, and pigeons
② Heaven and Hell
③ mistreated animals
④ noisy animals

11 How many stanzas does this excerpt contain?

① one
② two
③ three
④ four

12 Which type of music would best fit the rhythm and the meaning of this poem?

① a slow ballad
② a peppy show tune
③ an angry rap song
④ calming elevator music

13 The rhyme scheme of the first stanza is

① *a, b, b, a*
② free form
③ the same as that of the second stanza
④ *a, b, a, b*

14 What figurative language is used in lines 1–2?

① similes
② metaphors
③ personification
④ understatement

15 Which word from the poem best conveys the speaker's mood?

① Heaven
② Rage
③ Shudders
④ Calls

16 Each pair of lines in the second stanza is organized

① in chronological order
② in cause-and-effect order
③ in comparison-and-contrast order
④ from large to small

17 Which word from the first stanza is a homonym for the word *sea*?

① see
② Sand
③ Eternity
④ hour

WHICH CHARACTER HAS THE MOST CONTROL?

1   The country is India. A large dinner party is being given in an up-country nation by a [British] colonial official and his wife. The guests are army officers and government attachés [assistants] and their wives, and an American naturalist.

2   At one side of the long table a spirited discussion springs up between a young girl and a colonel. The girl insists women have long outgrown the jumping-on-a-chair-at-sight-of-a-mouse era, that they are not as fluttery as their grandmothers. The colonel says they are, explaining that women haven't the actual nerve control of men. The other men at the table agree with him.

3   "A woman's unfailing reaction in any crisis," the colonel says, "is to scream. And while a man may feel like it, yet he has that ounce more control than a woman has. And that last ounce is what counts!"

4   The American scientist does not join in the argument, but sits watching the faces of the other guests. As he looks, he sees a strange expression come over the face of the hostess. She is staring straight ahead, the muscles of her face contracting slightly. With a small gesture she summons the native boy standing behind her chair. She whispers to him. The boy's eyes widen: he turns quickly and leaves the room. No one else sees this, nor the boy when he puts a bowl of milk on the verandah [porch] outside the glass doors.

5   The American comes to with a start. In India, milk in a bowl means only one thing. It is bait for a snake. He realizes there is a cobra in the room.

6   He looks up at the rafters—the likeliest place—and sees they are bare. Three corners of the room, which he can see by shifting only slightly, are empty. In the fourth corner a group of servants stand, waiting until the next course can be served. The American realizes there is only one place left—under the table.

7   His first impulse is to jump back and warn the others. But he knows the commotion will frighten the cobra and it will strike. He speaks quickly, the quality of his voice so arresting that it sobers everyone.

8   "I want to know just what control everyone at this table has. I will count three hundred—that's five minutes—and not one of you is to move a single muscle. The persons who move will forfeit 50 rupees. Now! Ready!"

9   The 20 people sit like stone images while he counts. He is saying ". . . two hundred and eighty . . ." when out of the corner of his eye, he sees the cobra emerge and make for the bowl of milk. Four or five screams ring out as he jumps to slam shut the verandah doors.

10   "You certainly were right, Colonel!" the host says. "A man has just shown us an example of real control."

11   "Just a minute," the American says, turning to his hostess, "There's one thing I'd like to know. Mrs. Wynnes, how did you know that cobra was in the room?"

12   A faint smile lights up the woman's face as she replies. "Because it was lying across my foot."

—"The Dinner Party" by Mona Gardner

18 This piece of writing contains only one main event, so it's from a

① novel
② short story
③ poem
④ drama

19 What word best describes the hostess?

① fluttery
② nervous
③ brave
④ shy

20 From paragraph 2 to paragraph 4, the conflict shifts

① from men to women
② to people against nature
③ from internal to external
④ from external to internal

21 From what point of view is the story told?

① first person
② second person
③ third-person limited
④ third-person omniscient

22 The story is told mostly in

① narrative
② dialogue
③ figurative language
④ past tense

23 The story is set in India in the 1930s. How does the setting influence the conflict?

① There would be no cobra if it weren't set in India.
② A man today wouldn't claim that women lack nerve control.
③ India was the only place where a Briton would have servants.
④ An American wouldn't have as much control as the British hostess.

24 The most effective descriptive detail is given about

① the argument between the girl and the colonel
② the womans' behavior when the cobra touches her
③ the American scientist's search for the cobra
④ what the scientist says to the group

25 What statement best sums up the story's theme?

① The squeaky wheel gets the grease.
② People are more important than things.
③ Women are not inferior to men.
④ Envy makes people do crazy things.

26 To describe the amount of nerve control various characters possess, you could use

① chronological order
② cause-and-effect order
③ order of degree
④ example order

Questions 27 through 33 refer to the following passage and cartoon.

WHAT IS THE WRITER'S OPINION?

Kansas Evolves Back

1   Nearly five years into the 21st century, the Kansas State Board of Education has begun an earnest discussion of whether schools in that state should teach science that was obsolete [outdated] by the end of the nineteenth century. The board is holding hearings into proposed changes to its model science standards, changes intended to cast doubt on conventional evolutionary biology and inject into classrooms the notion of "intelligent design"—the idea that the complexity of life can be explained only by some conscious creator's having designed it.

2   Intelligent design is not your parents' creationism. It's a slick set of talking points that are not based on biblical inerrancy [truth] but framed, rather, in the language of science: molecular biology, the structure of DNA, and holes in the fossil record. Moreover, the ostensible [claimed] justification for the changes is a seductive one. Proponents [supporters] say they mean merely to ensure that schoolchildren are given a full sense of the scientific controversy over evolution so that they can make up their own minds. Who can object to that?

3   But there is no serious scientific controversy over whether Darwinian evolution takes place. Intelligent design is not science. Whatever its rhetoric [arguments], the public questioning of evolution is fundamentally religious, not scientific, in nature. That is not to say that wonder is illegitimate; it is a perfectly reasonable response to the beauty and enormity of the universe to believe that it could not have happened without a divine hand. But the proper place to discuss such belief is not the public schools. Biology classes need to be taught with sensitivity to the religious sensibilities of students but not by casting doubt on evolution. . . .

4   Evolution is a reality, no matter how much people may object to it. And denying or downplaying its importance to any serious examination of the biological sciences ill serves students who may wish to know how bacteria become resistant to drugs, how birds and dinosaurs are related, or why dolphins and sharks share certain morphological [structural] traits. How people reconcile their religious convictions with scientific reality is a matter for places of worship, not for science classrooms— or state boards that set standards.

—Excerpted from "Kansas Evolves Back," *The Washington Post*

27 The author's main purpose in this passage is to

1. entertain
2. inform
3. evoke emotion
4. persuade

28 What is the writer's main message?

1. The complexity of life can be explained only by the existence of a creator.
2. Intelligent design should not be taught in science class.
3. There is no reason to wonder at the beauty of the universe.
4. People must reconcile their religious convictions with scientific reality.

29 This passage is the type of informational nonfiction known as

1. an article
2. a report
3. an editorial
4. a business document

30 A strength of the author's argument is

1. the title of the piece
2. the justification for "teaching the controversy" in paragraph 2
3. the use of the term "divine hand" in paragraph 3
4. the list in the final paragraph of biological facts that evolution explains

31 The connotation of *serious* in paragraphs 3 and 4 is

1. positive in 3, negative in 4
2. negative in 3, positive in 4
3. positive in both 3 and 4
4. negative in both 3 and 4

32 Which words from the passage show bias?

1. *obsolete* and *slick*
2. *doubt* and *complexity*
3. *controversy* and *evolution*
4. *religious* and *illegitimate*

33 The cartoonist is comparing "intelligent design" to

1. the intelligence of Einstein and astronomers
2. astrology and other unscientific approaches
3. chemistry, neurology, physics, and astronomy
4. magic

Questions 34 through 39 refer to the following excerpt.

WHAT CELEBRATION DID THE AUTHOR MISS?

1   My birth mother never heard me laugh. Her name was Betty Jackson Monroe, and she was robbed of that moment, an immense loss for a Navajo mother. Christians have baptisms for newborn children, and Jews have brises or circumcisions for boys and naming ceremonies for girls. But, as my newfound sisters have told me, Navajos have a different ritual, a ceremony of their own for a new baby.

2   They wait. They watch. And they listen. They are waiting for the baby's first laugh. It has to be spontaneous and self-generated; no kitchy-kooing and no tickling allowed. It usually happens when the baby is a month or so old. And then they celebrate.

3   What an idea! From the minute I heard about that, I loved it. After all the new and strange things that I was struggling to understand, here was something that I grasped immediately. A baby is a great joy, and its laughter is a true blessing from whatever holy spirit you believe in.

4   Eyes on the road, I remembered the tradition I'd been told about. I thought of how it might have been, if I hadn't been stolen from my parents. When I laughed out loud for the first time, my older sisters would have run from hogan [house] to hogan, issuing invitations and spreading the word. Meanwhile, my mother would have been busy cooking. She'd have taken her wedding basket, the woven basket that was used in the marriage ceremony for her and my father, the basket with a circle, endless and unifying, painted in its center. She'd have filled the basket with food—corn cakes, tortillas, blue ears of Indian corn, whatever she chose.

5   My mother would have propped me up on pillows and placed the basket in front of me. And then people would have arrived to accept the gifts from the basket, a symbol of the gifts that this child was bringing to this world, a hope that the life of this child would always be blessed with laughter.

6   No such celebration was ever held for me. No one knows where I was when I gave my first laugh. No one knows who heard it. And for Navajos, famous among Indian tribes for their wit, their good humor, their love of practical jokes, that was a cause for great sadness.

7   Still, in my growing-up years, far from the people whose blood ran through my veins, I did have the blessing of laughter. However I got there, I was lucky to have landed in the arms of Beatrice and Lawrence Silverman, and they heard my laughter a lot. It was loud. It was long. It often gave me the hiccups.

8   My adoptive parents praised and pampered me. Why wouldn't I be laughing? They gave me love, a home, a religion, and an identity. Why wouldn't I be happy? They half-convinced me that being adopted was better than just being born.

9   "You're special," Bea used to say. "That's why we chose you."

—Excerpted from *Looking for Lost Bird: A Jewish Woman Discovers Her Navajo Roots* by Yvette Melanson

34 This passage is an example of

① a biography
② an autobiography
③ an essay
④ a critical review

35 The author's style

① uses big words and long sentences
② uses few adjectives or descriptive details
③ is personal and straightforward
④ is obscure and hard to understand

36 What can you infer from the passage and the book's title about what happened to the author as a child?

① She never learned how to laugh.
② She was kidnapped from her Navajo parents.
③ She was baptized as a Christian.
④ She grew up in the Southwest.

37 If you look up *hogan* in a dictionary, it will be on the page with the guide words

① *hoard* and *ho-hum*
② *hit* and *hockey*
③ *hogwash* and *hold over*
④ *hopscotch* and *house*

38 Which of the following are transitional words used to organize paragraph 4?

① *When, meanwhile*
② *first, run*
③ *circle, chose*
④ *remembered, endless*

39 "A baby is a great joy, and its laughter is a true blessing" is

① a fact
② an opinion
③ a description
④ a prediction

WHAT IS HELL?

Characters
Valet
Estelle
Garcin
5 Inez

GARCIN: Will night never come?
INEZ: Never.
GARCIN: You will always see me?
INEZ: Always.

10 [Garcin moves away from Estelle and takes some
steps across the room. He goes to the bronze
ornament.]

GARCIN: This bronze. [Strokes it thoughtfully.]
Yes, now's the moment; I'm looking on this
15 thing on the mantelpiece, and I understand
that I'm in hell. I tell you, everything's been
thought out beforehand. They knew I'd stand
at the fireplace stroking this thing of bronze,
with all those eyes intent on me. Devouring
20 me. [He swings round abruptly.] What? Only
two of you? I thought there were more; many
more. [Laughs.] So this is hell. I'd never have
believed it. You remember all we were told
about the torture-chambers, the fire and
25 brimstone, the "burning marl" [earth]. Old
wives' tales! There's no need for red-hot
pokers. Hell is—other people!

ESTELLE: My darling! Please—

GARCIN: [thrusting her away.] No, let me be.
30 She is between us. I cannot love you when
she's watching.

ESTELLE: Right! In that case, I'll stop her
watching. [She picks up the paper-knife from the
table, rushes at Inez, and stabs her several
35 times.]

INEZ: [struggling and laughing] But, you crazy
creature, what do you think you're doing? You
know quite well I'm dead.

ESTELLE: Dead?

40 [She drops the knife. A pause. Inez picks up the
knife and jabs herself with it regretfully.]

INEZ: Dead! Dead! Dead! Knives, poison,
ropes—all useless. It has happened already, do
you understand? Once and for all. So here we
45 are, forever. [Laughs.]

ESTELLE: [with a peal of laughter] Forever. My
God, how funny! Forever.

GARCIN: [looks at the two women, and joins in
the laughter] For ever, and ever, and ever.

50 [They slump onto their respective sofas. A long
silence. Their laughter dies away and they gaze
at each other.]

GARCIN: Well, well, let's get on with it. . . .

CURTAIN

—Excerpted from *No Exit* by Jean-Paul Sartre

40 *He swings round abruptly* in line 20 is

  ① dialogue

  ② characterization

  ③ a prop

  ④ a stage direction

41 How might lines 36–38 be written in a novel?

  ① Inez struggled and laughed. "But, you crazy creature, what do you think you're doing?" she demanded. "You know quite well I'm dead."

  ② But, you crazy creature, what do you think you're doing? You know quite well I'm dead, Inez said, *struggling and laughing.*

  ③ Inez struggled and laughed. *But, you crazy creature, what do you think you're doing? You know quite well I'm dead.*

  ④ Inez struggled and laughed. But, you crazy creature, what do you think you're doing? You know quite well I'm dead.

42 The plot is about

  ① two women and their brother

  ② three people trapped together in Hell

  ③ torture-chambers, fire and brimstone, and red-hot pokers

  ④ a man studying a bronze ornament

43 All the characters are laughing at the end of the play because

  ① they think suicide is funny

  ② they're happy

  ③ they've resolved their conflicts

  ④ if they don't laugh, they'll cry

44 The author, Jean-Paul Sartre, was a leader of the philosophical movement called existentialism, which emphasizes taking individual responsibility in a world where you don't know for sure what's right or wrong.

Given this background, what do you think Garcin means in line 53?

  ① Can't we all just get along?

  ② Estelle, let's ignore Inez.

  ③ There must be some way to hide.

  ④ It's our job to torture each other, so let's begin.

45 What do you predict will happen between Garcin and Estelle?

  ① They'll learn to ignore Inez.

  ② They'll fall in love.

  ③ They'll grow to hate each other.

  ④ One of them will commit suicide.

WHAT DOES THE REVIEWER THINK OF THE BOOK?

A Review of the Book *Marriage, A History: From Obedience to Intimacy or How Love Conquered Marriage* by Stephanie Coontz

1   Since antiquity [ancient times], conservative social critics have fretted over the crisis in marriage. Even the Roman emperor Augustus promoted a family values campaign, according to Stephanie Coontz in her new book, *Marriage, A History*. Augustus created a "wave of manufactured nostalgia for the supposed virtues of earlier times, when women were not allowed to drink wine and, according to the satirist Juvenal, wives were too tired from working at their looms to engage in adultery," she writes. Augustus didn't let his own divorce and affairs get in the way, just as President Ronald Reagan did not let his own divorce mar his family values campaign. . . .

2   The radical idea that people should marry primarily for love caused chaos in marriage. Until the eighteenth century, most people didn't have too many options. Family, government, and the church restricted one's choice in mates.

3   That is not to say that husbands and wives throughout history did not love each other. Coontz acknowledges that people fell in love, sometimes even with their own spouses. But for most of human history, "marriage was not fundamentally about love," she writes. "It was too vital an economic and political institution to be entered into solely on the basis of something as irrational as love."

4   To prove her point, she traces the developments in marriage from the Stone Age to President Bush's 2004 State of the Union Address. Coontz is quick to note that "many of the things now seen as unprecedented in family life are not actually new." Stepfamilies, out of wedlock births, even same sex relationships existed throughout human history. . . .

5   Despite the 2004 election and anti-gay marriage referenda on ballots in eleven states, homosexual unions are not the biggest threat to the primacy of marriage. It's people who are constructing meaningful lives outside of marriage and who see marriage as a choice. "Divorce, single parenthood, and cohabitation among heterosexuals have already reshaped the role of marriage in society and its meanings in people's lives," writes Coontz.

6   She does a good job of explaining how we got to where we are now. The journey is long and sometimes a slog for us to get through. Coontz stops at interesting points along the way, but she can also get bogged down in detail, especially in the chapters on medieval times. And even though the title and the first chapters hint at a global view of marriage, she narrows her focus to Western Europe and eventually the United States.

7   Still, this is a valuable historical survey. Although we are in uncharted territory, Coontz recognizes that the solution does not lie in mandating a return to the past. That isn't possible. We need to recognize how we really live today and embrace the freedom that comes with that.

—Excerpted from "Last Comes Love" by Elizabeth DiNovella

46 This piece is an example of

   ① fiction

   ② poetry

   ③ drama

   ④ nonfiction

47 What does the reviewer do to familiarize readers with this book?

   ① She tells them where to find the book.

   ② She discusses the book author's motives in writing it.

   ③ She quotes from the book.

   ④ She gives her opinion of its subject.

48 The reviewer's point of view about marriage is

   ① it can adapt to new realities

   ② it's outdated and will soon be extinct

   ③ it hasn't changed in centuries

   ④ it worked better when it was about money and politics instead of love

49 Context clues show that the word *unprecedented* in paragraph 4 means

   ① typical

   ② new

   ③ stepfamilies

   ④ historical

50 The best summary of paragraphs 6–7 is

   ① Coontz does a good job of explaining how we got to where we are now, although she can get bogged down in detail. The focus is not global. The book covers mostly Western Europe and the United States. Coontz recognizes that rather than trying to return to the past, we need to recognize how we really live today and embrace the freedom that comes with that.

   ② Coontz does a good but too detailed job of explaining how we got here. The book focuses on Western Europe and the United States, but it is still a valuable historical survey. Coontz says we need to recognize how we live today and embrace our freedom.

   ③ Coontz does a good job of explaining how we got to where we are now. The journey is sometimes a slog. Coontz stops at interesting points along the way, but she can also get bogged down in detail. And even though the title and the first chapters hint at a global view of marriage, she narrows her focus to Western Europe and eventually the United States. Still, this is a valuable historical survey. Coontz recognizes that the solution does not lie in mandating a return to the past. We need to recognize how we really live today and embrace the freedom that comes with that.

   ④ Coontz does a good job of explaining how we got to where we are now, although she can get bogged down in detail. The focus is not global (the book covers mostly Western Europe and the United States), but this is still a valuable historical survey. Coontz recognizes that rather than trying to return to the past, we need to recognize how we really live today and embrace the freedom that comes with that.

Posttest Evaluation Chart

After you complete the Posttest, check your answers with the Answer Key on page 171. Then use this chart to figure out which skills you need to review. In column 1, circle the numbers of the questions you missed. The second and third columns tell you the name of the skill and its number in the instruction section of this book. The fourth column tells you the pages to review. From the fifth column, use the pages from Contemporary's *GED Language Arts, Reading* book for further study if necessary.

Question Number	Skill Name	Skill	Pages	GED Language Arts, Reading
1	Main Idea and Details	1	18–19	15–30
36	Inference	2	20–23	47–56
6	Conclusion	3	24–27	53–56
49	Context Clues	4	28–29	31–37
31	Connotation and Denotation	5	30–31	57–58, 113–115
50	Summarizing and Paraphrasing	6	32–33	121, 125–128
39	Fact and Opinion	7	34–35	111–113
32	Detecting Bias	8	36–37	111–113
30	Strengths of an Argument	9	38–39	49
45	Prediction	10	40–41	47–49
38	Chronological Order	11	42–43	74–76
16	Cause and Effect	12	44–45	81–82
8	Comparison and Contrast	13	46–47	90–95
26	Order of Degree	14	48–49	72–74, 76–80
17	Homonym	15	50–51	
27	Author's Purpose	16	52–53	99–100
48	Author's Point of View	17	54–55	97–98
35	Author's Style	18	56–59	62–71
46	Genre	19	60–61	109, 165, 217, 249
18	Basic Elements of Fiction	20	62–65	165–192
19	Characterization	21	66–69	179–184
20	Plot and Conflict	22	70–73	172–176
21	Point of View	23	74–75	176–178
22	Dialogue and Narrative	24	76–77	185–192
23	Setting, Mood, and Tone	25	78–81	95–97, 166–171
24	Descriptive Details	26	82–85	113–116, 193–196
25	Theme and Symbol	27	86–89	197–211
44	Extended Synthesis	28	90–93	102–105
9	How to Read a Poem	29	94–97	217–225
10	Subject and Theme	30	98–101	225–229, 237–242

Question Number	Skill Name	Skill	Pages	GED Language Arts, Reading
11	The Shape of Poetry	31	102–105	223–229
12	Rhythm and Meter	32	106–109	222–225
13	The Sound of Poetry	33	110–113	218–219
14	Imagery and Figurative Language	34	114–117	230–237
15	Mood and Emotion	35	118–119	217–221
40	Drama as a Literary Form	36	120–123	249–254
41	Reading a Play or Script	37	124–125	255–258, 267–276
42	Plot and Conflict	38	126–127	260–261
43	Characterization	39	128–129	263–266
7	Types of Nonfiction	40	130–131	109–110
34	Literary Nonfiction	41	132–133	137–144
47	Commentary and Review	42	134–135	110, 148–159
29	Informational Nonfiction	43	136–137	110, 117–120
28	Editorial	44	138–139	
3	Workplace and Business Document	45	140–141	128–130, 132–136
5	Community and Consumer Document	46	142–143	131, 163–164
4	Business and Consumer Letter	47	144–145	
33	Cartoon	48	146–149	
2	Table and Graph	49	150–151	
37	Reference Source	50	152–153	

Answer Key

Page 157

❶ ③, ❷ ①, ❸ ④, ❹ ②, ❺ ②, ❻ ④, ❼ ④, ❽ ③

Page 159

❾ ②, ❿ ③, ⓫ ②, ⓬ ③, ⓭ ④, ⓮ ②, ⓯ ②, ⓰ ②, ⓱ ①

Page 161

⓲ ②, ⓳ ③, ⓴ ④, ㉑ ④, ㉒ ①, ㉓ ①, ㉔ ②, ㉕ ③, ㉖ ③

Page 163

㉗ ④, ㉘ ②, ㉙ ③, ㉚ ④, ㉛ ③, ㉜ ①, ㉝ ③

Page 165

㉞ ②, ㉟ ③, ㊱ ②, ㊲ ①, ㊳ ①, ㊴ ②

Page 167

㊵ ④, ㊶ ①, ㊷ ②, ㊸ ④, ㊹ ④, ㊺ ③

Page 169

㊻ ④, ㊼ ③, ㊽ ①, ㊾ ②, ㊿ ②

Answer Key

Skill 1: Finding the Main Idea and Details, page 19

1 ②, **2** ①, **3** ③, **4** ①

5 Supporting details: Ivan is the most powerful hurricane to hit Grenada in nearly a decade. Winds hit 140 miles per hour. Ivan killed at least 12 people. Ninety percent of homes on the island were damaged. Concrete homes were pulverized into rubble and hundreds of roofs were torn off. Ivan destroyed a prison, leaving criminals on the loose.

6 The devastation took place on Grenada (an island in the West Indies).

7 The hurricane hit on September 7, 2004.

8 At least 12 people died.

9 Hurricane Ivan demolished their houses.

Skill 2: Making Inferences, page 21

1 ③, **2** ①, ②, ④, **3** ①

4 **Possible answer:** A new printer will improve the work I do in my home office. I need this new printer.

Page 23

1 ②, **2** ④, **3** ①, **4** ④

Skill 3: Drawing Conclusions, page 24

1 true

2 false: Only Irish people have red hair. Sha-lin must be Irish.

3 false: All cats are stupid. Luna must be stupid.

4 false: Alligators have hollow bones. Alligators are birds.

5 false: Only humans know American Sign Language. Koko must be human.

6 true

Page 26

1 They probably live in a modern home because the husband uses a computer and the wife is his tech support.

2 They probably have children since they go around the dinner table telling what each has learned, which you wouldn't expect two people to do. The second paragraph refers to "the family."

3 Their nontraditional division of labor does seem to work. The wife solves the husband's computer problems and serves as his "total emotional support service package."

4 The husband may be a writer because he uses the computer daily. He may also be a stay-at-home dad who uses the computer for entertainment and to keep in touch with friends.

Page 27

5 ③, **6** ②, **7** ②, **8** ①, **9** ④, **10** ④

Skill 4: Recognizing Context Clues, page 29

1 ①, **2** ④, **3** ②, **4** ③, **5** ②, **6** ④

7 Cognitive science is the study of how people think and learn.

8 *Consciously* means "paid attention to" or "kept in the mind."

9 Disruptions are interruptions.

10 Internal information is knowledge in the mind, or head.

11 External information is knowledge in the world.

Skill 5: Understanding Connotation and Denotation, page 31

1 −, **2** +, **3** −, **4** +, **5** −, **6** +, **7** 0, **8** +

In the +, or positive, box: self-confident, peaceful, free-spirited, dedicated employee, fashionable, computer expert, brave, artistic, curious, focused

In the −, or negative, box: arrogant, dull, unreliable, workaholic, clothes crazy, computer geek, foolhardy, moody, nosy, obsessed

Skill 6: Summarizing and Paraphrasing, page 33

1 ④

2 **Possible paraphrase:** King George VI of England was shy growing up. He stuttered and he was afraid of crowds. His brother Edward was supposed to become king, but when Edward became involved with a divorced American woman, the British government forced him to abdicate the throne. George was crowned king and led his people through World War II.

3 ①

4 **Possible paraphrase:** The classic movie *E.T.* is about relationships. The cute creature from outer space is befriended by a little boy named Elliott, who helps E.T. escape from federal agents trying to capture him. The alien helps Elliott deal with his family. Elliott is brave enough to help his friend get home. This movie doesn't waste time on shootouts and chase scenes. Instead, it concentrates on feelings.

Skill 7: Identifying Facts and Opinions, page 35

1 F, **2** O, **3** F, **4** F, **5** G, **6** O, **7** F, **8** O, **9** G, **10** O

11 The Boston Red Sox beat the highly paid New York Yankees to win the World Series in 2004. The Yankees' owner is George Steinbrenner.

12 Italian food includes many different kinds of pasta. The tomatoes in spaghetti sauce are good for you because they contain lycopene, which fights cancer.

13 Malayan sun bears live in the tropical rainforests of Sumatra. They eat insects, small rodents, and fruit. At about four feet tall, they're the smallest bears.

14 Rembrandt van Rijn was born in 1606 in Holland. He was an artist who created many oil paintings, pencil sketches, and etchings, including prints about Greek myths.

Skill 8: Detecting Bias, page 37

1 **Examples of loaded language:** on the side of life; killers; "The Culture of Life"; killers and terrorists; reckless; murder weapons; destroys the right of victims.

2 **Examples of facts:** Bill S.397 protects gun dealers from being held accountable by victims; the bill is backed by the NRA; 30,000 lives will be lost to gun violence this year; the U.S. Senate's phone number is 202-224-3121.

3 The headline addresses senators. The text shows the ad is directed to consumers and urges them to call their senators.

4 The ad wants you to believe that Senate bill 397 should be defeated and gun sales should be restricted.

5 The ad wants readers to call their senators and tell them to vote against S.397.

6 coolest tunes (positive)

7 stuck, tired, old (all negative)

8 courage, experience (positive)

9 reward (positive)

Skill 9: Evaluating an Argument, page 39

1 ④; **2** ②; **3** ③; **4** ①

5 Opinions will vary.

Skill 10: Making Predictions, page 41

1 Anna will probably speak English.

2 Ruth will probably speak English, too.

3 Anna's grades will probably improve.

4 The mother will probably learn English so she can keep talking to her daughters.

5 ③, **6** ④

Skill 11: Using Chronological Order, page 43

1 Maathai started the Green Belt Movement in 1977.

2 After forests were cleared to make room for plantations and Kenyans used up nearby wood for fuel, women had to walk miles to gather firewood.

3 Maathai won the Hunger Project's Africa Prize for Leadership in 1992.

4 In 2002, the country made a peaceful transition to a democracy.

5 Maathai was elected to Parliament and soon after appointed as Kenya's vice minister of the environment.

6 Maathai won the Nobel Peace Prize in 2004.

7 4; 5; 1; 6; 3; 2

Skill 12: Recognizing Cause and Effect, page 45

1 The dam's failure was caused by a combination of too much rain and poor repair.

2 The flood killed more than 2,200 people and destroyed much property.

3 The wealthy owners didn't care much about the millworkers, who were too poor to have any power.

4 Typhoid was caused by crowded conditions and a lack of sanitation.

5 ③, **6** ③, **7** ②, **8** ②

Skill 13: Recognizing Comparison and Contrast, page 47

1 ④, **2** ④, **3** ①, **4** ②

5 *circle:* family fun, relaxation; *underline:* gravity-defying rides, watching fish

6 *circle:* ocean dwelling, good swimmer; *underline:* fish, covered with hair

7 *circle:* rooting for your team, cheering home runs; *underline:* eating hot dogs, getting a workout

8 *circle:* big city, crowded highways; *underline:* near Mexico, cold in winter

9 *circle:* is applied with a brush; *underline:* comes in all colors, highlights wood grain, goes on drywall

10 *circle:* quenches thirst; *underline:* contains Vitamin C, rots teeth, has no nutrients

11 *circle:* come in different sizes, go on feet; *underline:* protect from snow, are comfy in warm weather

12 *circle:* flowers, have petals; *underline:* bloom in spring, bloom in fall

Skill 14: Using Order of Degree, page 49

1 ①, **2** ③, **3** ②

4 ①, **5** ④, **6** ④, **7** ③, **8** ②, **9** ②

Skill 15: Understanding Homonyms, page 51

1 principle, **2** affect, **3** bored, **4** site, **5** buy, **6** whether, **7** stationary, **8** role, **9** patients, **10** precede, **11** your, **12** it's, **13** break, **14** passed, **15** their, **16** who's

17 **a.** a type of fish; **b.** a type of guitar

18 **a.** a time interval of 60 seconds; **b.** tiny

19 **a.** street and city of residence; **b.** make a speech

20 **a.** a gift; **b.** introduce

Skill 16: Identifying Author's Purpose, page 53

1 ②, **2** ④, **3** ①, **4** ①, **5** ②, **6** ④

Skill 17: Identifying Author's Point of View, page 55

1 ③, **2** ②, **3** ③, **4** ①

Possible answers:

5 Usher's new CD is <u>cool</u> and <u>first class</u>. When I hear him sing, I feel <u>mellow</u>.

6 Usher's new CD is <u>boring</u> and <u>repetitive</u>. When I hear him sing, I feel <u>like screaming</u>.

7 Hockey is a sport that <u>appeals to</u> me. It's <u>exciting</u>, and the fans are <u>enthusiastic</u>.

8 Hockey is a sport that <u>appalls</u> me. It's <u>brutal</u>, and the fans are <u>bloodthirsty</u>.

Skill 18: Identifying Author's Style, page 58

1 ①, **2** ②, **3** ④, **4** ②, **5** ①, **6** ③

Page 59

7 Author C, **8** Author A

9 imagery, figurative language, modifiers

10 interruptions, long sentences

11 short words, short sentences, interruptions

Skill 19: Identifying Genres, page 61

1 fiction, **2** drama, **3** nonfiction, **4** poetry, **5** nonfiction, **6** drama, **7** fiction, **8** fiction, **9** poetry, **10** nonfiction, **11** nonfiction, **12** nonfiction

13 ④, **14** ②, **15** ①, **16** ④

Skill 20: Recognizing Basic Elements of Fiction, page 64

1 ②, **2** ①, **3** ②, **4** ④, **5** ②, **6** ①, **7** ①, **8** ③

9 N, **10** S, **11** N

Page 65

12 ③, **13** ①, **14** ③, **15** ④, **16** ③, **17** ②, **18** ④

Skill 21: Understanding Characterization, page 68

1 ③, **2** ①, **3** ②, **4** ③, **5** ③, **6** ④, **7** ①

Page 69

8 ②, **9** ③, **10** ④, **11** ①, **12** ③, **13** ②

Skill 22: Identifying Plot and Conflict, page 73

❶ ①, ❷ ②, ❸ ③, ❹ ③, ❺ ③, ❻ ④

❼ This exposition is much shorter—only one paragraph as compared to four paragraphs.

❽ The dwarfish Santa is the first character.

❾ Santa's conflict is with the world, or people in general.

❿ The climax is in the very last line when the narrator sees the word *SPREAD*.

Skill 23: Understanding Point of View, page 75

❶ ②, ❷ ①, ❸ ③

❹ This passage is first person point of view.

❺ The narrator refers to herself as *I*.

❻ The reader knows only the narrator's thoughts.

❼ The passage would emphasize that the mother was just trying to help by shrinking the daughter's clothes. It might suggest that the daughter was ungrateful. It would leave out the explanation in paragraph 2.

Skill 24: Recognizing Dialogue and Narrative, page 77

❶ ④, ❷ ①, ❸ ④, ❹ ②, ❺ ③

❻ Elaine thinks that Andrea perceives her as old.

❼ Elaine starts off disliking the reporter but gradually warms up to her. The author shows this by having Elaine say something she knows will annoy Andrea in paragraph 2 and correct her in paragraph 6. Then in paragraph 14 Elaine thinks, "I'm softening up" and realizes that Andrea could be worse.

Skill 25: Identifying Setting, Mood, and Tone, page 80

❶ ③, ❷ ④, ❸ ①, ❹ ②, ❺ ④, ❻ ①

Page 81

❼ The setting is the suburbs of Cambridge, Massachusetts, in the present.

❽ Cambridge and Northeastern University are specified. The hints that it's a suburb include no sidewalks, no streetlights, no mass transit, and few stores.

❾ She has a Toyota Corolla and eats Rice Krispies, so you know it's not very far in the past or future.

❿ The mood is distressed and unhappy.

⓫ ②, ⓬ ②, ⓭ ①, ⓮ ④, ⓯ ②

⓰ The author describes a saint in every church, the ivory caskets, the jewel-studded coffins, the gold and silver shrines lit night and day by a thousand candles.

Skill 26: Recognizing Descriptive Details, page 84

❶ ②, ❷ ④, ❸ ①, ❹ ③

Page 85

❺ The author uses two similes: the bottle leaps in her hand "like a frog, like a still-beating heart in the hands of a surgeon."

❻ Vivid verbs: gripped, clasped, steadied (line 11), flew (line 16), gathered, turned, and flew (line 24), blocked (line 28), surmounted (line 30), encased (line 31).

❼ Specific nouns: bottle (lines 3, 18), glass (line 4), dust-spots (line 7), frog (line 9), heart (lines 10, 12), splinters (line 13), swarming (line 18), exhalation (line 19), woodsmoke (line 21), cinnamon (line 21), sulfur (line 21), incense (line 22), leather (line 23), cloud (line 24), paisley or comma (line 25), foot (29), gold (line 32), snakeskin (line 33).

8 These lines evoke a feeling of astonishment and perhaps also fear or foreboding.

9 ②, **10** ①, **11** ②, **12** ③

13 Vivid verbs in paragraph 1: shrinks, gorge, ripen, burst, hum, die.

14 Specific nouns in paragraph 3: June, monsoon, wind, water, sunshine, children, countryside, boundaries, fences, walls, vines, poles, creepers, banks, roads, boats, bazaars, fish, puddles, potholes, highways.

15 Adjectives in paragraph 4: slanting, silver, loose, old, steep, gabled, low.

16 The weather in May (paragraph 1) is hot but dry ("the river shrinks," "dustgreen trees"), but in June (paragraph 3), there is water everywhere ("the countryside turns green," plant life grows wild, "flooded roads," "boats in the bazaars," "fish in the potholes").

17 Paragraph 3 evokes a feeling of fertility. The water makes everything grow and turn "an immodest green." It even causes fish to appear.

Skill 27: Discovering Theme and Symbols, page 89

1 ②, **2** ④, **3** ④, **4** ③

5 The scarcity of cats suggests that something has happened that killed off a lot of animals (tame cats as well as wild animals) and maybe humans, too.

6 Anders wants to pretend the gorillas are still alive because he loves them.

Skill 28: Understanding Extended Synthesis, page 92

1 ②, **2** ①, **3** ③, **4** ④

Page 93

5 ②, **6** ④, **7** ②

Skill 29: Learning How to Read a Poem, page 96

1 ③, **2** ②, **3** ④, **4** ②, **5** ①, **6** ①, **7** ③, **8** ②

Page 97

9 ③, **10** ④, **11** ②, **12** ①, **13** ①, **14** ②, **15** ③

Skill 30: Identifying Subject and Theme, page 100

1 ②, **2** ①, **3** ①, **4** ③, **5** ④, **6** ③, **7** ①

Page 101

8 ②, **9** ②, **10** ④, **11** ①, **12** ③

13 The "brighter fire" is the joy in life that the speaker has always felt was more important than the reasonable knowledge that everyone dies.

14 Their flow mimics the flow of the snake "all spring through the green leaves before he came to the road."

Skill 31: Appreciating the Shape of Poetry, page 104

1 ④, **2** ③, **3** ②, **4** ④, **5** ①

6 Lines 34–35 show the mother behaving heroically. She rescues her daughter's hair just before it catches fire from the candles.

7 They predict that she'll always have to pay her dues, to put up with the tedium of life before she gets rewards (cake).

Page 105

8 ①, **9** ④, **10** ②, **11** ②, **12** ②, **13** ③

Skill 32: Understanding Rhythm and Meter, page 108

1 ②, **2** ④, **3** ①, **4** ④, **5** ②, **6** ②

Page 109

7 Lines 1, 6, 12, and 18 show repetition.

8 It suggests they're both "one art." That is, they're the same type of loss, with about the same degree of importance.

9 The poem has a regular rhythm.

10 This poem's rhythm is irregular. The stressed and unstressed syllables don't alternate evenly, and the line lengths vary.

11 *Remember* (in title and lines 1, 3, 4, 5, 7, 10, 11, 14, 17, 19, 20, 21, 22, 23, 24); *earth* (lines 12-13); *you* (lines 19-21) are examples of repetition.

12 Line 11 stresses *Remember, earth, skin,* and *are.*

Skill 33: Listening to the Sound of Poetry, page 112

1 ①, **2** ④, **3** ③, **4** ①, **5** ①, **6** ①, **7** ②, **8** ③

Page 113

9 T, **10** F, **11** T, **12** T, **13** F

14 The second and fourth lines rhyme; the sixth and eighth lines rhyme.

15 These are examples of alliteration.

16 These are examples of alliteration.

17 These are examples of consonance.

18 These are examples of end rhyme.

Skill 34: Using Imagery and Figurative Language, page 116

1 ②, **2** ②, **3** ④, **4** ③, **5** ①, **6** ③, **7** ②, **8** ④, **9** ③

Page 117

10 T, **11** T, **12** F, **13** F, **14** T, **15** T, **16** T

17 Stanza 1 appeals to sight, smell, touch, and hearing.
Sight: "It was bare and bright," "we looked into a fire," "underneath the moon," "the dawn came."
Smell: The ferry "smelled like a stable."
Touch: "we leaned across a table," "We lay on a hill-top."
Hearing: "the whistles kept blowing."

18 Stanza 2 appeals to taste: "you ate an apple, and I ate a pear."

19 The figure of speech in line 12 is a metaphor: "the sun rose dripping, a bucketful of gold."

Skill 35: Analyzing Mood and Emotions, page 119

1 ②, **2** ④, **3** ①, **4** ②

5 It suggests that the contents of the poem are unimportant, that it's just a quick, tossed-off note.

6 It suggests guilt over stealing his partner's breakfast and perhaps regret at his selfishness.

7 He seems to want his partner to know just how good the plums would have tasted. The lines suggest that he doesn't really mean line 8 ("Forgive me") or feel any guilt or regret.

Skill 36: Reading Drama as a Literary Form, page 122

1 ②, **2** ④, **3** ③, **4** ④, **5** ③

6 The character list describes Winnie as "sweet and charming. Always," which could be annoying. Also Lon calls her "my helpful little helpless wife" and complains about her giving parties for her "charity groups," especially on their anniversary.

Page 123

7 Four acts are listed.

8 Act I takes place in the park at Sorin's estate.

9 It is sunset when the play begins.

10 Jacob and the other workmen are coughing and hammering as they build a stage for amateur theatricals.

11 The first scene is about Masha and Medvedenko talking.

12 They are waiting for the play to start.

13 Medvedenko says, "But I don't go round like someone at a funeral."

14 Medvedenko talks about money and his love for Masha.

15 Masha says, "What rubbish," and seems unmoved by his words.

Skill 37: Reading a Play or Script, page 125

1 ③, **2** ③, **3** ②, **4** ①, **5** ④

Skill 38: Identifying Plot and Conflict, page 127

1 ③, **2** ①, **3** ②

4 This play has three acts.

5 Act III has one scene.

6 Act II, Scene 1 takes place on the courthouse lawn.

Skill 39: Understanding Characterization, page 129

1 ③, ④, ⑥

2 ①, ⑤, ⑥

3 ①, ②, ⑥

4 The cab driver's description of his passengers reminds Veta of Elwood's good qualities and makes her realize the cure might change him for the worse.

5 The cab driver has a negative opinion about what he considers "normal" behavior for humans (lines 29–35).

Skill 40: Identifying Types of Nonfiction, page 131

1 ②, **2** ④, **3** ③, **4** ①, **5** ②, **6** ③

7 informational, **8** visual, **9** literary, **10** informational, **11** informational, **12** literary

13 speech, **14** consumer document, **15** personal essay

Skill 41: Analyzing Literary Nonfiction, page 133

1 ①, **2** ②, **3** ③, **4** ①, **5** ②, **6** ④

Skill 42: Interpreting Commentary and Reviews, page 135

1 ④, **2** ③

3 O, **4** F, **5** O, **6** F, **7** F, **8** F, **9** F

Skill 43: Analyzing Informational Nonfiction, page 137

① Four C.I.A. officers were on trial.

② They were charged with lying to their superiors and to lawmakers about a secret antidrug operation in Peru.

③ A Peruvian Air Force jet shot down the plane because they thought it was carrying drug smugglers.

④ American missionaries were on the plane.

⑤ Bryan Sierra, a Justice Department spokesman, announced that there would be no prosecution.

⑥ ④, **❼** ①

Skill 44: Interpreting Editorials, page 139

① ①

② The editorial was persuasive because it explained how consumers can be cheated by credit card companies in South Dakota and Delaware.

③ Nearly all of the letter is factual. Some fact are: The Millennium Ecosystem Assessment measures the decline in the earth's functioning. More than 1,300 scientists from 95 countries have contributed to the report. Ecosystems must be able to filter water, provide food, and pollinate crops.

④ Knowing who commissioned the report and who worked on it gives the letter credibility and makes me more likely to agree with its conclusion.

⑤ Yes, it supports her conclusion. I don't see any errors or false assumptions.

Skill 45: Understanding Workplace and Business Documents, page 141

① ③, **②** ④, **❸** ②

④ This form gives an employee notice of a problem that needs corrective action.

⑤ No, dress code violation is not a reason for corrective action.

⑥ The employee and his or her supervisor must sign the form.

Skill 46: Understanding Community and Consumer Documents, page 143

① ②, **②** ④, **❸** ②

④ *2 BR apt.* means the apartment has two bedrooms.

⑤ No; the ad says utilities are included.

⑥ The phrase *pkg. gar.* means parking garage.

❼ It probably means that it's an old building and it may be run down.

❽ To rent this apartment, the tenant will have to pay first and last months' rent at $900 per month, or $1,800, at the beginning of the lease.

Skill 47: Using Business and Consumer Letters, page 145

① Alma Cisneros wants to get the police to support her neighborhood's anticrime efforts.

② Alma's tone is cooperative because the police chief is more likely to be cooperative.

③ Alma is complaining about a crime-ridden neighborhood filled with drug dealers, where the police don't patrol often and are slow to respond to emergency calls.

④ Alma wants an officer to give advice to her group, and she wants the police to respond to 911 calls in ten minutes or less.

⑤ ③, ⑥ ②

⑦ Ms. Patel is the human resources director for Citywide Auto Service.

Skill 48: Interpreting Cartoons, page 148

❶ ②, ❷ ④, ❸ ④, ❹ ① ❺ ①, ❻ ③,
❼ ②, ❽ ④

Page 149

❾ ③, ❿ ②, ⑪ ①, ⑫ ④

⑬ ③, ⑭ ④, ⑮ ②, ⑯ ①

Skill 49: Interpreting Tables and Graphs, page 151

❶ ①, ❷ ③, ❸ ③, ❹ ④

❺ ④, ❻ ②

❼ The graph is about fluctuations in oil prices.

❽ This graph shows light sweet crude oil.

❾ The source of the information in this graph is the U.S. Dept. of Energy.

❿ In May the price of oil fell below $47 per barrel.

Skill 50: Understanding Reference Sources, page 153

❶ ②, ❷ ①, ❸ ②

❹ Yes, because *keyboard* comes between those two words alphabetically.

❺ The noun usage of *keyboard* came earlier (1819); the verb usage dates only to 1961.

❻ ②, ❼ ④, ❽ ③

Glossary

alliteration in poetry, the repetition of consonant sounds at the beginnings of words. For example, the *s* sound in "see the sights of the city."

assonance in poetry, the repetition of vowel sounds within non-rhyming words. For example, the *i* sound in "time out of mind."

author's point of view the author's opinion or way of looking at his subject. He may state his point of view clearly, or *explicitly*. Or the reader may have to figure out the author's *implicitly* stated point of view.

author's purpose the author's reason or goal for writing. For example, an author may want to entertain, inform, or persuade his readers.

author's style the author's unique way of using language in his writing. Author's style is also called *voice*.

autobiography life story of the writer told in first-person point of view

bias a slanted, often prejudiced, viewpoint that a writer wants you to believe

biography factual record of the life of an individual told in third-person point of view

business documents written materials that employees may encounter at work; may include employee handbooks, training materials, and memos

cartoon visual communication that uses images and humor to make a point

cast list list of characters in a play that may reveal their ages, occupations, physical descriptions, and personality traits

cause and effect organization used in a sentence or a passage that gives the reason for an action or event and the result of that action or event

characterization the way an author reveals the personality of the fictional characters in a story

chronological order sequence, or the time order in which things happen

climax the turning point of the plot; the high point of the action

comedy a play that ends happily for the main character

comparison and contrast organization used in a passage that tells how two or more things are alike or different

conclusion combining what you read with what you already know to figure out what the text means

conflict internal or external problems that a character in a story must solve

connotation the meaning of a word with the positive or negative emotions that the word makes you feel. For example, the wind can be *brisk* (positive connotation) or it can be *freezing* (negative connotation).

consonance in poetry, the repetition of consonant sounds within words. For example, the *k* sound in "a stroke of luck."

context clues clues for the meaning of unknown words. The clues are found in nearby words or sentences.

criticism nonfiction in which the writer discusses a writer's or artist's entire works, or a style of art or writing

denotation the basic, dictionary meaning of a word

dialogue conversation written on the page

drama a category of writing with dialogue for actors and acting directions to be performed on stage

editorial short piece of nonfiction that is designed to persuade the reader to share the opinion of the writer

essay nonfiction writing that presents the author's opinions and observations on a subject

euphemism word with a positive connotation that is used in place of a word with negative connotation. For example, *pre-owned* may be used instead of *used*.

exaggeration overstating something for emphasis or comic effect. For example, *If I've told you once, I've told you a million times.*

extended synthesis reasoning that integrates new information from outside a passage with what you have learned from the passage to reach a new understanding

fact a statement that can be proved. For example, *Austin is the capital of Texas* is a fact that can be proved.

fiction a category of writing that tells about events that happen to imaginary characters

generalization a statement that is a judgment rather than a provable statement. A generalization is usually false because it does not allow for any exceptions. For example, *All Californians are blonde* is a generalization.

genre a category of writing based on its content, form, and style. The four major genres are fiction, nonfiction, poetry, and drama.

graph organization of information for easy access and understanding. Common graphs are the line graph, bar graph, and circle graph.

homonyms words that sound alike but are spelled differently. Homonyms include both homophones (pronounced alike but different in meaning and spelling) and homographs (spelled alike but have different meanings). For example, *to, too,* and *two* are homonyms.

imagery word descriptions that appeal to the reader's sense of sight, hearing, touch, taste, or smell; also called *sensory details*

inference the use of information that is stated directly to figure out a message that is unstated

informational nonfiction writing, such as business documents or speeches, that conveys useful information

literary nonfiction writing that uses creative techniques like dialogue and lyrical language to tell a true story

main idea the most important idea in a paragraph or a passage

metaphor a comparison that doesn't use *like* or *as*. For example, *Lisa has a heart of stone.*

meter the rhythm of language in a poem, consisting of stressed and unstressed syllables in words

nonfiction a category of writing that includes useful information and true stories, such as biographies

onomatopoeia in poetry, words that suggest the sounds they describe. For example, *Bees buzz.*

opinion a statement that expresses feelings, beliefs, or personal judgments. An opinion cannot be proved, but it can be supported with facts or statistics. For example, *Spring is the most beautiful season* is an opinion.

order of degree organization of a piece of writing that puts things in an understandable order. For example, you might write about the members of your family and put them in order from oldest to youngest.

paraphrase restate a passage, telling the main ideas as well as the supporting details. When you paraphrase, you put the passage into your own words.

personification descriptive writing that gives human qualities to an animal or object. For example, *The sun smiled on us all day today.*

persuasive writing writing that attempts to influence the reader to share the writer's opinion

plot the action in a story. The five stages of a plot are the exposition, rising action, climax, falling action, and resolution.

point of view the perspective from which the narrator tells a story. The three basic points of view are first person, third-person limited, and third-person omniscient.

prediction an educated guess about what will happen in the future based on your observations and past experience

rhyme the use in a poem of words that sound alike. Rhymes can occur within a line or at the ends of lines.

rhythm the beat of a poem, or the pattern of sounds created by the rise and fall of syllables

sensory details words and phrases used by the author to appeal to the senses: sight, hearing, touch, taste, and smell; also called *imagery*

setting place and time of the story

simile a comparison that uses *like* or *as*. For example, *My hands are as cold as ice.*

stanza division of a poem with several lines grouped together somewhat like a paragraph. Stanzas are separated by a blank line.

summarize restate a passage, telling only the main ideas. When you summarize, the summary is much shorter than the original passage.

symbol a person, object, or place that stands for something besides itself. For example, lions symbolize strength.

synthesis reasoning that puts together several bits of information to reach a new understanding

theme the main idea or underlying message of a story or novel

Index